VIETNAM: PEASANT LAND, PEASANT REVOLUTION

Vietnam: Peasant Land, Peasant Revolution

Patriarchy and Collectivity in the Rural Economy

Nancy Wiegersma
Associate Professor
Fitchburg State College, Massachusetts

St. Martin's Press   New York

First published in the United States of America in 1988

Printed in Hong Kong

ISBN 0–312–01358–2

Library of Congress Cataloging-in-Publication Data
Wiegersma, Nancy.
Vietnam: peasant land, peasant revolution/Nancy Wiegersma.
p.   cm.
Bibliography: p.
Includes index.
ISBN 0–312–01358–2 : $39.95
1. Peasantry—Vietnam—History.   2. Farm tenancy—Vietnam–
History.   3. Vietnam—Rural conditions.   I. Title.
HD1537.V5W54 1988
305.5′63—dc19   87–27352
                                                                      CIP

To the memory of Oscar J. Wiegersma,
an American farmer

Contents

vii

List of Tables

Tables

Figures

Preface

On the tenth anniversary of the end of the Vietnam War, the US Secretary of State George Shultz stated, 'Our goals in Central America are like those we had in Vietnam.' Others have also noticed the many similarities between the US political, economic and military interventions in Vietnam in the 1960s and in Central America in the 1980s. Even some of the details of interventionary policy are the same. Roy Prosterman from Washington State University, for example, wrote the land-to-the-tiller laws for both Vietnam and El Salvador. Because of the current US involvement in Central America, there is renewed interest in understanding issues raised by American intervention in Vietnam in the 1960s and 1970s. Americans are continuing to be concerned about what happened in Vietnam, why we failed (probably because the USA failed) and what has happened there since the US involvement.

The Vietnamese revolution was not an aberration and this point becomes clearer as we view similar scenarios in Central America. Despite the continuing importance of understanding Vietnam for an appreciation of contemporary world politics, most Western observers do not understand the development of Vietnamese socialism and the forces behind the Vietnam War.

I have tried in *Vietnam: Peasant Land, Peasant Revolution*, to promote a deep understanding of the development of revolutionary forces in Vietnamese society and the way that US involvement influenced these forces. By focusing on the village community and the peasant family as the fundamental building blocks of Vietnamese society, the book first presents a clear picture of traditional Vietnam and then shows the dynamics of change during French Colonialism, the American Intervention, and the present socialist period. The focus on peasants and on their land brings out the basic differences between the various governments and their policies concerning the great majority of Vietnamese – the peasants. I hope therefore that the reader can find answers to questions about Vietnamese 'hearts and minds' which have been unanswered by the voluminous journalism of the Vietnam War Period.

I worked on the Southeast Asia desk at the US Department of Agriculture, Economic Research Service, from 1969 until 1972. I travelled to Vietnam in 1972, during my tenure at the Department of Agriculture, and worked with a team of economists on a book published by the US Department of Agriculture entitled *Agriculture in Vietnam's Economy*. Since 1972, I have published numerous articles on Vietnam and worked on the present book while holding a college faculty position in economics, currently at Fitchburg State College.

My interest in rural Vietnam dates from the mid-1960s, prior to my working for the US Department of Agriculture in Vietnam. I began writing on Vietnamese land tenure and economic development while I was a graduate student at the University of Maryland in the mid-1960s. It was in this period, also, that I first joined the peace movement which later became known as the anti-Vietnam War movement. Even as a federal employee in the late 1960s and early 1970s, I continued my active involvement in this movement.

Many people who were part of the US anti-war movement in the 1960s have been disillusioned and disappointed in the policies of reunited Vietnam in the post-war period. The Cambodian invasion, the flight of the 'boat people' and the mistakes that the bureaucratic Communist Party has made in southern Vietnam are some of the reasons. I hope that the argument in this volume concerning divergence in social, political and economic developments of the northern and southern regions in Vietnam will offer insight into some of these issues. The composition, leadership and policies of the National Liberation Front in the south in the 1960s were very different from those of the northern-dominated Viet Minh in the 1940s and 1950s.

The US government in the 1960s and 1970s used arguments about north–south differences to justify US intervention in Vietnam. Probably because of this history, Western intellectuals have shown a tendency to be unwilling to recognise the importance of north–south differences in Vietnam and their impact on contemporary Vietnam. The anti-war activists who expected post-war Vietnam to reflect the mass-based pro-peasant politics of the National Liberation Front were very disappointed. The northern Communists were more bureaucratic, hierarchical and pro-Soviet than their southern contemporaries. These differences, seen in a political–economic context, contribute to an explanation of contemporary policies in Vietnam.

In my own personal experience, I have lived through the transition from a family-based mode of production on the farm where I grew up, to the marketised capitalist economy, in which I have participated as an adult. From the togetherness, interconnectedness and integration in my background, I have moved to an individualised modern family where each person goes his or her own way in the economic world. In the more individualised modern family, there is more flexibility in gender roles. The sense of wholeness or togetherness which accompanies family-based production, however, is missing in the modern economy. Because of this background, I have not approached the study of Vietnamese peasants from the perspective that they have traditional values and patriarchal family structures and that we, in the West, do not. Rather, I have the perspective that there are profound differences, but also some important similarities, in both the positive and negative aspects of family farms everywhere.

Acknowledgements

This work has been considerably influenced by a number of people, none of whom would probably agree with all of my conclusions. Several of my graduate professors at the University of Maryland inspired my work. Professor Robert Bennett first introduced me to the field of economic development and economic research. My graduate advisor, John Q. Adams, first interested me in economic anthropology and directed me toward village study materials in analysing the political economy of rural Vietnam. Professors Allan Gruchy and Dudley Dillard helped me to develop a non-traditional, institutionalist, approach to political economy.

Christine White, Institute for Development Studies, Sussex, England, and Cornell University, has aided me considerably in researching Vietnamese sources. She has directed me toward numerous studies and has profoundly influenced my reading of the political economy of North Vietnam.

The statistical information and perspective on US intervention which I gained while working for the US Department of Agriculture's Economic Research Service was invaluable. Individuals who particularly helped me with my research were Rex Daly, Harry Walters and Joseph Willett.

Groups of people who have given me considerable help and feedback on parts of the manuscript are the New England Women and Development Group and the New York Women and Development Group, especially Carmen Diana Deere, Nancy Folbre, Jeanne Henn, Laurie Nissonoff, Jeanne Pyle, Nola Reinhardt and Sharon Stricter. I also benefited from presenting some of this work to the North-east Feminist Scholars' meetings.

I received a Professional Development Grant from Fitchburg State College for research expenses pertaining to the last few chapters of this book. I am grateful to Vice-President Patrick Delaney and others at Fitchburg State College who have encouraged me in this work.

The patience, understanding and competence of Karen Thatcher of Words-Worth, in Amherst, has been very important to me. I gratefully acknowledge her contribution.

Lastly, and very importantly, I benefited from the comments of individual people who read parts of this manuscript. These individuals are Christine White, Morton Sobell, Robert Sherry, David Dellinger, Daniel Clawson and Peter Bohmer.

NANCY A. WIEGERSMA

Author's Note

Parts of Chapter 3 were first published in an article entitled 'The Asiatic Mode of Production and Vietnam', *Journal of Contemporary Asia*, vol. 12, no. 1, 1982. Reprinted by permission of the editors.

Parts of Chapter 3 and Chapter 6 were first published in an article entitled 'Women in the Transition to Capitalism: Nineteenth through Mid-twentieth Century Vietnam', *Research in Political Economy*, ed. Paul Zarembka, vol. 6, 1981. Reprinted with permission of the publisher, JAI Press, Greenwich, CT.

Parts of Chapter 11 were first published in an article entitled 'Regional Differences in Socialist Transformation in Vietnam', *Economic Forum*, vol. 14, Summer 1983. Reprinted with permission of the editors.

Glossary

Land Tenure Terms

bon thou dien: an endowment to the village from a family with the agreement that the notables would perform certain ceremonial duties.

cong dien: communal rice land protected by the state from usurpation or alienation and redistributed periodically to villagers

cong tho: communal land other than rice land, lands which were used for crops other than rice and the settlement lands

duong loa: a portion of patrimony devoted to care of a living member of the previous generation

huong hoa: a part of the family patrimony (in rice fields and other property) which are set aside to pay the expense of maintaining an ancestor's cult

khau phan: the individual share in the division of *cong dien*

ky dien: a family worship property to be used to celebrate the anniversary of the death of an ancestor

thien back nien chi ke: a property for which a purpose has been designated, literally, 'to make the work last for hundreds of thousands of years'

tu dan dien, tu dan tho: communal land over which the central government had no controls; this land was often set aside for ritual purposes

tu dien: private rice fields, rice fields which were the patrimony of families

tuyet tu: a family worship property, devoted to the cult of a relative who died without heir

Other Terms

corvée: public labour obligation, the obligation to devote a certain amount of labour to public purposes, under the direction of village or central government authorities (a French term)

dia bo: traditional land taxation list

xviii

dien co: a credit agreement which gave the use of land as a pledge; not permanent possession

dinh: house of the village spirit, housed the spirit of some revered person, usually the founder of the village, meeting house

giap: neighbourhood, *giap* is usually translated as 'Hamlet' but this translation gives the wrong connotation because a hamlet is a small village, a *giap* is an integral part of a village, a division of a village

ho: extended family

hoa: Vietnamese term for the Chinese minority

hui: a mutual credit society

mai-lai-thuc: option to repurchase

mau: 0.36 hectare; 0.9 acre

nghia thuong: common reserve granary of the village

ngoai dinh: non-registered person, a person not registered on the tax list of the village

ngu-cu, dan-lau, or *dan-ngoai*: alien persons who simply reside in the village , those not registered on the village list (*so hang xa*)

sao: one tenth of *mau*, 0.09 acre

so dinh: the list of persons registered in the village who are called upon to pay personal taxes, usually males between the ages of 18 and 60. The right to a share of public land is granted to persons on this list

so hang xa, *so lang*: the village list, the list of persons who are registered in the village

thoc: one fifteenth of a *sao*, 0.006 acre

truong toc: the administrator of *huong hoa*, the family cult land, usually the eldest son

xa: village

1 Peasants and Socialism

'The Vietnamese revolution is in the main a revolution to liberate the peasantry.'[1] (Nguyen Khac Vien (ed.) *Vietnamese Studies*, Hanoi)

Volumes have been written about the American intervention in Vietnam and mistakes Americans made there. Journalists have written in great detail about the dependence of the Saigon government and its corruption. We have vivid pictures of the moral degradation accompanying US intervention – the drugs, prostitution and atrocities. Millions of Americans were awakened to the realities of what US intervention in other countries means. Our sources told us much about the USA and its political system but little about Vietnam, so that our picture of Vietnam and the Vietnamese is still clouded.

To the average Westerner, Vietnam is an agglomeration of huts in the countryside with rice paddies and graveyards or a Saigon city slum. Vietnam is 'Charlie', an elusive and effective fighter. Our stereotyped picture of Vietnam tells us nothing which could inform us why Vietnam became socialist. The appeal of the National Liberation Front (NLF) is usually explained in terms of the NLF being the only alternative to a corrupt and dependent US-supported government. The deep-seated reasons why the Vietnamese supported a communist-led revolution have not yet been fully explored.

The strength of the Vietnamese resistance to American intervention was based, predominantly, on the Vietnamese peasantry and the National Liberation Front's programme which mobilised and united them. The Saigon government controlled most cities until the very end of their regime while the NLF was most successful in the countryside. The reasons for the peasants' strong allegiance to the NLF will be analysed in the following chapters of this study. Briefly, many of the NLF's structures were similar to collective institutions in the pre-colonial (traditional) Vietnamese village and this encouraged peasant support. Most importantly, the Vietnamese peasants' support of the NLF was based on the Liberation Front's support of the peasants' rights to land as opposed to the landlords' claims in the countryside. This book offers answers to questions about Vietnam's transformation to socialism based on an analysis of the Vietnamese system of landholding in the countryside and how this system was

1

affected first by French colonialism and, later, by American intervention. The historical transformation of property and production in the
Vietnamese village is the key to understanding the Vietnamese
transition to socialism.

THE VIETNAMESE

The Vietnamese have been permanent settlers of the Red River Valley
since 200 BC. Throughout their long history they have cultivated rice
in the lowlands. As sedentary people, they developed a deep
attachment to their respective communities and the land their
ancestors tilled. Within the geographic boundaries of Vietnam there
are also various ethnic minorities who are predominantly highland
rice-cultivators. Some of these people, for example, the Meo, practice
slash-and-burn agriculture. They migrate into a forested area, burn off
the vegetation, use the soil until its fertility is exhausted, and then
move on. The institutions of these mountain peoples are not within the
scope of this study, although they may show us some insights into the
origins of Vietnamese society.

We are concerned here with the ethnic Vietnamese who comprise 90
per cent of the population of Vietnam. Unlike the mountain tribes, the
Vietnamese have historically been a unified people, both culturally
and politically. Their basic social structure has varied little throughout
the country, the most important groupings being the patriarchal
extended family, the neighbourhood and the village or commune.
Village organisation and land tenure have been similar everywhere.
The Vietnamese language has been a unifying element, and although
there are several dialects, the people from north to south can
understand one another.

Throughout most of their history, the Vietnamese have been
centrally administered with subdivisions down to the village level
implementing administrative decisions. From the fifteenth century
until the nineteenth, this central administration operated through the
institution of the mandarinate. Only during a short period in the
precolonial history of the Vietnamese was regionalism effective in
dividing the country – for 150 years, from 1620 to 1774, the Trinh
family in the north and the Nguyen family in the south ruled
separately. Late in the nineteenth century the French, for their own
administrative purposes, ignored the traditional Vietnamese unity and
divided the country into three states, Tonkin, Annam and Cochinch-

ina. This division was a colonial intervention with no precedent in Vietnamese history.

Centralised control in the Vietnamese context was very necessary and important because the canal and dike system had to be maintained throughout the country. The Emperor had to be an organiser of water-control projects in order to protect his people from floods and ensure agricultural production. A strong central control was also necessary for military reasons. There were dangers from the large Chinese empire to the north, from the hill tribes in the mountains and from lowland Indo-Chinese people such as the Cham and the Khmer to the south. A large centrally controlled army had to be maintained to guard against these dangers.

The emperor was the symbol of unity of the Vietnamese people. He was a protector-figure but more a figure of fatherly concern for his people than one of aloofness. As protector of agriculture he would actually plough the first furrow each year. He was responsible for caring for his people and ensuring that the crops were good. If his people were prospering this was his responsibility. However, if for whatever reason the Vietnamese were not faring well, the emperor was held accountable. Droughts, floods or bad crop years were blamed on him. If the period of hard times continued, the emperor would lose the backing of his people and they would support the overthrow of his dynasty. This change of heart was expressed as the loss of the emperor's 'heaven-given mandate' but there was nothing metaphysical about the active support given to contenders for the throne during hard times. A Vietnamese historian, Le Thanh Khoi, described the emperor's position:

> The central power is embodied in the person of the emperor, the son of heaven who is invested with a 'mandate' to maintain the universal order. But the emperor reigns only for the good of his subjects. When he fails in his mission and causes misery and disorder, by his injustice or his tyranny, then he loses the mandate of heaven and the people assume the right to revolt.[2]

Vietnamese society, despite a strong central control, has always had its base in the rural village economy. From 85 to 90 per cent of the Vietnamese lived in rural villages before the arrival of the French and the colonial period did not change these proportions substantially. Therefore, devolopment of modern Vietnamese institutions can be understod only when studied within the context of the rural village economy where the large majority of the people have lived and where almost all production has been organised. The basic foodstuff, rice has always been produced in flooded paddy fields and the community has determined the use of most of the village fields and controlled water distribution among them. The control of production of handicraft items has also been shared between families and the village but the relative shares of control are variable and indistinct to the observer. We have a much clearer historical view of the production of agricultural goods, particularly rice, in the Vietnamese village and the collective property relations underlying this production.

Traditional rights, which were shared between the village and the patriarchal family, have formed the basis for social structures in the modern period. The Vietnamese have strong historical traditions of collective and family work at the village level, on which Vietnamese socialists currently rely.

THE USA ENCOUNTERS SOCIALISM IN VIETNAM

The US government was not able to develop an explanation of the success of the NLF in Vietnam for most of the war period. The friction of outside intervention through 'communist aggression' and 'invasion from the north' was the only establishment explanation of the war. For as long as possible, the US government ignored the mass support of southerners for the programmes of the NLF (sometimes called the *Viet Cong*) and they relied on allegations of aggression from the Communist north. According to the domino theory of communist aggression, the north had already 'fallen' to communism, presumably because of aggression from somewhere else, like the Soviet Union or China. This theory postulates that communism spreads like an aggressive disease unless checked by military aid combined with developmental aid from non-communist governments. The US government feared that unless it was checked in Vietnam, communism would spread throughout the rest of Southeast Asia and beyond.

The domino theory and the assumption that there was no local southern Vietnamese support for the Viet Cong was challenged in the USA by the media, by anti-war activists and by a segment of the US government itself. After the war had dragged on for years, the popularity of the NLF became increasingly apparent.

A new theory, developed to accommodate the new liberal view of reality, explained the success of socialism as an alternative course for an underdeveloped country encountering the modern world from the perspective of their revolutionary experience and nationalism. An urban-based government in South Vietnam which was ineffective, and whose US government sponsors were not particularly helpful, caused a vacuum in leadership which was filled by the communists. For an understanding of their failures in Vietnam, Americans turned to the French experts on Vietnam for answers. The works of Pierre Gourou and Chares Robequain were consulted and the perspectives of Paul Mus were relied on. The teachings of Mus reached Americans mostly through the interpretation of his American student, John McAlister. McAlister and Mus developed an analysis of the reasons for the success of Vietnamese socialism in their book, *The Vietnamese and Their Revolution*.[3] This book showed considerable insight into the success of communism in Vietnam. Theirs was the best of the liberal establishment analyses.

These authors did not question the basic legitimacy of the US intervention or the legitimacy of French Colonialism. The problem they addressed was the American and French lack of understanding of Vietnam and Vietnamese traditions. A more complete understanding, on the part of the communists, of Vietnamese history and culture, led to their greater success. The failure of those Vietnamese groups supported by the French and Americans was a failure of knowledge and political policy.

According to the writing of Mus and McAlister, there were three alternative political forces within Vietnam: the pro-Western urban-oriented governments, the village-based revolutionaries, and the religious sects (the *Hoa Hao* and the *Cao Dai*.) The sects were interested in abolishing modern ideas and this made them unacceptable to most Vietnamese. Traditional Vietnamese political patterns called for the integration of new ideas in a comprehensive new form, not for their complete rejection, and this accounted for the sects' ultimate lack of success.

Mus and McAlister saw the Marxists as having produced a solution for Vietnam which incorporated Western ideas into the communal and egalitarian ideals of the people. According to these scholars, this solution was more viable than that of the sects but the potential problem with this plan for the traditional Vietnamese political pattern was that there was no supernatural dimension to the NLF solution.[4] Socialism involved a new political contract of the people with one another and heaven did not enter into it.

It seemed that the Vietnamese were actually able to accept a more human-centred, non-metaphysical, approach. Probable causes of this outcome were the humanist basis of the Confucian philosophy and the extent of modernisation in Vietnam. Frances Fitzgerald was, in fact, proved correct in her perception that the moral nature of the socialist solution was sufficient and heaven need not play a part.[5]

In comparing the success of village-based NLF revolutionaries with the urban-oriented pro-Westerners, McAlister and Mus used three criteria, (i) the comprehensiveness of their strategy, (ii) their use of the traditional idiom, and (iii) their awareness of the traditional concept of revolution and what it entailed. They first showed how the Marxists were successful by these criteria and they then developed a pro- gramme for the Western-oriented group to change their strategy and reverse their losses.

In terms of the comprehensiveness of their programme the Marxists had a well-defined concept of order and an inclusive political programme with answers to questions ranging from individual behaviour to the realm of state power. Each village in the liberated areas had associations for soldiers, workers, peasants, women, and old people. There were programmes for education and health as well as projects which increased agricultural production. The Marxist organ- isation of society was as comprehensive as the Confucian organisation. By contrast, the programmes of the Western-dominated governments had been partial, solving some problems and bringing about others. These programmes did not fit into the traditional pattern of an encompassing social philosophy and a comprehensive programme which fitted this world view.

Another reason for the Marxists' success was that they made use of the traditional Vietnamese idiom in expressing their concepts of socialism, thus tying together the new and the old. For example, Ho Chi Minh used the words *Xa Hoi Hoa* to symbolise the word socialism or to 'put in common'. *Xa* refers to the traditional village or commune, *hoi* is a word for society and *hoa* connotes the action of putting society under a new system or 'virtue'.[6] The implication, not stated directly by Mus and McAlister, was that the Western-oriented governments, by not linking their programmes to the traditional Vietnamese idiom, failed to make themselves understandable to the villagers.

Closely related to the point about the importance of an inclusive political programme is the Vietnamese concept that one cannot change a part of society without changing the whole. According to Mus and McAlister, the Vietnamese have no concept of evolutionary change. The peasants put up with all kinds of abuses from government and landlord classes until a time of social crises when they decide they will put up with no more and there has to be a change in the system (which McAlister translated as a new 'virtue'). At this time there must be a new 'mandate from heaven', a comprehensive new programme for society because the old leaders cannot be successful.[7] This traditional concept of revolutionary change seems to coincide with the Marxist theory of revolutionary change. The post-1945 attempts of the French and the later attempts of the Americans to influence Vietnam were simply too close to the colonial solution to be viable. The Vietnamese were ready for a new 'virtue' and what they saw from the Western-oriented governments was more of the old.

The demonstration of similar political patterns in Confucianism and Marxism by Mus and McAlister was convincing, but only to a point. The Marxist concept of revolution and the Confucian concept of periodic uprisings and the rise to power of a new dynasty have similarities but there are also profound differences. Marxist revolution connotes change in the basic social structure. Revolution followed a cyclical pattern in Vietnamese history and with the exception of the estalishment of the Le Dynasty in the fifteenth century, dynastic changes meant redistribution within the same basic societal structures. The periodic revolutions which established a new dynasty and distributed property of supporters of the old dynasty among the peasants did not challenge the basic Confucian system. The Le Dynasty's imposition of a completely structured mandarin system on a wide basis at the expense of the nobility and Buddhist clergy was the only change in recorded precolonial Vietnamese history which could be considered a revolution in the Marxist sense. The Marxists in Vietnam organised a revolution which involved much more pervasive institutional change than the traditional revolutions which replaced an old with a new dynasty.

The traditional political patterns pointed out by McAlister and Mus aid our understanding of the success of the NLF in Vietnam. What Mus and McAlister did not make clear was why the US-supported Saigon government did not simply adopt the same traditional patterns. Reading from their analysis one might conclude that failure to do so was simply a result of a failure of analysis, of political acumen. The traditional patterns, however, could not have been adopted wholesale by the US-supported Saigon government. In omitting analysis of the dynamics of the establishment of capitalist markets in Vietnam in the colonial period, Mus and McAlister miss the introduction of individualism and individual property rights. A comprehensive and collective solution for the Vietnamese state and Vietnamese village came into fundamental conflict with the institutions of individual property rights which were established during the colonial period. A capitalist property system with a comprehensive set of rights held in the hands of individuals was established at that time. The preservation of these individual property rights by the US-supported governments made it impossible to adopt the collective power and comprehensive programmes which were suggested by Mus and McAlister. The Saigon government could not support the continued development of capitalist private property and still support comprehensive collective policies of the order necessary to be consistent with Vietnam's traditional political patterns.

The war persisted, despite the influence of the more liberal Americans on Vietnam political policy. As with the French before them, the Americans seemed to be unable to initiate policies which would produce expected results. One example was the introduction of new high-yielding varieties of rice. Production increased with the use of these hybrids but the distribution of income became more skewed, resulting in even less support for the Saigon government and US aid programmes among most of the peasantry. US and Saigon government military policy met with similar frustrations. Individual commanders thought that they saw 'a light at the end of the tunnel' but, generally, it seemed that the war would never end.

In 1972, Frances Fitzgerald, another author strongly influenced by Paul Mus, wrote an indictment of the US involvement in Vietnam which became a national best-seller. Fitzgerald took Mus and McAlister's argument one stage further and determined that the US-sponsored government was incapable of a complete change on the order of Vietnamese revolutions of the past. Only with the withdrawal of American troops would such a revolution be possible. Along with some wishful thinking about the possibility of a coalition government, Fitzgerald took the clear position that anti-Americanism had developed to such an extent in Vietnam that no permanent political solution in Vietnam was possible while American intervention continued. This was a justification for withdrawal which Americans wanted to hear.

A problem with Fitzgerald's perspective was her explanation of the development of socialism in Vietnam. She saw the Vietnamese as changing more through psychological manipulation than through change in their own economic and political structures. She presented traditional peasant psychology as meek and self-effacing, particularly with respect to the peasant's behaviour towards landlords. Fitzgerald saw the changed attitudes and behaviour of the peasants toward landlords in the modern period as the work of the NLF's agitation and propaganda campaigns. According to her, the NLF's solution was mainly a psychological one – the Vietnamese peasants had internalised their anger towards their landlords and the NLF taught them how to express their anger outwardly.[8]

Fitzgerald's psychological explanation neglected the social and economic transformation of the Vietnamese village during the colonial period – the development of private property and markets – and its effects on the attitudes of the Vietnamese peasants. Her analysis did not differentiate between two very different types of landlords. Traditional landlords were often elderly village residents who rented out their land because they were too old to farm and these landlords were respected in the village. Landlords in the second group were new since the colonial period. They were created in the process of concentration of landholding by capitalist market forces. They were large (often absentee) landlords whose identification was with the city, not with the village, and they were scorned by the villagers. Lacking this differentiation, Fitzgerald thought that the landlords left the village solely because of *Viet Minh* and *Viet Cong* influence on villagers' attitudes.[9] In fact, changes in peasant attitudes were primarily caused by changes in rural property relations and the creations of large-scale estates. (The transformation of the Vietnamese countryside through the development of private property and a land-market will be discussed in Chapters 4–7.)

Fitzgerald suggested that the NLF used not only the peasants' hatred of the landlords, but also the psychology of the family to reverse the traditional relationship of father–son dominance used by former leaders such as mandarins. According to her, cadres treated the villagers as parents instead and received from them the permissive attitudes which Vietnamese mothers reserve for their children:

> Whereas Vietnamese mandarins had always taken the formal, Chinese father–son relationship as the model for statehood, [this front officer] seemed now to be offering the Vietnamese mother–child relationship as a substitute. Because to him the soldiers came from the people – as a child comes from his mother's womb – so they should not live in a state of repressed conflict with the people, showing only their 'self-control'.[10]

Later in her analysis, Fitzgerald developed another reason for the good relationship between NLF cadres and the villagers. The NLF cadres depended on the villages for material support and had to treat them with respect while the Saigon government cadres got their rations from the Americans and were therefore not dependent on the villagers. This was a more important factor in the NLF cadres' good relationships with villagers, and the psychological explanation which Fitzgerald presented first is over-stated.

Fitzgerald underestimated land reform as an issue in Vietnam and this contributed to her misunderstanding of the NLF. The US government's argument was that the Saigon government had most support where the landlords were most powerful. It could not be land reform which made Vietnamese support the NLF because the NLF had the most support where landlords were weakest. Fitzgerald did not attack the fallacies of the government argument or its conclusions. Instead, she depicted the NLF as a force which was generally reactive to the Saigon government support of foreign and landlord interest.[11] The positive decision of the stronger centralised villages of the Central Lowlands, with fewer landlords, to support the NLF programme and the NLF's strong land reform were therefore not given the emphasis in her analysis which these factors deserved. In not emphasising the impact of market capitalism and changes in landlord-tenant relations in the Vietnamese village, Fitzgerald missed much of the basis of the revolution she described. Her analysis of the Vietnamese personality was separated from any analysis of the changing Vietnamese social structure.

CONTEMPORARY REASSESSMENTS

There are a number of scholars who have recently introduced analyses of the failure of the USA and the success of the NLF in Vietnam. Historians Alexander Woodside and William Duiker have analysed the period previous to US intervention and traced the success of communism from this earlier period.[12] A political scientist, James C. Scott, and an economist, Samuel Popkin, have analysed peasant motivations and attempted to understand peasant choices favouring the NLF.[13]

Contemporary historians' explanations of the success of the NLF seem to hinge on the assumption that Vietnam was already 'won over' to communism when the US intervention started. The really important battles between the capitalist and communist alternatives are perceived as being earlier, in the 1920s, 1930s and 1940s. From this perspective, the lack of any viable nationalist, anti-communist, movement in the earlier period with the strength of Ho Chi Minh's Vietnamese Communist Party predetermined the later outcome of US intervention.

Insights from events in the 1930s and 1940s certainly inform us about the Vietnamese allegiance to socialism. The drift of contemporary thinking of authors like Alexander Woodside, in *Community and Revolution in Vietnam*, and William Duiker, in *The Rise of Nationalism in Vietnam 1900–1941*, seems to be that the early communists linked themselves more satisfactorily to Vietnamese traditions than did the non-communists.[14] These authors followed in the traditional analysis of Paul Mus in this respect. The unique aspects of their analysis came with their stress on the international connections of the the communists. Connections with the international communist organisation, the Comintern, aided the Vietnamese Communists greatly, both financially and politically, in establishing their legitimacy. The international legitimacy provided by the Comintern connection was seen by Woodside as similar to the earlier legitimising of Confucian scholars by China.[15]

The implication is that if there were *competing communist organisations* in Vietnam without the Comintern connection, they would not have fared as well as Ho Chi Minh's party. (In fact, the Trotskyists groups did not succeed.) This is a valid but moot point. The importance of the legitimising influence of the Comintern is questionable when comparisons are made with non-communist organisations. If there had been a viable non-communist nationalist movement in Vietnam, links could have been developed with nationalist movements in China, India or elsewhere. The USA was certainly interested in financing nationalist, anti-communist movements in the 1940s.

The works of Woodside and Duiker are important in providing information about the development of communism in Vietnam. Historical analysis which centres on the northern part of Vietnam in an earlier period, nevertheless falls short of providing a comprehensive analysis of the success of the NLF in the south in the 1960s and 1970s.

Recent attempts to explain the actions of Vietnamese peasants have come from two contemporary analyses of Vietnamese peasant motivation. James C. Scott has explained Vietnamese peasant behaviour in terms of a moral imperative that was not understood by the Americans. The peasants chose the NLF programme because of their subsistence welfare concerns which were not part of the programme of the American supporters. In refuting Scott, Popkin insisted that rationality, in the neoclassical economics sense, was the real criterion by which the Vietnamese peasants chose communism. The communists simply offered the peasants a better deal. Presumably, if the US advisors had used neoclassical economic analysis more extensively, and social, psychological and political analysis less, US policy in Vietnam would have been more successful.

Scott's major contribution in his book was a perspective on colonialism, its arbitrariness, and the massive deterioration of traditional class relations that it engendered. He wrote about the 'blind rigor' with which colonial taxes were imposed by administrations which ignored local crop failures or other extenuating circumstances.[16] He clearly showed some of the fiscal causes of the cruelty of the colonial administration and the consequences of their impact on the Southeast Asian peasants.

The most illuminating part of Scott's description is his understanding of the newly-opened-up areas of cultivation in Vietnam and Burma. These areas were tied in closely with the market economy from the first when the colonialists aided in bringing them under cultivation.[17] In these areas Scott found that, at least for some time after they were opened up, the income of the cultivators did not decrease; in fact, they were better off than producers in the past and producers in other parts of the country. The problem in these areas was the eventual deterioration of rural class relations – the peasants lost power to a small class of large landlords. The landlord–peasant relationship also lost its traditional patronage aspects and became very arbitrary. This was not seen as a severe problem as long as the price of rice was high and subsistence was not too difficult. When the depression hit and the price of rice fell, the arbitrary aspects of the new landlord–peasant relationship fell into stark relief and there was agitation against the new system.

The major problem with Scott's work is his generalisation of the concept of 'peasant' and his Western bias in his understanding of rural life. In his introduction and at many points throughout the book he assumed a direct relationship between European peasants and the Southeast Asian peasants about whom he was writing.[18] He saw no essential difference between the French peasants of the eighteenth and nineteenth centuries who still might have had some common grazing land and the peasants of Vietnam with their periodically distributed common cultivated land and with their village- and regionally-controlled irrigation and drainage systems. The French peasants to whom he referred were very individualist compared with the Vietnamese peasants of a century and a half later. The French peasants were small holders with extensive private property rights and they chose to support a leader, Napoleon, who was interested in preserving the rights of small holders of property. The Vietnamese peasants supported a quite different political movement and this choice came from their perception of their own interests which were quite different from the interests of the French peasants of the eighteenth and nineteenth centuries.

To Scott, the individual patriarch, or family head, was the universal decision-maker in Vietnam both before and after the colonial intervention. This patriarch, according to Scott, had to contend with the flexible taxes of the traditional regime and later the arbitrary taxes of the colonial regime, but it was he who made all of the production decisions for the rural population. Scott underestimated the role of the village government and the neighbourhood in an agricultural system where power and decision-making was actually shared by these groups. The village notables controlled the distribution of water and the distribution of communal lands and the heads of neighbourhood groups controlled the reciprocal labour exchanges. None of this division of responsibility was included in Scott's analysis.

Scott's individualistic analysis of the Vietnamese peasant family and his emphasis on the decision-making of the family head, with his neglect of the importance of village and neighbourhood, led to many mistakes in his analysis. The advantage of the traditional government system over the colonial system, according to Scott, was its flexibility and lack of rigidity in response to local problems and crop failures. This was, in fact, only part of the traditional social security system. Land and produce were shared in the village through an elaborate system which insured against individual, family or neighbourhood disaster. (This system is described in Chapter 3 of this book.) During precolonial times, the state organised large-scale water-control systems with large dams and networks of canals on the regional level. The central government collected stores of grain in good years which it distributed in poor harvest years.

Another problem is Scott's use of the concept 'morality' to describe peasants' views of their rights and responsibilities. In most cases, peasants' views of social justice are based on their view of equity and of tradition, and not on 'morality', which connotes a religious mysticism. 'Morality' seems to have very little to do with 'subsistence', which Scott argued is what peasants were predominantly concerned with. Survival is, in fact, a very material concern for those who are on the very edge of it.

Even if we concern ourselves only with Scott's subsistence argument, and leave out morality, there are great problems with his analysis. His view was that the peasants see social justice as a subsistence guaranteed to them by a magnanimous upper class. Peasants, like everyone else, have ideas about social justice which go beyond mere tactics for survival. Social justice for the Vietnamese peasant includes standards concerning equality of remuneration for equal amounts of labour and standards regarding public control of property in land. Labour in the pre-colonial village was exchanged in reciprocal patterns. In the traditional village, public control of land and the distribution of water was in the hands of the village notables who were elected by the village patriarchs. In the more modern village, recently under capitalist economic relations in the south, hired labour gangs worked in a socialised way on land held individually by the rich. Small tenants farmed land which they rented from larger absentee landlords. These landless labourers and tenants joined a resistance against the landlords and rich peasants and transformed their villages on a more egalitarian model consistent with the Vietnamese collectivist past.

By neglecting collectivity and public decision-making in the Vietnamese rural economy, Scott opened the way for attack by a neoclassical economist who contended that the rationality of neoclassical utility analysis is appropriate for understanding the motivation of Vietnamese peasants. Samuel Popkin challenged Scott's perspective that subsistence is the central factor in peasant calculations and that when peasant subsistence is challenged, peasants rebel.[19] He showed that sometimes peasants rebel when their subsistence is squeezed, sometimes they do not. The prime factor which determines whether peasants will rebel or not is whether a viable alternative presents itself. In the case of Vietnam, the viable alternative was the Vietnamese Communist Party and the peasants made the 'rational' choice of supporting them.

Popkin saw Vietnamese peasants in the period of US intervention as being essentially small-enterprise owners. He saw corporate villages, with their restrictions on private land ownership, as an historical phenomenon with no contemporary relevance. Popkin's modern peasants lived in open villages and engaged in market activities within a legal framework where private property and western-style contracts were established.

Whereas others have seen peasants, including Vietnamese peasants, as a group caught in between new and old realities, Popkin saw them as small farmers operating according to new economic rules. Popkin viewed capitalism as having become fully established in Vietnam. He saw this establishment as largely to the benefit of Vietnamese farmers. Popkin made the same implicit assumption as other analysts with respect to capitalist alternatives. Presumably, if there had been a viable pro-US opposition, peasants could have made a different choice. The contradiction between US support of capitalist enterprise in Vietnam and the social and economic necessity of collective decision-making in rural Vietnam was not seen by either Scott or Popkin.

Economic decisions were not made either 'rationally' or 'morally' by Vietnamese peasants. Decisions were made by the village leaders and the family patriarchs in the context of traditional and modern realities. In this book I shall show peasant motivations as predominantly determined by the mixture of old and new political-economic interrelationships and old and new technologies.

A VIETNAMESE VIEW

The Vietnamese themselves have views of the success of socialism in Vietnam which are different from the perspectives of Americans. The perspectives of Nguyen Khac Vien on the subject are internationally known. They reflect a Marxist approach to Vietnamese history.

To Vien, the pre-capitalist stage of Vietnamese history, which he called the feudal period, was actually divided into two parts. First was the pre-fifteenth century of decentralism and control by the local nobility. The second period began when the Le Dynasty imposed a more centralised mandarin-style administrative structure with the emperor's representative being chosen through competitive examination of the Confucian classics. Strong, decentralised villages and peasant ownership of land were features of this second system. Of the two periods, Vien definitely preferred the Confucian period and he wrote approvingly of the defeat of the nobility and the rise of the mandarins and a peasant class of owners.

To Vien, transition to socialism in Vietnam had its roots in Confucian traditions. Confucianism was divided into popular and official Confucianism and the defenders of these traditions were the village scholars on the one hand and the highly-placed mandarins on the other. He described Confucianism as a humanist philosophy with two theses, the *ly* and *khi*. The *ly* was the primacy of the principal objects and those mandarins who believed in the primacy of the *ly* tended to believe in the celestial origin of royal power, while those village scholars who believed in the *khi*, the primacy of the substance of things, were more likely to attribute the origin of royal power to the people. The *ly* mandarins enacted strict legislation and put down peasant uprisings. The village scholars, on the other hand, were likely to be leaders of peasant revolutions to overthrow the current dynasty in hard times.[20]

In the colonial period, modern village scholars tried to follow the traditions of popular Confucianism. They failed because they lacked modern weapons and a political doctrine adapted to the new times. The scholars in traditional Vietnam had fought on the basis of humanism; they always wanted to replace an inhuman king with a more humane one. With Western ideas came the concepts of democracy and science. The concept that people should participate in politics came to Vietnam through the writings of Rousseau and Montesquieu. Technical knowledge came from French engineers and scientists. The study of science and machines as well as democracy were not the province of the traditional scholar. They were the province of the modern, French-educated scholars.[21]

Nguyen Khac Vien described the first Marxist cadres as being similar, in many respects, to the Confucian village scholars. They were 'petty intellectuals' who had not finished their baccalaureate degrees and who worked as clerks in the colonial administration and in factories and on plantations, Some were, in fact, village teachers. They carried on the tradition of old-time revolutionary scholars by living in the villages and teaching and organising peasants over a period of time.[22] But what they taught included principles of political participation and they had a knowledge of modern weaponry.

As an explanation for the development of Marxism in Vietnam (ahead of its development in most Christian and Moslem countries), Vien pointed to the humanism of the Confucian tradition. Confucians concentrate men's thoughts on political and social problems rather than on concerns of heaven or the 'other world'. Furthermore, the Confucian man accepts collective discipline which is important in socialist systems. Individualism and personal interests, along with individual interaction with a 'superior force', are concepts of philosophies in other parts of the world which provide a stumbling block for socialist thinking.[23] Vietnamese tradition, on the other hand, put the Vietnamese people in an advantageous position for receiving a humanist philosophy.

The identification of traditional Vietnam so closely with Confucianism, even popular Confucianism, must be questioned. The traditional village operated within a mandarin structure where Confucian values were important but property relations and distribution mechanism in the village were also fundamental in maintaining a value system which was only partly Confucian. The traditional village in Vietnam was different from the village in China. We miss that difference if we look at rural Vietnam mostly through the philosophy of Confucianism. For example, mutual assistance through neighbourhood groups was important in Vietnam although Confucian values focused on the patriarchal extended family as a source of labour. Strong peasant proprietors were necessary for the preservation of the patriarchal obedience structure in Confucianism. The periodic redistribution of large percentages, and in a few villages, all the village's land severely limited the power of the individual patriarchs in Vietnam. These specifically Vietnamese neighbourhood and village institutions influenced their Buddhist and Confucian philosophies and their animistic beliefs. Confucianism was the dominant but not the exclusive philosophy of the later pre-colonial period in Vietnam.

It was the system of property and methods of production in the pre-colonial period which lay at the base of the Vietnamese emphasis on that part of Confucian philosophy which attributed the source of royal power to the people. Collective institutions at the village level and the strength of the village as a production unit provided the village scholars with a strong base. It was this traditional collectivity which was later broken down by the imposition of capitalist markets and private property.

Capitalist markets led, through a process described later in this book, to the creation of a powerful class of large landlords who controlled most of the land and rented to a large group of dispossessed peasants. Wage labour replaced collective labour and renting replaced communal land and peasant holdings. Marxism united the peasantry with urban workers in its fight against the landlords and foreign interests. Marxism was popular in Vietnam for reasons discussed by Vien, but also, and more importantly, from its appeal to the tenants, organised rural labourers, and workers operating in the capitalist sector of the Vietnamese economy.

THE VIETNAMESE VILLAGE IN TRANSITION

The strength of the National Liberation Front and the weakness of the Saigon government are much more based on differential programmes in the villages of Vietnam than indicated by any of the work on Vietnam reviewed in this chapter. When property, production and distribution in the Vietnamese villages is analysed and we look at the process of change, we can see the inegalitarian effects of the establishment of capitalist markets in the colonial period. We can also see the inequality of small-scale capitalist innovation in agriculture when this is added to market penetration in the modern period. The NLF was able to organise a cohesive village structure which enforced reduction in inequalities. They were also able to organise water control, which was a solution to some production problems in the village.

This study focuses on the Vietnamese village and the patriarchal family in traditional and modern periods, and shows the process of change in property relationships and politics. Close analysis of the villages and families as building blocks of Vietnamese society exposes social relationships more clearly than if we look mostly at political and administrative centres and trade networks. The village in Vietnam has long participated in organising production along with the neighbourhood and the patriarchal family. The study of changes over time within the village forms an important basis for understanding economic and political changes in Vietnam which formed the roots of the development of socialism.

The chapters of this book alternate between descriptions of change in the broader political economy and a focus on production and distribution in the actual villages. Analyses of the microeconomy of the village are developed for traditional times, for the post-colonial period in the south and for the 1960s collectivised village in the north. These specific descriptions of the effects of overall political, social and economic change on village institutions illuminate the analysis of the process of change. Because of these descriptions of the microeconomies, the impact of national political policies can be better understood.

Studying precolonial Vietnam is a starting-point for describing the process of change and resistance to outside interventions in the modern period. Through looking at Vietnam in the traditional period, we can more carefully identify the significant structural changes in Vietnamese society coming with colonialism, US intervention and then socialism. We can also see how the basic self-sufficiency and cohesive strength of the traditional village made possible resistance to certain capitalist institutions supported by the French and the Americans.

Analysis of traditional Vietnam is also a means for understanding the basic structures of property, production and exchange which existed in some parts of Vietnam until very recently. During the colonial period the North and Central parts of Vietnam were merely protectorates of the French rather than colonies, and penetration of capitalist institutions was not nearly as pervasive as in the South. Resistance to colonialism and American intervention were strongest in the areas where traditional institutions had survived. These areas have played a very important part in the building of socialist movements in the modern period.

The dynamic of change in property relationships in the traditional period was a circular process. There were periods of strong central government control over land tenure and water control alternating with periods of failure of the central government in the upkeep of dikes and dams and failure to provide protection against usurpation of communal land in the villages. A dynasty would gain power and change the distribution of wealth in the villages through a land reform which usually consisted of nothing more nor less than the distribution of land expropriated from supporters of the previous dynasty, among the poor peasants. The new dynasty would organise massive water-control and drainage projects to protect agricultural production and expand areas under cultivation. Then, as the dynasty grew older, it tended to slacken off in upkeep of the water-control system and the protection of communal land in the village. Rival political factions would develop, usually in underground or secret-society fashion. Then, after a period of destructive typhoons or drought, lack of sufficient attention to the water-control infrastructure would become obvious to the peasants suffering from famine. At that time one of the new political factions would challenge the dynasty and receive the support of the peasantry in setting up a new dynasty. I have already mentioned the peasants' tendency to support a revolutionary new political movement under these conditions.

Looking at the traditional village, we see a centrally administered collective unit with closely controlled water distribution, an essential part of wet rice cultivation. Communal land was part of the community life which was rich with celebrations and village-wide activities. Basic welfare needs of the villagers were preserved through a system of communal land and village and state stores of rice. Within a structure of redistributive exchange of land and agricultural products, and reciprocal exchange of labour, production and distribution were managed in the village on a relatively equal basis.

Yet the pre-colonial village was not a Utopia and it was not egalitarian in several respects. One class of people particularly, the women, were not even second-class citizens; they were not considered citizens at all. The village leaders, called notables, were chosen by the male members of the village and they held considerable power over everyone in the village. Most males, including young boys and old men, but excluding new residents, were inscribed on the village list of citizens. New residents were generally not considered citizens for their life times but their sons could become citizens. Later, with Western intervention and colonialism, restrictions on residence were lessened and a substantial number of non-inscribed people entered the villages. With colonialism, also, a significant number of males lost their rights to communal land and their membership in the village. An underclass of males with no political rights was then established. In the traditional period the citizens on the list chose their notables on the criteria of age, which reputedly brought wisdom; wealth, which brought free time to devote to village activities; and mandarin title, which brought prestige.

Colonialism

In the mid-nineteenth century the French colonised the southern part of Vietnam and gained control of the north by the end of the century. With the French promotion of trade and commerce, colonialists entered Vietnam and looked for owners, someone with whom to make contact, someone with title to the land. The 'owners' found or created by the colonial government often belonged to the traditionally powerful classes of mandarins and notables who had some understanding of what the colonial leaders were looking for. The land was surveyed and titles were issued to a class of newly-designated 'owners'. The traditional system of rights was abrogated by those who most readily adapted to the new market economy and saw the advantages of coming under the control of the colonial administration.

Where the colonialists decided that the peasants had a majority of rights in land, ownership later became concentrated by market forces. Hla Myint has described the process which accompanied the introduction of production for market exchange in pre-capitalist economies in two phases which correspond precisely to the Vietnamses situation.[24] In the first phase, people produced their own subsistence needs and for the new export markets only on a part-time basis. Later in the second phase, they began to specialise devoting all or most of their resources to market production. They were now also committed to buying their subsistence rations on the market. The peasants became fully involved with market economies with their lives guided by fluctuating market prices. Given their ignorance of rapidly changing market conditions, they frequently became heavily indebted. Where land was alienable, as in the southern region of Vietnam, they lost their land in default of loans and were reduced to the status of tenants or landless labourers. Money-lenders and landlords then collected a large portion of the crop and sold it to exporters.

The characteristics of the system established during the colonial period were different in the South from those in the Central Lowlands and the North. The South completed the second phase of the opening-up process already described, while the Central Lowlands and the North were, for the most part, still in the first phase. There was little change in methods of production in agriculture in the South. After an initial expansion of cultivated area through improvements in the water-distribution system, there was also little increase in total production of rice. Large amounts of rice exports were maintained through an increased inequality of income as three-quarters of the peasants were forced off their land and became tenants. The landlords fed the export market with their share of the produce from the expropriated land. With available cultivable land completely in use and increasing population growth, increased inequality of incomes was especially devastating to the peasantry of this area. The peasants could not combat these problems through the traditional method of extending the canal system to provide sufficient water control for double cropping. Private property prevented the kind of centralised village control necessary for this solution.

In the Central Lowlands and the North, in contrast, the cohesiveness of the village was not destroyed and the water-control system and double croppings were preserved. Absentee landlords with large holdings were the exception rather that the rule. These areas remained in the first phase of the opening-up process. There was some production for market exchange, but this was secondary and supplementary to the traditional mechanism of exchange in the village agriculture in these regions. Concentration of landholding which did occur here came about more through the traditional methods of usurpation of communal land than through the market mechanism. The practice of usurpation by those in power in the villages was encouraged by changes in administrative structures brought about under the French and their lack of enforcement of traditional laws against this practice. Increased property inequalities were more the result of the breakdown of the traditional system than of the imposition of market forces. Inequalities were consequently increased but were not as extensive as in the southern area.

Population continued to increase in the Central Lowlands and the North as well as the South. With the closing of the frontier, the problem of overpopulation could not be alleviated in the traditional manner by setting up new villages. Although the traditional village structure did not entirely break down in the Central Lowlands and the North, usurpation of communal lands, heavy colonial taxation and demands for corvée as well as population increases continuously decreased the welfare of the villages. The villagers were not able to put up stores of rice for poor harvest areas and the colonial state did not provide for disaster relief. Caught in this dilemma, the peasants were more than ready for communist solutions to their problems.

Vietnamese Resistance

Peasant revolts and isolated violent acts were committed against the French from the beginning of colonialisation. Despite this, only after 1925 was there an organised resistance movement which was capable of fighting a Western enemy which possessed technical sophistication. The form the movement took was a product of the historical period in which it was formed and the ideological education of its founders. The 1917 revolution in Russia and the formation of a world-wide anti-imperialist movement influenced Vietnamese youth who were looking for an anti-colonialist theory. The develoment of a socialist movement in France had a great impact on the resistance youth who were able to work and study there. These youths brought back Marxist–Leninist theory to Vietnam and they organised among Vietnamese peasants and workers.

During the First World War native industry had been built up in Vietnam using Western technology, since imported goods were so difficult to obtain. Workers' organisations were formed in these industries and these groups worked with similar organisations on French rubber plantations and in French mines. These worker organisations came together with Marxist–Leninist youth groups to form the Indochinese Communist Party in 1930. The Party then undertook the task of organising the majority of the Vietnamese not yet represented in their organisation – the peasantry. They cooperated with existing peasant groups and helped to form new mass peasant organisations during this period of depression, low agricultural prices and poor weather conditions in Vietnam. The Party was associated with the many peasant revolts during this period.

During the Second World War the Communist Party undertook a 'united front' policy, uniting peasant and worker organisations with anti-colonialist landlords and native capitalists who were anti-French. The united front organisations and the *Viet Minh* were led by the Party, which was now called the Vietnam Communist Party. The *Viet Minh* fought the War of Independence against the French (1945–54), and they were able to win permanent control of the northern half of Vietnam (including the North and part of the Central Lowlands), but not the southern half (the South and the rest of the Central Lowlands), which came under US influence when the French pulled out their troops.

Although the *Viet Minh* understood village collective institutions and the necessity for cooperation and village-level involvement in production decisions, they underestimated the strength of the peasant patriarchy. The *Viet Minh* eliminated the threat of landlords and distributed property to the individual families. When the communists then moved toward collectivisation, village middle-level peasant patriarchs acted to undercut cooperation on the order that the Party envisioned. As a result, in the present period, the Party has had to step back from its egalitarian goals and allow considerable family level private enterprise in order to build self-sufficiency in food production.

During the period of American intervention, another stage in the political-economic development of southern Vietnam began. Technological changes which developed in this period were made possible because of the resistance to landlords staged first by the *Viet Minh*, and later by the NLF. The *Viet Minh* had distributed land belonging to the French and French-supporting landlords in large areas of the south which they controlled during the War of Independence. The NLF continued and extended this policy in areas they controlled. Since the landlords had lost power in the countryside, the peasants were able to gain control of income which had formerly gone to rent payments. Many invested this income in new technology, and this was the beginning of a process of technical innovation in the rural economy. The introduction of chemical fertilizers came first and then the water-pump and new high-yielding rice varieties. These innovations were spread through the market system. Some richer farmers were able to acquire the essential amount of capital to use these innovations and other poorer farmers were not. A substantial amount of water control and a large amount of fertiliser were necessary to make use of the new rice varieties. A class of capitalist farmers developed in the countryside. They were, for the most part, former rich peasants who were able to take advantage of all of the new innovations. The situation in which some peasants benefited much more from the new technology than others, encouraged not only the enlargement of capitalist farms but also the adjunct of an increased use of the wage labour of former peasant-farmers who could not afford the innovations.

The NLF organisation in the South differed from the *Viet Minh* organisation in the North because of the different historical period in which it was formed, and the effects of greater capitalist development in the south of Vietnam. The Communist Party played less of a vanguard leadership role in organising the NLF than it had in organising the *Viet Minh*. The NLF was more truly an association of peasant, worker, intellectual and women's organisations. The northern peasants had been attracted to the collective ideals espoused by the Communist Party because of the similarity of these ideals to the traditional pattern. The southern peasants, in the modern era, were mostly rural workers who had much less recollection of the traditional patriarchal village. The rural workers in the South were much more able to understand the socialist message directly, rather than through the filter of Vietnamese tradition. They were more capable of organising themselves for participation in a modern socialist organisation. The participation of women, especially, was vastly increased in the NLF because of the destruction of the traditional form of patriarchal control in the village in the South. Women were therefore prominent in the leadership of the NLF at all levels in both military and civilian roles.

The NLF controlled large areas of the countryside during the war of national liberation waged against the USA and the Saigon government it supported. In the NLF areas, most of the profits from new innovations in agriculture were taxed away. The use of the new technology was less extensive than in the American influenced areas, but there was more extensive canal-building and canal-repair in the more administratively centralised villages of the NLF areas. Total prodution in NLF areas was therefore not very different from US controlled areas but the benefits were more equally distributed and no capitalist farmers were established.

First the *Viet Minh* and then the NLF were formed in the atmosphere of discontent which arose among the Vietnamese peasants as a result of the changes associated with colonialism and American intervention. These successful movements appealed to collective traditions which had developed in Vietnamese communities over the centuries. Chapters 2 and 3 analyse, in detail, traditional property relations and political power. Chapters 4–6 cover change during the colonial period, while Chapters 7–10 describe the period of socialist development in the north of Vietnam and American intervention and the NLF in the South. Chapter 11 analyses the integration of the country in the modern period.

2 Collective Property and the Rise of the Confucian Patriarchy

The early history of the Vietnamese is based partly on legend and is therefore conjectural but it is very important to the Vietnamese identity. It is only through a strong sense of their own past that the Vietnamese have been able continuously to fight off foreign intervention. With this strong identity the Vietnamese were able to survive and resist assimilation during over 1000 years of Chinese rule (111 BC to 940 AD).

According to the Vietnamese, their early history had many matriarchal aspects.[1] The brave attempts of women leaders to fight off Chinese rule over its first four centuries would tend to support these claims. In this chapter we will encounter the struggle which the Vietnamese women and men waged against the imposition of a rigidly hierarchical Confucian patriarchy by the Chinese.

Recounting of the early history of the Vietnamese illustrates the importance of collective institutions at the village level. Some of these institutions were preserved and even further developed by the Chinese – to their own ends. Communal landholding is the most important form taken by the early Vietnamese collectivism. Periodically redistributed communal lands remained very important in Vietnam until French colonialist intervention in the nineteenth century. In the north and central parts of Vietnam communal lands were important secondary forms of landholding until the *Viet Minh* revolution. Particularly since the importance of early Vietnamese collectivism has been undervalued by Western observers, this chapter details the history of communal landholding arrangements in Vietnam, citing government regulations and other evidences of traditional concern for the collective ideal.

PRE-CHINESE HISTORY OF THE VIETNAMESE

The history of Vietnam is that of a people rather that a geographical area. Before they were conquered by the Chinese in 111 BC, the

Vietnamese had permanently settled in a unified area but migration gradually shifted the centre of gravity of Vietnamese society toward the South. The first Vietnamese kingdom did not emerge before 1000 BC and most likely appeared around 500 BC. The Vietnamese practised an early form of irrigation and had a developed social and political system before the Chinese era. From 500 BC to 111 BC the state of Nam Viet occupied an area that is now part of southern China and northern Vietnam.

The pre-Chinese economy of the Vietnamese is thought to have been similar to the system of Thai and Muong tribes which now reside in the area. In these tribes the local leader allows most of the land area to be cultivated by the families but keeps a certain amount for himself. This land is cultivated through a system in which each labourer has to work for a certain period each year on the chief's land.[2] The rest of the land is periodically divided among the families with certain advantages for the dignitaries who receive additional shares.

Although it is difficult to make definitive statements about the social organisation of Vietnamese society before the Chinese period, we can make some suppositions. Since all land not held by notables was redistributed periodically, there seems to have been no individual peasant family landholding in this period. Nguyen Khac Vien contends that a class of peasant landholders arose later, as a result of Chinese influence.[3] The work of cultivating the fields was done by common labour, not family labour. The neighbourhood work teams, important in later periods, were probably even more important in this early period.

The status of women in early Vietnamese society was more equal to men than in subsequent periods of Vietnamese history up to (and possibly including) the present era. Women fought in the Vietnamese military in this early period. In fact it was Vietnamese women military and political leaders who mounted attacks on the Chinese in the first several centuries of Chinese rule. In addition to the famous rebellion by Trung Trac and Trung Nhi which was temporarily sucessful against the Chinese in 40 AD, there was another insurrection against the Chinese led by a woman military leader, Trieu Thi Trinh, 200 years later.[4] After this, the anti-Chinese leaders were men and this change reflected the influence of Confucianism on Vietnamese society. In addition to these indications of high female status, there is considerable contemporary cross-cultural evidence, presented by Esther Boserup, that the more 'primitive' farming systems are female and that men gain ascendancy in agricultural societies only after the introduction of the metal plough. The Vietnamese may have had a primitive version of a plough before Chinese intervention but the Chinese claim to have introduced an improved metal plough into Vietnamese agriculture.[5]

Women were the early agriculturalists in Vietnam and are reputed to have discovered rice cultivation. A woman named Sao Chi is supposed to have introduced rice cultivation into Vietnam: 'One day, she discovered a grass with white grains, She picked off the grains and scattered them on the mud. More plants grew from them and then more grains.'[6] There were temples erected to the women discoverers of other crops also, for example Lady Soya, Lady Mulberry and Lady Bean.

In this early Vietnamese society, children did not know their fathers and even later, after several centuries of Chinese influence, did not bear the name of their fathers. There was no parental interference with their progeny's marriage decisions in this early period, since this epoch was before the establishment of private property and there were no economic factors for the parents to consider. The husband, when married, went to live with the wife in her family home.[7]

A form of pantheistic religion was practised at this time, and there were many female and male gods. The world of divinities was presided over by three goddesses, the Goddesses of the Heavens.[8] This high regard for women in religion later influenced Buddhism and Taoism, when they were introduced in Vietnam. There were several female Buddhas in Vietnam who were worshipped equally with the male Buddhas and they are still worshipped to this day.

Political leadership, in this early period, was in the hands of notables or dignitaries who were both male and female. The dignitaries held considerable power on the local level, making the centralised leadership of Nam Viet weaker than in subsequent periods. Chesneau suggests that the Vietnamese were, in fact, governed as a loose confederation of tribes previous to Chinese rule.[9]

CHINESE RULE 111 BC–940 AD

During 1000 years of Chinese rule, the Vietnamese adopted many elements of Chinese civilisation but they were never assimilated. The Vietnamese identity was maintained because the Chinese were never able to change completely the character of the Vietnamese village. The Chinese promoted more centralised villages and a centralised state, ruled by a mandarin system of administration. The Chinese institutions were superimposed on a pre-existing Vietnamese social structure and the eventual result was a specifically Vietnamese form of centralised State and a stronger Vietnamese village which was controlled by a patriarchal élite.

When Vietnam was first conquered, the Chinese adopted an administrative policy of complete non-interference with local institutions. The revolt of the native aristocracy led by the Trung Sisters in 40 AD changed the perspective of the Chinese about their policy of non-interference. The Trung sisters became joint Monarchs when they succeeded in driving out the Chinese. Two years later the Chinese re-entered Vietnam and re-established their rule. The Chinese then defeated the local Vietnamese dignitaries, this time killing most of them.

The new administrative structure then set up was almost completely Chinese. This leadership, however, did not stay loyal to the Chinese empire for long. The first Chinese officers who conquered Vietnam were soon joined by political refugees of the Han dynasty in China. More native participation was also gradually allowed in the new administrative system. Because of the numbers of political refugees and the increasing amount of Vietnamese participation, a Sino-Vietnamese upper class was eventually formed with interests which differed from the interests of the Chinese empire. The administrative system in this period was not a complete transformation of the previous system but an integration of the Chinese and Vietnamese systems. The structure was quasi-hereditary and quasi-mandarinal. While many positions required scholastic degrees, many positions were passed down in the same family.

Along with the opening-up of trade between China, South east Asia, and India, Buddhist pilgrims came to Vietnam and spread their new ideas. Buddhism found almost immediate widespread adherence in Vietnam and this allegiance was particularly strong among women. The Vietnamese enthusiastically adopted Buddhism as a religion of consolation after having been defeated many times in their attempts to attain independence from China. Buddhism gave the Vietnamese a non-aggressive way of resisting the imposition of Chinese rule and Confucian institutions upon them by providing them with an ideological basis for passive disagreement with the Chinese. In many respects, Buddhism was a reactive religion. Its tenets first reacted against the hierarchy and aggressive behaviour fostered by Hinduism in India in the fifth century BC, when the religion was founded.

Buddhism later challenged Chinese Confucian hierarchy when the religion reached China and Vietnam in the first and second centuries AD. Buddhist doctrine was against castes or classes in society and the grasping and aggressive behaviour which accompanied the accumulation of wealth by the higher classes or castes. Buddhists preached that the devoted could be saved through mysticism and rebirth. This must have appealed to the Vietnamese, who had been defeated in their many attempts to throw off the Chinese yoke. Buddhism became intertwined with the traditional and nationalist feelings of the Vietnamese, and Buddhists honoured Vietnamese national heroes like the Trung Sisters.

Gradually, despite the popularity of Buddhism among the lower classes, an upper class of Vietnamese mandarins and dignitaries was formed with strong allegiance to Confucian principles. Many Vietnamese peasant men also developed allegiances to Confucian societal structures when they were given adminstrative privileges in the Vietnamese village and control over communal lands. In return for these privileges, the emperor and his mandarinal representatives expected loyalty, taxes and military service, from the Vietnamese peasant males. This new allegiance, based on privileges, was not very consistent with Buddhist pacifism and the Buddhist renunciation of grasping and accumulating property. The result of this conflict was the the women of the village became the mainstay adherents of Buddhism. Although there were Buddhist 'monks' as well as 'nuns', most loyal practitioners of Buddhism were women.

The method by which the Chinese were gradually able to change the Vietnamese village, was through introducing new methods of production, like more efficient methods of water control, the improved metal plough, and the water buffalo. In handicraft production also, Chinese rule resulted in the Vietnamese increasing their technical sophistication. Vietnamese were sent to China to learn new skills and handcrafts and upon returning they taught their skills to others in the villages. Changed methods of production eventually led to profound institutional changes in Vietnamese society. The use of an improved plough and the water buffalo gave men a more important place in agricultural production than they had previously had. Men were in charge of the ploughing, which greatly increased the yields of crops in this period. With this change in productivity and the strong support of patriarchial power in Confucian philosophy, the modern patriarchal peasant family developed and became entrenched as an institution in Vietnamese society.

The Chinese also supported a strongly centralised village ruled over by the peasant patriarchs. Improved water control meant that there was a need for increased village control of water distribution and the administration of construction and repair projects. The village as a unit became more cohesive in the process of carrying out these tasks. That is, the village became a stronger and more centralised institution than it previously was.

The traditional neighbourhood associations, local nobility, and Buddhist clergy were challenged by the growth of these new institutions in the Vietnamese countryside. These older groups gradually lost power as the new institutions developed. Changes were not sudden, however, and the mandarinate and the class of peasant patriarchs gained power but did not reach full ascendancy in their respective spheres until after the period of direct Chinese rule. (The process by which they achieved their victory will be described in the next section.)

With the production and adminstrative changes described above, there were changes in the landholding system favouring individual peasant landholding. The Chinese nevertheless preserved certain collective institutions such as village-held communal land and the periodic redistribution of these lands. These institutions were consistent with Confucian philosophy and Chinese history. In fact, ancient Chinese writings referred to a system of land tenure whereby the political authorities controlled the allocation of land among all families according to their size. Reallocation took place at regular intervals. In the book of rites called the *tcheou*, compiled in the eighth century BC, and in subsequent writings through the centuries, this form of tenure was described. Vietnamese historian, Vu Van Hien elaborates:

> all the states in China, both royal and seignorial estates, were divided in the form of a *tsing (tinh)*, that is to say in large squares which in turn were divided into nine smaller ones. Eight of these were cultivated by eight peasant families under the name of *sseu-tien (tu dien)*, or private fields. These families also had to cultivate the ninth lot in the center, called *Kong-t'ien (cong dien)*.[10]

The leader received only what came from the centre lot. The families received the produce from the lots assigned to them. In his parenthetical additions Vu Van Hien points out the similarity between Chinese and Vietnamese terms for private and public land. In Vietnam, *cong dien* means 'public rice field' and *tu dien* means 'private rice field'. *Tu dien* and *sseu tien* should not be confused with private ownership. The peasants of a single *tsing* did not cultivate their fields individually, but rather they cultivated all nine lots in common.[11] There is some dispute over whether this organisation of Chinese society ever existed exactly in the form described. Regardless of this, it is important from the Vietnamese perspective because of the influence it had on Confucian philosophy which made reference to it.

When Confucian social structures and philosophy were promoted in Vietnam, the Chinese developed the new category of peasant private property which was controlled by the peasant patriarchs. The Chinese also sanctioned many of the communal aspects of the village, however, by preserving some categories of public land and encouraging the periodic redistribution of this land among the male villagers. Chinese terminology was obviously adopted for the new private and public categories of land, which were henceforth differentiated as *tu dien* and *cong dien*.

Vietnamese peasants were heavily burdened, in the period of Chinese rule, by a taxation system which not only supported Chinese officials in Vietnam but also provided tribute to China. As a large part of the Sino-Vietnamese upper class began to judge their interests as very different from the interests of China, they sought alliance with Vietnamese peasant patriarchs, against Chinese domination. After centuries of moving closer to the Vietnamese peasants in search of their support, the upper class was also influenced by Vietnamese institutions as they had survived in the village.[12] The alliance between the Sino-Vietnamese ruling group and the peasantry, when their interests were finally combined, was sufficient to throw off Chinese rule.

POST INDEPENDENCE – THE TENTH TO THE FIFTEENTH CENTURY

In the period immediately after the overthrow of Chinese rule, the influence of Confucianism reached a low point in Vietnam. The Vietnamese were interested in returning, as much as possible, to their native institutions, The mandarins lost power and influence as local aristocrats gained political power and economic strength throughout Vietnam. The position of women in the aristocracy, and in society in general, was also heightened in this period.

In 979 AD, when the king was assassinated, the mother of the young 6 year-old king was crowned, along with her son, as regent to the throne. Upon hearing about this woman leader, China immediately sent an expeditionary force to attack Vietnam. Untrained in military strategy herself, the queen selected a young male general, Le Hoan, to lead the national resistance, She then married him, and had him crowned king, thus inaugurating the early Le Dynasty. The Confucians thought it outrageous that a woman should rule and doubly outrageous that a king's wife should remarry.[13] Nevertheless their opinions appear to have not held much sway in Vietnamese society in this period. Even two centuries later, when King Ly Hue Ton had no sons, he left the throne to his daughter who became Queen Ly Chien Hoang.

Women in the villages held property rights in this period. They could make transactions on their own, rather than through their husbands or their fathers. Many donations of property to pagodas, inscribed in this period, were in women's names.[14]

In this post-independence period also, property-holding arrangements gave considerable power to the local aristocracy to directly exploit lands in the villages. Members of the royal family and loyal followers of the emperor who had fought against the Chinese held special rights to estates which were cultivated through a system of labour requisitioning. These lands were the equivalent of the lords' lands in the ancient Chinese *tsing* system and the chief's land in the tribal system of the Vietnamese highlands. The incomes of the local aristocrats came from the harvests of these lands which the French later called 'domainal' lands. The villages which were under the direction of these local dignitaries also had responsibilities to the Emperor for labour conscriptions and taxes.

A system of appanages which gave even more power to the local aristocrats was also in force in some areas in this period. Under this form of landholding, the aristocrat had more control over the peasants in his area because the peasants paid no taxes to the emperor and did not participate in state labour conscriptions.

Under neither of these forms of tenure did the aristocrat have an automatic right of inheritance since the property reverted back to the emperor when the dignitary died. This factor differentiates the Vietnamese landholding system of this period from the Western feudal system which in some other respects this system resembles. The property which was held by a dignitary was a gift of the emperor which returned to him on the death of his beneficiary. The emperor usually decided to allow the family to keep part of the property, but the portion generally decreased with each generation.

Despite this early period of a powerful Vietnamese aristocracy, the influence of the Chinese social system and the mandarin class had not ended with the defeat of Chinese rule in 940 AD. Some of the greatest institutional changes caused by the Chinese intervention occurred several centuries after the period of direct Chinese rule, when the mandarin administrators finally won ascendancy over the local aristocrats. Buddhism, as we have seen, was a religion which challenged Confucian values and Confucian influence in Vietnam. The division between Buddhism and Confucian philosophy was sharpened in the fourteenth and fifteenth centuries. This difference was the spiritual and intellectual aspect of a struggle for power between the two administrative classes in Vietnam, the nobility and the mandarins. The dignitaries supported Buddhism and were allied with the Buddhist clergy. The mandarins held to their guiding philosophy, Confucianism.

As part of their strategy in defeating the interests of the Buddhist clergy and the aristocracy, the mandarins allied themselves with forces which had gained power in the countryside, the peasant patriarchs in the village. This developing class of small peasant landholders undercut the power of the local aristocrats while bolstering the strength of the village as a unit. The peasant patriarchs gained control of village administration and strengthened village services. The mandarins, who were often small landholders as well as public administrators, were able to win the confidence of other small landholders in the village. Through the unity of small landholders and mandarins operating in a strong village, these forces were able to challenge the power of the local aristocracy successfully.

The mandarins could then move further, through the Emperor, to limit the power of local nobility. Some of the first regulations dealing with land tenure cited by French and Vietnamese source were instituted under the Tran dynasty and were aimed at the power of local nobility. An edict was promulgated in 1397 which limited to ten *mau* the maximum area of rice fields that could be held by a person who was not of royal blood.[15] This regulation preserved the privileges of the royal house while it decreased the power of the lesser aristocracy. In the next year all landholders were ordered to declare all areas belonging to them to the administration and to mark them with poles bearing their names. Fields not so designated became communal lands *(cong dien)* to be administered over by communal authorities. In this manner, land formerly belonging to local aristocrats and cultivated by labour conscription was converted to *cong dien* controlled by the village.

THE MANDARINATE AND THE LE CODE

At the beginning of the fifteenth century the regent Ho Qui Ly, having supported the mandarins in their struggle against the aristocrats, deposed the Tran Dynasty and declared himself emperor. The relatives and retainers of the Tran Dynasty then petitioned China to intercede and China again conquered Vietnam and ruled for a short period, from 1407 to 1429.[16] Le Loi, a rich landlord who was against the strategy of turning to the Chinese, led a peasant rebellion against the Chinese which was successful in throwing them out. Le Loi was proclaimed emperor and a dynasty of strong and influential emperors was established. These emperors promulgated a code of laws for a more centralised and militarily stronger Vietnamese society.

As we have seen, a general redistribution of land and political rights over land followed wars throughout Vietnamese history. These changes expressed new political power relationships and rewarded soldiers who fought with the winning side. The distribution which took place when the Le established their dynasty was particularly significant because this distribution expressed the final ascendancy of the mandarinate and Confucian thought over the local aristocrats and Buddhism. The latter institutions lingered but were no longer powerful in Vietnam. They were superseded completely by a mandarin-style administration with a strong central government and strong villages.

The ascendancy of the mandarinate as a ruling group, however, did not mean that Vietnam became a smaller version of the larger empire to the north. The Confucian tradition coming from China had emphasised strict hierarchy reinforced by ritual. The remoteness and aloofness of leadership in the Chinese model did not carry over into the Vietnamese context. Hierarchy was mitigated by the necessity, in Vietnam, of the mandarinate and the emperor aligning themselves with the peasantry to defeat the nobility and also to ward off intervention from the north. Lacking any large foreign ally to come to their aid against the Chinese, the Vietnamese emperor and his mandarin administrators depended on mobilising large numbers of

Vietnamese peasants to resist invasion. In this new period of strong centralised control the Vietnamese peasant patriarchs continued to see their emperor as a protector-figure. The mandarins, for their part, frequently had to put their patriotic duty of serving their country ahead of their interest in safeguarding and extending their own privileges because they were continuously aware of shared interest with the peasants as opposed to the Chinese or the Indochinese Kingdoms further south on the peninsula.

Immediately after the new dynasty was established in 1428, a general census of population and cultivated land was ordered. By law land was to be allocated to individuals in equal shares. The administration of this law took a somewhat different form, however. Much of the land was divided among soldiers and their families and supporters of the new administration and the rest became communal land. The lands that were divided were fallow lands formerly belonging to the state, large estates which had developed during the Chinese occupation, and estates belonging to powerful families who supported the preceding dynasty. When the new regime was consolidated, those who had collaborated with the Chinese dispersed to China or the frontier, leaving their lands to be distributed.[17]

Beginning with the Le Code, Vietnamese imperial laws regulating landholding patterns are a major source of information about traditional landholding and local political economy. These laws, however, were not always administered down to the village level. Because of a strong tradition of village autonomy, we cannot assume that what the law prescribed existed in all the villages in Vietnam. Strong emperors were able to carry out their decrees more effectively than monarchs who did not have much support. If we interpret the laws and discussions of exceptions to these laws within a general historical framework, they provide us with valuable information about landholding patterns and the changes that took place. They represent standards if not uniform practices.

The Le Code established the supremacy of the central government over the communal lands known as *cong dien*. The administrative procedure of the distribution of this *cong dien* was prescribed by the code. Articles 384 and 346 of the code stated that all those inscribed on the village rolls should participate in the distribution of *cong dien* from the age of 15.[18] The inscribed at this time were practically all male residents of the village over 15. Parcels of *cong dien* which were equal in size were to be redistributed every three years to these inscribed men.

The village officials who carried out the distribution were nominated by the state in the fifteenth century. The official who had charge of the distribution was not the head notable in the village but one of lower rank. (The French were later confused about this and called him the 'mayor'.) In the fifteenth century, registers of distributions were drawn up by this official and copies of them were sent to the capital for the emperor's approval.

As previously mentioned, the fifteenth century was a period of strong central control, and all this centralised power was needed to enforce Article 346 of the Le Code which provided that there should be a redistribution of collective lands among the villages. Local administrative authorities were authorised to confiscate some collective lands from villages with a low population density relative to cultivable land and allocate these collective lands to villages with a high population density. Vu Van Hien, a Vietnamese scholar who wrote about communal property in Tonkin, believes that this intra-village redistribution was at least partially carried out.

Communal property and public lands were protected by many provisions in the Le Code. Article 347 prohibits the creation of farms (*chang*) or private estates. These *chang* were land areas large enough to require continuous hired labour or renting of property. Article 341 protects communal property from being sold or mortgaged. According to law, all those plots illegally alienated would have to be restored to redistribution and the state would claim the price paid for the land. In articles 342 and 371, individuals, and specifically officials, were absolutely forbidden to usurp communal property. Land illegally usurped would be reclaimed and the value of the harvest confiscated. These provisions definitely asserted the inalienability of communal and public property.[19]

Under the Le Code, the peasant's right to *cong dien* did not allow him to leave a parcel of land fallow. Article 349 of the code states that when neglected, lands are to be immediately reassigned.

During the early Le period, the tax that the inscribed man had to pay to the public granary was less than 10 per cent of the produce from his *khau phan* (share of *cong dien*). He became personally subject to the tax at the time he was inscribed on the list of receivers of *khau phan*. By law, the inscribed would lose a tenth of a share of *cong dien* and be given eighty blows of the *troung* (stick) if he were late with his tax payment.[20] Since the tax payment amounted to less than 10 per cent, it seems that in this period the institution of *cong dien* was used to provide a basic minimum income for families in the village in addition to providing tax revenue.

An aspect of the creation of peasant private-property-holding and the patriarchal peasant family was the subjugation of peasant women. The originator of the Le Code, Le Thanh Ton , also regulated family matters in such a way as to ensure that women would be the private property of their husband's or their husband's family. A 1470 edict stated that all marriages must be decided on by an intermediary and that after the betrothal ceremony and the welcoming of the bride ceremony, the bride must greet her parents-in-law and prostrate herself before her husband's ancestors' altar. This regulation was to wipe out all final traces of a previous matriarchal marriage system, such as the bride living at her mother's home after the marriage. This was still a popular custom in rural Vietnam before the fifteenth century. Le Than Ton also ordered that a married woman must obey her husband and that if she failed to accomplish her duties as a wife, her parents would be punished.[21]

The Confucian regulation on education stipulated that only men could take advantage of private or public education and that only men could participate in local and national politics. Women were educated within the families and taught the Four Virtues: frankness, modesty, politeness and fidelity. They were also schooled in the Three Obediences: obedience to their fathers when young, to their husbands when married, and to their sons when widowed. Women were thus confined to the private household sphere with no basis in ideology or legal right to participate in the administration of the larger society.

SEPARATION OF THE COUNTRY – THE RISE OF THE TRINH AND THE NGUYEN DYNASTIES

The Le developed a bureaucracy which was effective in administration for two centuries. The dikes were kept in repair and the frontier was extended by the Vietnamese 'march to the south'. Vietnamese control of land was extended along the western coast of the Indo-Chinese peninsula for nearly 1000 miles from the Tonkin Delta southward. It eventually became possible for the Nguyen, a family of high officials, to carve out their own southern domain because the bureaucracy had grown too large for the Vietnamese peasantry to support.[22] Taxation increased to support the bureaucracy and the Nguyen took advantage of the popular discontent over the growing tax burden.

Intermediary power of local officials arose in the villages and regions as the Le Dynasty weakened. Family heads with large patrimonies gained power in the villages and began to usurp communal lands. By

1664, the central administration had weakened to such an extent that the establishment of village registers was left to the villages themselves. Village officials who carried out the distribution were now appointed by the village. In effect, the management of land was taken from the central authority and put under the communal governments with only indirect supervision from representatives from above.

From the 1620s to 1673 there was fighting between the Trinh family of administrators with power in the north and the Nguyen family in the south, with the Nguyen winning independence. One hundred years of separate political existence followed in which there was considerable breakdown of centralised authority in both regions. The Trinh and the Nguyen exerted military control in their respective regions, giving only formal allegiance to the Le Dynasty which was essentially held in captivity by the Trinh.

Thus, for a total of nearly 200 years (1620 to 1801) there was no central authority strong enough to hold together all parts of Vietnam. During this period areas far from the capital in the north, as well as in the south, would break away and lead their own political existence for brief period of time. The ideal of Vietnamese political unity was never lost, however, as the various leaders of the areas breaking away fought to unify the state under their own power; but each time they would be put down by the Trinh or the Nguyen.

The different parts of the country did not develop unique institutions during the period of political separation. The Nguyen in the south developed the same kind of structure and legislated the same kinds of laws as the northern state. The 'immutable' Vietnamese village preserved the cultural homogeneity of the Vietnamese during this period, despite the breakdown of central authority.

French sources cover only the changes in property regulations of the northern part of the country during the separation period, but we can assume that conditions in the south were not very different from those in the north. Regulations of the seventh year of the Emperor Vinh-Trinh (1711) made several changes in the Le Code. The period of redistribution of village lands which had been extended, in practice, to six or more years in many places was now consecrated by law in Article I of the new regulation. Reflecting the decline in effective central administration, this regulation gave a greater initiative to the village. In addition, administrative initiative was legally given to villages to follow their particular customs in the methods of the distribution of *khau phan*. Even the indirect supervision of the central government was henceforth withdrawn.[23]

Along with the state administered and centrally regulated distribution of *cong dien* communal property, the distribution of strictly village communal property had always been maintained in the communities. This village communal property was neither regulated nor controlled by the emperor or his officials. Customs had developed in the villages surrounding the distribution of these lands and when the central distribution of *cong dien* was relaxed, it was these local traditions that could be called on in the villages to control allocation of *cong dien*.

The exclusion from the distribution of *cong dien* of those already provided with resources was another important change in the laws of this period, compared with the Le Dynasty. Articles 11 and 12 of the regulation of 1711 contained these restrictions:

> individuals, functionaries, or titulars of honorary posts to whom privileges in the form of taxes to be collected from a certain number of the villages have been granted are no longer included in the distribution.[24]

The regulations went on to say that residents who possessed rice fields by themselves or through their wives no longer had any right to a share of communal property, *khau phan*. If their personal property was small, they were allowed a smaller part of the *cong dien* to increase their rice fields to the rationed amount. There was but one exception to this law: soldiers could participate in the distribution of *khau phan* even when they received other privileges. This regulation was an attempt to stem the tide of increasing power in a few hands in the village by distributing the remaining *cong dien* more equitably; however, events show that its effects were limited.

The regulation of 1711 asserts the inalienability of *cong dien* except where the sale of communal lands was current practice. Earlier laws dealt with the inalienability of *cong dien* but no exceptions were made. This part of the regulation was a clear recognition of the deterioration of collectivity and centralised control in the village.

EAST–WEST CONTACT IN THE EIGHTEENTH CENTURY

The changes which occurred in the rural economy in the eighteenth century cannot be directly tied to Western contact but such contact was an important indirect factor. A greater amount of legislation concerning land contracts and the regulation of money-lenders certainly appeared after Western contact. We can, at this point, only make general statements about East–West contact before Colonial rule was established and the immediate effects of this change.

East–West trade before the French conquest was not very large, but it was important because imports were mostly in the form of munitions. The central government and government officials were the major buyers of Western goods because the ruling families of the north and the south were very interested in obtaining Western munitions to aid them in their civil wars. It is doubtful that the separation of the country could have lasted so long had it not been for the advanced munitions acquired by both sides.

In order not to endanger their chances of obtaining weapons, the Vietnamese leaders were lax, at times, in letting people they considered social and political revolutionaries – the Catholic missionaries – enter their country. Missionary conversions were generally made among the lower ranks of the rural population and not among the mandarinate. It is significant that most conversions were made in groups, that is, villages or hamlets rather than individual persons were converted. This reflects the collective character of the Vietnamese village. Catholic communities and their missionaries were discriminated against by the rest of Vietnamese society and at times they were persecuted.

Vietnamese mandarins feared and distrusted the missionaries for the social disruption they caused. The mandarins well understood the difference between Christian and Confucianist doctrines regarding the relations between individuals and the state. Buttinger states:

> To reject the existing moral and civic code with reference to one's own conscience was a revolutionary act of greater consequence than an armed rebellion for the redistribution of land. The concept of public order was one of a moral relationship patterned after the Confucianist family, with its strict adherence to natural duties and its absolute parental authority. To act by one's conscience if such action violated the principles on which society rested was to act immorally. The standard accusation against the missionaries, in fact, was that the existing social order was being corrupted by their work.[25]

The immediate result of Catholic influence on the rural economy was that the many communities with Catholic hamlets discriminated against them in the distribution of land. More subtle effects appeared only in time through the seeds of social discord that the missionaries planted.

THE TAY SON AND THE ASCENDANCY OF THE NGUYEN DYNASTY

Peasant revolts coincided with the weakening of centralised power under the Trinh and the Nguyen. These revolts were, in part, reactions to the increased taxation in both the north and the south and the seizure of communal land by local officials. The uprisings were only sporadic in the seventeenth century but they gained momentum in the eighteenth.

Conditions in the villages in the North were very poor and there were three revolts which had at least temporary success. In the first one, which lasted from 1740 to 1751, insurgents succeeded in controlling several provinces in the Tonkin Delta. Another uprising developed in the lower part of the Delta and this one lasted from 1739 to 1769. A third revolt, active from 1738 to 1779, had a base in the highlands and controlled two lowland provinces.[26] Despite these revolts the Trinh were eventually able to regain control through the use of force aided by Western munitions.

It was in the central part of the area controlled by the Nguyen, Binh Dinh province, where the final successful revolt began. This revolt was called the Tay Son revolt, from the name of the home village of the brothers who initiated it. The Tay Son were merchants and were supported by the new commercial interests in the towns which had grown up with the opening of trade with the West. The Tay Son revolt was a peasant revolt, in that most of the participants were peasants, but it was also a revolt which included the interests of commercial groups.

Peasant women had traditionally been the local traders in Vietnam and larger-scale trading was handled by mandarins' wives or the Chinese. The Confucian prejudice against trading, as an occupation had influenced Vietnamese society for centuries. The patriarchs had shunned trading until the eighteenth century when the profits from trading became more important in relation to those from the agricultural sector. Chinese aliens were accumulating fortunes in Saigon towards the end of the eighteenth century and in reaction, some nationalist Vietnamese males threw off their Confucian bias and began to move into trading and money-lending.

In the course of their struggle against the established order the Tay Son were aided by all forces in society which were alienated from the crumbling and corrupt mandarin officialdom supporting the Le, the Trinh or the Nguyen. Of course, the poverty-stricken and dissatisfied peasants supported the Tay Son. The Buddhists and Taoists had been awaiting their time to support an alternative to the Confucians, who had suppressed them, and they joined forces. Some of the national minorities, which had been conquered by the Vietnamese, also joined in the struggle.

Women were also important participants in this struggle. After nearly 1300 years of inactivity as leaders in the military, a woman again led an army of the Tay Son. Bui The Xuan was an upper-class woman who had led a unit of 5000 soldiers against the Siamese invaders. She later fought against the Nguyen in the south and the Trinh and the Le in the north in support of the Tay Son. Peasant women in the villages also participated in the uprisings, as some were later reported as having been punished for their exploits.[27]

The Tay Son overthrew the Nguyen by 1771 and were subsequently able to overthrow the Trinh and unify the country. At first the Tay Son paid homage to the Le emperor. However, when the Le family turned toward China for help, the youngest Tay Son brother, Nguyen Hue, set himself up as emperor in the northern part of the country while his brothers administered other sections. Nguyen Hue successfully fought off the Manchu invaders from China in 1787 but he died two years later and his brothers died the following year, leaving relatives of lesser stature to rule.

The Tay Son regime was true to its nationalist, commercial and anti-Confucian backing. The Vietnamese language supplanted Chinese as the language of the court and this greatly offended the Confucian mandarinate. The establishment of new merchant enterprises was also promoted by the Tay Son. More that 100 mines were opened up in the north during the reign of the Tay Son and shipyards, military workshops, paperworks and printers were established.

The greatest failing of the Tay Son was their lack of attention to peasant concerns. In the process of the conquest, the Tay Son had taken merchandise from rich villagers and given it to the poor. While in power, however, they never carried out the redistribution of land which previous dynasties had correctly seen as the very foundation of lasting redistribution of wealth and power in rural Vietnam. Probably because they were merchants, the Tay Son had little understanding of the importance of agricultural production in the country they were ruling.

As the peasant support of the Tay Son waned, representatives of the Nguyen dynasty were able to regain power by reinstating a reactionary government. French assistance was relied on to effect this overthrow and the return to power of the defeated dynasty. The traditional pattern of a more popular dynasty being established after a period of hardship and discontent was thus ended because of the impact of Western assistance.

Gia Long, the new Nguyen monarch who ruled from 1801 to 1820, was interested in asserting Confucian values untempered by Vietnamese traditions. His son, Ming Mang (1820–41), followed the Confucian structure even more rigidly. Codes of law adopted Chinese social structure much more exactly than previous dynasties' law codes. As a result, these codes were difficult to administer in the Vietnamese context.

Gia Long attempted to institute changes in landholding patterns through changes in laws. The amount of *cong dien* in the villages had decreased considerably during the insecure centuries, so that in the first half of the nineteenth century, there was considerable legislation aimed at increasing *cong dien* in the villages. This legislation was implemented, at least partially. Some private lands were transferred to communal lands by an 1802 regulation of Gia Long in which land occupied by former rebels was ordered to be transferred to *cong dien*.[28]

Some lands that would traditionally have been village communal lands (*bon thou dien*) and *tu dan dien* were also transferred to *cong dien* during this period. The difference between state communal land and village communal land was therefore reduced. The following categories of land were legally designated *cong dien* instead of village communal lands: lands which had been the beds of streams, lands abandoned by their owners, and land left by persons without descendants.

In the 1800s there was further legislation regarding the administration of *cong dien*. A law of 1804 regulated periodic distributions with greater uniformity than had previous legislation. Vu Van Hien believed that this regulation restricted the realm of application of the law and that the communities acquired more freedom in administering *cong dien* because this law could not be easily administered.[29] The village notables continued to conduct the operations entailed in the distribution during this period and as a result, there was greater village autonomy in the distribution of *cong dien* as compared with the Le Dynasty period.

Other laws enacted under Gia Long adopted the essence of former legislation but with smaller changes. A partition was required to be equal in size, as formerly, but also to be equal in fertility of land. In order to ensure this, the land was to be divided into three classes according to fertility, and the inscribed was to have a parcel from each class. It would seem that these regulations also could only be administered with great difficulty.

Gia Long's law codes reflected much of the previous Vietnamese collective traditions but they also show the impact of an increasing influence of private property, trading and markets which accompanied Western contact. On the one hand, the regulations of the nineteenth century reproduced the prohibitions against the alienation and prescription of *cong dien* legislated in earlier centuries. On the other hand, renting of *cong dien* was officially allowed for the first time, with the proviso that this should occur only when public interest permitted and only for a period of three years.

The status of *cong dien* had been evolving for centuries. Divergent local customs had been encouraged when the representative of the central government ceased to directly administer the distribution of *cong dien*. The notables could always present reports to the higher administrators which did not reflect what was happening in the village. The decline in central power and the later land-tenure laws helped to change the status of *cong dien* from state-controlled communal land to something very much like village communal land. The only difference between these categories that the French perceived when they arrived in Vietnam was that *cong dien* could not legally be sold, even for obligations contracted in the name of the village, but that village communal land could be disposed of in any way the village notables desired because it was alienable.

There were additional major legal changes taking place in the nineteenth century which can be directly linked to Western contact and capitalist forms of sale and contracts. This was the introduction of Western-type sale contracts, that is, legislation involving the complete sale of land. An ordinance of 1840 stated that when a final sale was made, this fact had to be clearly indicated in the contract. In the same year another law limited the common sale-with-repurchase contract. This law stated that after thirty years, repurchase would not be authorised.[30] These laws were a reflection of changes occurring in society as a result of Western trade and religious influences. They eased the way for property transactions in the future to be made increasingly according to a capitalist private property format.

The Nguyen also tried to impose rigid Confucian standards with respect to the status of women in society. A new law stated that daughters had no rights in inheritance. According to previous law codes and longstanding tradition, daughters had inherited from the family patrimony in equal proportion with sons except for the eldest son. This new law was not always enforced among the peasantry and it was sometimes not even enforced among the mandarin class, but is was enforced often enough for it to be reported that women frequently committed suicide over the division of the inheritance.[31]

The Nguyen Dynasty's push toward Confucian orthodoxy plus lingering allegiances to the Tay Son caused this dynasty to fail to establish its authority at the village level.[32] Serious local uprisings started in the 1820s and 1830s, becoming worse thereafter. By the 1880s the central administration was so negligent in its duties that there were repeated breaches in the Red River dike system. The hardship resulting from this added to the already existing discontent. It was at this moment that the French decided to mount an invasion in the southern part of Vietnam (Cochin China). The weak Nguyen dynasty was caught in a cross-fire between the French forces and their own peasantry and they were defeated.

ORIGIN AND DEVELOPMENT OF COMMUNAL LAND

There is much disagreement among French writers about the sequence of development of communal land in Vietnam. Confusion exists as to how communal land arose in new villages and the mechanisms which varied the amount of communal land in older villages. The first French observers who wrote about Vietnam in the Colonial period were convinced that communal land was an old form of tenure that was dying out before the French arrived in Vietnam. They postulated that new villages were set up on a communal land basis but that as the villages grew older and more settled, communal lands gradually became private lands.[33]

Actually, the village institutions which developed after the Chinese period of innovation and change in Vietnam encouraged communal land and centralised communal power. Because of the increased need for coordination of water control activities, the village as a unit was stronger and more tightly organised than the pre-Chinese village where there had been no private family property but only collective property.

The early French theory of decreasing communal land was not borne out by the facts as they were later gathered. Vu Van Hien contended that increases in communal land were a normal development of village tenure institutions as villages became older and more crowded.[34] This statement is supported by the fact that *cong dien*, at the beginning of the Colonial era, was more plentiful in the more populated areas and less plentiful in the thinly settled areas. In Tonkin, there was less *cong dien* in the upper part of the delta where the population was less dense. Areas of maximum density of population corresponded with areas of maximum density of communal land: 'In the *phu* of Xuan-Truong of Nan-Vinh, the greatest density of *cong dien* (77.5 per cent of the total area) corresponds to the maximum density of the population (1000 to 1500 inhabitants per square kilometer)'.[35] Pierre Gourou measured the concentration of population and communal land in Tonkin in the 1930s (see Maps 2.1 and 2.2). It is evident from his maps that high percentages of *cong dien* are correlated with heavy population densities. Gourou did not include the extra plots allotted to functionaires and notables in his definition of *cong dien*, therefore the percentages of communal land are systematically underestimated on the maps but relative proportions can still be seen.

In late precolonial Vietnam, communal land was set aside when villages were established:

> On free areas, colonists are first permitted to settle where they please ... The administration and local authorities interfere only when the village founded by the settlers has been well established. They grant the settlers an exclusive right to the lots which they have cleared, and at the same time also, upon fixing the territorial limits of the village, foreseeing the growth of its population, they allocate to them a part of the free land as *cong dien*.[36]

Communal land was added to this initial allotment through the operation of village institutions. It was the custom in Vietnam for alluvial lands to be collective property. (Alluvial lands are those which have been recovered from salt waters or have been left by streams which have changed their course.) Because of this, the density of communal land was particularly high in areas which bordered rivers.

Communal land was also increased through the process of endowments. Endowments were given by individuals to the pagoda, various societies, associations, and the community. In return for the endowment of a parcel of land, the endower usually expected some ritual to be undertaken on his behalf. Endowments were sometimes established by a written agreement stating the quantity of offerings to be presented at each religious occasion in return for the endowment.

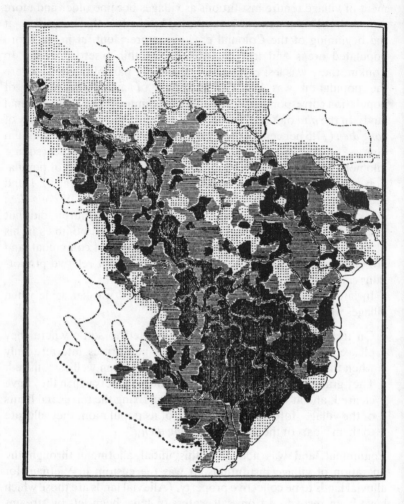

Map 2.1   Population density Tonkin Delta (schematic map)

▨   Medium density (400–599 inhabitants per square kilometer)

▦   Below medium density (less than 400 inhabitants)

▮   Above medium density (more than 600 inhabitants)

Scale: 1/1,000,000
Source: Gourou, *Peasants of the Mekong Delta*, pp. 814–16.

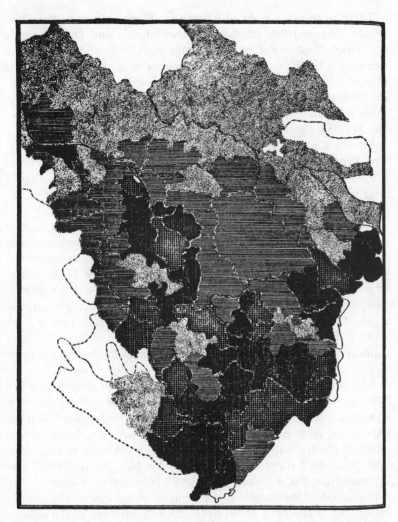

Map 2.2   The communal lands of the Tonkin Delta (percentage of the total area by *phu* and *huyen*)

from 1–10
percent

from 10–
20 percent

from 20–
40 percent

more than 40
percent
Scale:1/1,000,000

Source: Gourou, *Peasants of the Mekong Delta*, pp. 814–16.

There were other ways in which the village collected lands. The village inherited land that was without heirs, and part of newly developed lands went to the commune. Confiscations were also carried out by the commune if the owner did not pay taxes. After a change in dynasties. as we have seen, confiscations of large landholding families were carried out by the central government. Under these many rules and procedures, communal land would regularly accumulate as villages grew older.

Transfers were also made from communal land to family patrimony. This happened mainly through conversion by those with power and influence. Although imperial law consistently forbade alienation of *cong dien*, the multiplication of these laws throughout the centuries indicates that these principles were frequently violated.

What the French saw when they arrived in Vietnam, and described as a tendency for a decrease in communal land, was actually a tendency for communal land to become private land at times when the central government was weak and could not protect the village. In the course of development of the traditional society, this was a circular process and poor conditions in the villages would lead to unrest and eventually political agitation and the overthrow of a dynasty. The new dynasty reasserted village rights by confiscating large landholdings of those supporting the old dynasty and giving this land to the villages to be used as communal land.

According to the circular process described in this chapter, the Tay Son should have been able to establish a strong, centralised, new dynasty which would expand communal land and village control at the expense of large private holdings. We have seen the factors which changed the traditional pattern. The East–West trade in munitions and the French support of the unpopular Nguyen dynasty, led to increased conflict between rulers and peasants in Vietnam. The introduction of the complete sale contract in the nineteenth century reflected the influence of Western property interests in the village. The French described the Vietnamese social structure at the moment they encountered it. The process which was in force was decreasing communal controls with decentralisation and disorder which led to local landlord power. This was not traditional Vietnam but traditional Vietnam as influenced by the West.

3 Land and Economy in the Traditional Village

The village described in this chapter existed in Vietnam from the fifteenth to the mid-nineteenth centuries. This model of the village economy is constructed from laws and regulations of the period and from accounts and observations made in the early to mid-colonial period (1853–1935). The model depicts the distribution of property rights and the relations of productions and exchange in the Vietnamese village in this period.

STATE AND VILLAGE AUTHORITY

In pre-capitalist Vietnam, the emperor's interest in village resources co-existed with the rights of village and family heads. Village output was divided between villagers and the central authority in prescribed proportions according to law and custom. In addition to rights over village resources, the emperor and his representatives possessed all rights to land that was uncultivated in the country. When new villages were founded on this land, they received a guardian spirit from the emperor, representing the protection of the throne. The citizens of the village in turn were obliged to pay taxes to the emperor, serve in the army and serve on public work teams organised to construct and maintain the irrigation system.

Family heads and the village had explicit rights to land conditional upon cultivation and payment of taxes, that is, the central authority claimed all rights to land held by a family or village which failed to pay its taxes.[1] In practice, however, the emperor and his representatives generally dealt not with families but with whole villages and the village itself was held responsible for tax-collection and the cultivation of any fallow land. The central administration depended for revenue on both personal and land taxes, but all taxes ultimately depended on output from the village fields. The personal tax, the major source of revenue for the emperor, was levied uniformly on all men of the village who were listed on the tax rolls, usually those between the ages of 18 and 60. Everyone on the tax rolls was given a parcel of rice land as part of a redistributive sequence and the personal tax took only a small part of

51

the product of that parcel. Revenues were collected to the centre by a fairly elaborate government apparatus depending heavily on the administrative and accounting skill of the mandarinate and village officials. Taxes were assessed by the central government according to the number of registered males and registered parcels of land, but taxes were usually collected by the villages according to their own practices.

In times of hardship taxes were lowered. When famine broke out the emperor sometimes cancelled taxes and distributed alms. In later pre-colonial Vietnam, taxes were adjusted in the event of crop damage from storms, floods, droughts, or insects. A version of the following schedule was applied to relate taxes to crop losses:[2]

Loss of crops (%)	20	30	40	50	60	70
Tax reduction (%)	0	20	30	40	50	60

There were vital economic services which the central administration organised for the village economy, which included a complex system of dams, canals and hydraulic works administered at district, province and interprovince levels. The construction and maintenance of these facilities were carried out by labour recruited from the villages on a regular basis under the supervision of mandarins. The monarchy also conquered and colonised new land for the constantly growing population. This expansion, often called the 'march to the south', consisted of a series of displacements in sufficient numbers to form communities similar to those that had been left behind.[3] Families from overcrowded villages were organised to go to the frontier and all young family heads, except for eldest sons in charge of ancestor-worship in the original village, could migrate with their families. The new communities were led by mandarins who were allowed to keep tax-collections from the village for their lifetimes.

THE VILLAGE ECONOMY

Relying on accounts of traditional land-tenure regulations and the first-hand descriptions of later French and Vietnamese observers, we can reconstruct the property patterns in the villages and add some comments on related social and economic characteristics.[4] Important connections existed between villages and the state, but internally the village possessed a high degree of autonomy. The villages administered themselves to a large extent, collecting taxes and settling disputes among inhabitants. The central government did not deal with citizens, it dealt with villages. *Phep vua thua le lang* (the law of the ruler yields to the custom of the village) is a proverb often quoted.

The village leaders, called notables, were chosen by the male members of the village. Women were barred not only from the council of notables but also from membership in the village. The *so hang xa* was the list of members of the village which included even young boys and old men but never women. Most males in the village, except for new residents, were inscribed on the village list. In addition to the criterion of male sex, notables were chosen according to wealth, age and mandarin title. Age was respected in the Vietnamese village because wisdom was reputed to come with age. The greater accumulation of wealth by some members of the commune was rewarded by high status and a place on the council of notables. Mandarins, upon retiring, would certainly also find a place awaiting them on the village council in their home villages.

The governing decisions of the commune were made by the male members in the *dinh*, or house of the guardian spirit of the village. The *dinh* was an important area of ceremony, as well as political decision-making and women were not allowed to participate in *dinh* ceremonies. A ritual central to village life involved the division of a ceremonial feast of glutinous rice and meat among the male villagers in order according to rank on the village list. This symbolic division reflected the actual division of communal land resources which will be discussed in the next subsection.

The traditional village was predominantly agricultural, and rice production was of the greatest importance. Secondary production included areca nuts, bananas, beans, and peanuts. Some vegetables and fruit trees were planted in kitchen gardens within the settlement. Secondary crops were usually planted on lands that were incapable of raising rice because rice land was highly valued and it was around this that elaborate tenure institutions developed.

THE VILLAGE LANDS

The following paragraphs describe the role of land in traditional Vietnamese society and concentrate on the way in which the village holdings were divided among families and various communal purposes. The community controlled all the land within its confines, that is, it had some rights to all sections of the land. In simplest terms, the village area was divided between family and communal lands, and there were numerous subcategories of each. The most important land of the village was the rice land called *dien*. Other productive land, where acrea nuts, bananas, beans and peanuts were planted, was called *tho*.

Patriarchal families held rights to land conditional upon the payment of taxes and performance of other communal duties. *Tu dien* was a family heritage or patrimony where most rights belonged to the family patriarch. The extended family lived together until three years after the death of the father, at which time the patrimony was divided equally among all male and female siblings except that the oldest son got an extra amount called *huong hoa* for continuation of the cult of the ancestors.

The Vietnamese patriarch's attachment to his landed patrimony can be partially understood in the light of the practice of ancestor-veneration. Ancestor-worship is a religious practice where immortality is achieved through descendants and their remembrances rather than through survival in spiritual form. Human memory is the essential ingredient in this worship and the passing on of ancestral patrimony is connected to ceremonies which ensured the veneration of the deceased. With this outlook attachment to the ancestral patrimony is great, 'The Annemese peasant does not like to part definitively with the fields which his ancestors worked for years and in which the latter still lie in the earth ... [in] their coffins.'[5]

Vietnamese tenure customs ensured the perpetuity of landed patrimony. The usufruct of family-worship property could be leased or put up as a pledge on loans, but the patrimony belonged to the ancestors and descendants of the peasant's family and therefore the lands themselves could not be forfeited. The patrimony did not have to be a large property; its importance lay in it religious significance and not in its size.

The oldest son was made *truong toc* and put in charge of the part of the *tu dien* which was the family worship property called *huong hoa* .[6] This portion of the family lands was devoted to the practice of the cult of the ancestors and to the upkeep of their graves. It was the oldest son's duty to carry out the appropriate ritual obligations and he could not move from the village. The younger brothers could stay and claim their shares of family land or they could migrate to the frontier. Although the oldest son had charge of the worship property, he could not dispose of it. He took in all the produce from the property and from this he provided for suitable ceremonies and the upkeep of graves. These ceremonies were supposed to be conducted for five generations after the death of a patriarch.

The *tuyet tu* was another kind of family-worship property which was devoted to the cult of the relative who died without direct heirs. It was maintained by kin but the devotional expenses ceased with the second generation. The *tu dien* could be further divided, even beyond the property which was currently set aside for worship expenses. *Duong loa*, for example, was a portion of the patrimony devoted to care of one or more living members of the previous generation who presumably could no longer care for themselves.[7]

The income from the *tu dien* plots was divided as the patriarch wished, but family rights in land were limited by the rights of the emperor and the rights of the village. The patriarch had to pay taxes and see to it that his family performed services for the village and the central authority. Also they could not leave their *tu dien* uncultivated since rights in land were always linked to social obligations.

If a family should leave the village, the villagers reassigned cultivation rights to another patriarch. If the first family returned, however, they could reassert possession over their patrimony. The community could prevent any prospective new family from acquiring land within its confines. This was a question for the notables of the village to decide. When any family line became extinct a large percentage of the patrimony reverted to the village and a small proportion went to another family to take up the cult of the deceased family.

There were two types of land over which the patriarchs of the village commune held most of the rights in collectivity. These communal lands were the *cong dien* over which the emperor retained substantial control, and the *tu dan dien*, over which the village held superior rights. Both the *cong dien* and the *tu dan dien* were redistributed periodically among the male village inhabitants according to special rules. That is, usufructuary rights were granted but the community held the ultimate rights of reallocation and administration.

The basic operational principle was straightforward. All communal rice fields were assigned traditional purposes and became *thien back nien chi ke*, which literally means 'to make the work last for hundreds of thousands of years'.[8] Once a field had been committed to a special purpose it would not be shifted to another, unless substantial changes had taken place in communal feelings and needs of the village. The community's regulations for the distribution of communal income were, therefore, expressed not in terms of rice or coins but in terms of *mau* or *sao* of rice land.[9] The division of village rice output reflected the prior distribution of communal lands among various communal purposes. The income from a field was used for the purpose designated, and the field was known by the name of its function.

The portion of communal land called *cong dien* served the principal purpose of providing a ration for all villagers who were inscribed on the village tax list, usually all males in the village between the ages of 18 and 60. The individual shares of *cong dien* were called *khau phan*, or ration. Extra shares of *cong dien* were also given to mandarins, to notables and to functionaries of the village to reimburse them for their services.

The *tu dan dien* usually served to provide income for village ceremonies, rituals, and celebrations. It seems that those in charge of the cultivation of *tu dan dien* for a particular year would obtain the articles required for the ceremony. The division of the produce tended to vary with the generosity and piety of those charged with the particular offering. Although the land was allotted to individuals, responsibility for offerings was given to groups, or neighbourhoods, called *giap* or *zom*.[10]

The division of land among ceremonial purposes was highly refined. The following example of a traditional pattern was recorded in the village of Ha Lo in the 1920s or 1930s.

a rice field is set apart for the feeding of the pigs of the Chung group, another for the feeding of the pigs of the *Nam* group (the sacrifice of these pigs being a ritual ceremony), a piece of land pays for the purchase of joss sticks and oil for the lamp of the *dinh (den huong dien)*, a rice field is set aside for the breeding of the cocks for the sacrifice, another is earmarked for the purchase of chickens and the payment of musicians *(nhac dien)*, another to buy glutinous ricecakes (*Oan dien*), a rice field is attributed to those who celebrate the rites (*quan vien*), another meets the expenses of the cult from the first to the fifteenth of the month (*soc vong*), a piece of riceland is devoted to the ceremony of the new ordinary rice (*com moi*), a field is devoted to the celebrations of the anniversary of the village spirit (the *dan*), another to the costs of the wrestling contest (*danh vat*), another to the costs of dancing contests (*thi con cho*), a lot is specifically assigned to the celebration of the fifth of the month (*trung ngu*), another to the celebration of the tenth of the month (*trung thap*), another to the fifteenth of the eighth month celebrations (*vong nguyet*), another to the spring festival (*xuan te*).[11]

THE VILLAGE LISTS

The allocation of the communal lands among cultivators was resolved by reliance on lists of village precedence, enforced by custom and sanction. The *cong dien* and *cong tho* and the *tu dan dien* and *tu dan tho* were distributed in strict accordance with such lists. These rosters ranked all male villagers and thereby indicated unambiguously the order in which persons would select their fields. As ranks did not change quickly, probably only a fraction of the *cong dien* actually changed hands during each distribution, but over a longer period substantial changes could occur.

Two types of village roll were used, the *so hang xa*, or village list, and the *so dinh*, or tax list. The *so hang xa* had no official character in regard to the central authority; it was a village established list. All male members of the community were included, even the very young and very old. Admission to the list occurred automatically for children of persons already registered. Those non-inscribed, but residing in the village (*ngu cu, dan lau*, or *dan ngoai*) became inscribed with consent of the notables and sometimes by offering a money payment (*ngu cu*).

The *so hang xa* was used in the distribution of *tu dan dien* and *tu dan tho*. As explained earlier, *tu dan dien* and *tu dan tho* provided funds for ritual purposes. The use of these lands rotated among all those listed on the *so hang xa*. The recipients of these fields were responsible for bringing offerings for the feasts and ceremonies of the coming year. The *so hang xa* was also the list used to distribute that part of the *cong dien* used for special functions and to pay the notables. The *so hang xa* designated everyone's position in the hierarchy of the commune. The exact position one held was based on age, education, service, and responsibility.

The tax list, or *so dinh*, was used to determine other divisions of communal lands. The distribution of *khau phan* (ration) was in equal-sized plots to everyone on the *so dinh* – males between the ages of 18 and 60.[12] The equal distribution of *khau phan* was an established principle but the equality was one of the measured area, not of fertility. The individual chose his *khau phan* in the order of the communal hierarchy, as expressed in the *so hang xa*. The greatest differences would occur when some land was single-cropped and another was double-cropped.

In most villages *khau phan* was given only to those who were registered on the personal tax register (*so dinh*). In other areas, however, some other categories included in the village list were also included in the distribution of *khau phan*. In these areas widows, children and the aged participated in the distribution but received smaller shares.[13] In some villages which allocated *khau phan* by hierarchy, the *cong tho* (non-rice lands) were allocated in reverse order. The people lowest on the list could choose the best *tho* lands.[14]

The following quotation is an example of the quantities involved in the distribution of *cong dien* and *tu dan dien* in the village of *Duong-Lien* at Hadong, established in June 1914:

> out of 431 *mau* of *cong-dien*: (1) 349 *mau* 9 *sao* are distributed every six years among the inhabitants (or two *sao* per inscribed); (2) 51 *mau* reserved for soldiers; (3) 1 *mau* 4 *sao* entrusted to the guardian of the temple to give light and incense, 3 *mau* allotted to the class of old people for the preparation of the holiday of Thuong-tau, 2 *mau* to the aged 70 years of age and over, to buy clothing, 2 *mau* to each of the four *giap* for the ceremony of the day of the fifteenth of the first year of the Annamite year, one *mau* to the *ly-thruong* and *pho-ly* (mayor and vice mayor), for the expenses of service, 5 *mau* to the *giau-thu* (teacher), 6 *sao* 10 *thuoc* to the *tu van* association for the Temple of Confucious; (4) 10 *mau* rented to the benefit of the communal fund.[15]

A GENERALISED DESCRIPTION OF LAND USE IN VILLAGE VIETNAM

Figure 3.1 is an idealised picture of the distribution of land in the traditional village. It indicates the division of village land into family and communal sections, it shows the further subdivision according to specific function, and finally, it suggests how groups might select certain pieces of land to cultivate under share arrangements. The parcels were not this evenly distributed or uniform. Lands of like purposes are here grouped together for convenience.

In section I of the figure *tu dien* lands are shown. Regular *tu dien* patrimonies are indicated by the letter P. These could be divided into various family needs and purposes. The letter W identifies the *huong hoa* and other family worship lands. Income from this land was used specifically for religious purposes, although there was a deep attachment to all the patrimony.

Section II of the diagram shows the lands of the cults (C) and the mutual assistance associations (A). These included lands designated for cults of teachers and administered by student societies. In one

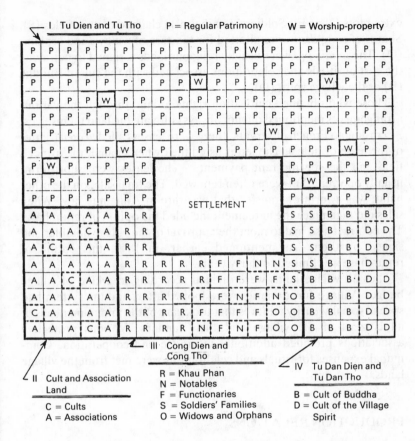

Figure 3.1 An Idealised Version of Land Distribution in the Traditional Vietnamese Village

village Gourou counted sixty-six of these societies.[16] The mutual assistance associations often had religious functions. There were also associations which were organised to take care of contingency expenses such as burials and weddings and others were a type of guild. Land could be held by all these associations or societies and the usufruct could be held by each member in turn, or the land could be rented.

Shown in sections III and IV are the communal lands. The *cong dien* and *cong tho* lands provided the individual shares, *khau phan* (R). The notables and functionaries, such as watchmen or guards also chose extra plots (N or F). Soldiers' families also claimed certain fields (S). Shares of *cong dien* were allotted for the care of widows and orphans (O). The *tu dan tho* were usually religious lands assigned to defraying the cost of rituals and celebrations associated with the cult of Buddha (B) or the village spirit (D).

Those who obtained cultivation rights to land through the various arrangements mentioned did not always cultivate the land themselves. According to French observers, there were leases called *ta dien* ('letter of the lease of field'). The letter listed the owner's name, the owner's field and the specific rent payment.[17] The leases were short-term, usually one year, but were often renewed. The final sale, on the other hand, was a form of transfer that was rare in Annamite law. When sales did take place the agreement included the option of repurchase. The contract also had to meet the approval of the village notables and signed by them. As mentioned earlier, in 1840, this option of repurchase was limited to thirty years.

Thus all village lands were divided according to a kind of village budget. Village functionaries were looked after, and the system had special social security features that took care of the minimum needs of all citizens of the village and their families. Various protective associations provided additional insurance and cooperation. Communal expenses for rituals and celebrations were met from the village lands.

PRODUCTION RELATIONS

Production management was through actions of the village notables, minor government officials, male family heads and male and female heads of mutual assistance teams. The notables administered the water resources and, in part, the usufructuary rights in land and the public works. One notable specialised in the collection of taxes and in keeping the village rolls which determined the allocation of public lands, and another controlled the village treasury. A notable supervised public works essential for agriculture, such as irrigation facilities, roads, and communal buildings. Improvements on public works and their maintenance were carried on through a labour requisition system under his direction.

The male family head was responsible for supervising the ploughing and preparation of the fields using male labourers. He used equipment and oxen which he owned or hired from another patriarch. Ploughing was the only part of the agricultural production process which was individualised, or not accomplished in groups. It was the very essential first part of the process which the patriarchs carefully guarded as their preserve. The patriarchs also organised labour during the harvesting period but then labour consisted of neighbourhood mutual assistance groups (and some hired labour) including both women and men.

Household labour was supplemented by adding children, either biologically or through adoption. If the patriarch became an official, or was particularly successful at farming, he might also supplement his household staff through polygamy. Another reason for polygamy would be if the husband and his first wife were unsuccessful in producing children. Generally, however, polygamy was the preserve of the very rich and high-level officials in traditional Vietnam.

Women's spheres and female powers were separate and greatly inferior to men's spheres and male powers in the village. In agriculture, women controlled the transplanting of rice since this function was linked to beliefs in the fertility of women being transferred to the plants. Women worked in neighbourhood work-groups headed by women for the rice planting. Another women's sphere was in marketing local products and this activity was led by an old woman in the market-place who controlled the market and settled disputes. Women also controlled, managed and worked in the village households and kitchen gardens.

Although the periodically redistributed *cong dien* land was allotted to a male inhabitant, it was not cultivated by the individual. The nature of rice-cultivation was such that not even the extended family could handle the entire task at various times during the year. All the plots of rice land in the village were cultivated by techniques that required intensive labour in certain periods and the labour force was therefore organised to work in sizeable groups in order to perform the required tasks. Since the work load was concentrated in the transplanting and harvesting seasons, two sources of labour power were relied upon to meet the extra labour demands. At planting time, reciprocal exchanges of labour were a means of augmenting family labour and at harvest-time migrant labour was also used.

The transplanting of rice seedlings was done through mutual assistance by women members of several familes working together. These groups of women were often united by bonds of worship and neighbourhood and sometimes also by common ancestry. Replanting was carried out in groups because once the seedling nursery was drained, the work had to be done quickly to ensure that the young plants would not suffer. Not all the nurseries had to be drained at once, however, and there was a week or so in which the work could be done. Groups worked on one nursery at a time until all were replanted in paddy fields. The men prepared the seedlings and brought them to the fields while the women performed the actual transplanting of the young plants.

At harvest-time conditions were different and there was little margin of time since the harvesting had to be done when the paddy was fully ripe. Labour migrated from one area of Vietnam to another during the harvest-season because harvests took place at different times between villages with different harvesting-times. Regular exchanges of workers occurred between villages or in some cases labour was recruited in market-places.

In addition to land and labour, water was an essential input for successful cultivation of rice. An adequate flow of water had to reach the fields at the proper time. Irrigation was not left to the individual family heads; instead the village and the central government handled these matters. On the village level, as mentioned earlier, the water supply was managed and allotted by the elected (male) notables. At the time of the feasts at the *dinh*, the inhabitants of the village were classified in tables. The following is a partial record of the communal law of the village of the Tho Duc:

> Eight inhabitants of the third table shall be designated to insure the irrigation of the rice fields. If in case of, or as a result of, negligence they shall have allowed too much water to be used, and as a result, it would not be possible to go forward with the transplantation of the lowest lands, all of the inhabitants of the third table shall be punished with a penalty of five ligatures per person.[18]

VILLAGE INDUSTRY

In many villages handicraft industries supplemented agricultural production and occupied villagers' time when they were not needed in the paddy fields. Some villages were almost exclusively industrial, and these were usually located in highly populated areas. Village custom, perhaps reaching back to the Chinese occupation when people had been selected from various villages to go to China and learn skills, determined the type of item to be manufactured. The industries were based for the most part on family labour. Apart from the universal crafts, villages specialised in various products and the complexity of the division of labour between villages was great. Gourou writes:

> It often happens that villages which produce native gold and silver ingots do not themselves prepare the bamboo strips (*nau*) which are used for the framework of these articles, and they buy them from the villages which, for the most part, do not produce any ingots.... The villages which make flat *latia* – leaf hats for women – do not make the hemispheric linings indispensable to hold the hat on the head; the linings are woven by other villages ... The potters of Bat Trong ... in preparation of the enamel for their potteries, make use of the ashes which they buy from the potters of Dinh Xa ... Nger Truc ... weaves large round bamboo baskets but does not weave the covers for these baskets; these are made at Ninh Xa.[19]

Even if the practice of the craft took the artisans out of the village, as for example with hairdressers and musicians, there was specialisation by village. The division of crafts by village was kept intact through the solidarity of the villagers. The knowledge of the procedures of production for a certain craft would remain in the control of the villagers, and they would keep this secret from people from other villages.

There was thus a complex organisation of specialisation of craft manufacture, not by family or guild, as in the West, but by village. Industrial villages required that other industrial villages have production and sales outlets for their partly finished products. For partly finished goods, it seems that producers traded directly with other villages and they probably arranged for transactions and transportation in a cooperative manner by village or neighbourhood.

Vietnamese males did not generally engage in trading since merchant activities were considered too lowly an occupation for male family heads or their sons. Government service or farming ranked above merchant activities in the Confucian hierarchy of occupations. Because of this prejudice, local buying-and-selling of agricultural and industrial goods was handled by peasant women, usually widows. The long-distance trading was often the occupation of wives of officials since these women had more funds with which to purchase larger stocks. Chinese merchants also handled much of the long-distance trading.

Another reason why trading was a woman's occupation was that village men were often more restricted in their travels because of the suspicion of officials about the potential for rebellion when there were contacts between citizens which did not involve the official hierarchy. Vietnamese men would be stopped along the road and their citizenship checked on the mandarin's rolls. If they were not registered, they were considered to be vagrants or vagabonds. Women were not citizens and were not considered important enough to be dangerous. Women, therefore, had more freedom of travel which was essential to their merchant activities.

MARKETS, MONEY AND CREDIT

Market-places are described by writers of early and middle colonial times and also existed in traditional Vietnam. Food products and handicraft items were exchanged in the markets and the commercial life in the market-place was active although the turnover was usually small. According to Gourou, walks from the village to the market were a welcome diversion for the peasants.[20] Markets were spaced at intervals between villages but for the most part, were not set up within the villages because they were not part of the community life:

> In the great majority of cases they [the markets] are not set up within the villages but in the open fields, along sides of a road, at the crossing of paths which link several villages. Indeed, the peasants mistrust the vagrant and the foreign population which the markets attract and would view the penetration of the sacred compound of the village by these strangers with alarm.[21]

Exceptions to this pattern are the specialised markets for products of industrial villages. These markets might be set up in the village but would be separate from the general purpose market and only the village product would be sold by the villagers.

The Vietnamese in precolonial times used money in a variety of ways. Coins, as a medium of exchange, were developed during the Chinese occupation. In the thirteenth century banknotes were issued. Paper money, however, was not used widely – if it remained in existence at all – at the time of the French conquest. French sources refer mainly to coins, and exchange rates are stated in coin equivalents. Money was used within the village for payments of fines as an alternative for certain goods in obligatory gift-giving, and sometimes for payment of taxes. Coins were also used in the rural market-places.

Most credit institutions that existed in traditional Vietnam cannot properly be regarded as providing capital funds for investment. Most borrowing was not for the purpose of increasing production or income but was a last resort in times of poor harvests or when other calamities befell the peasants. The French later commented unfavourably on the additional use of borrowed money for celebrations and gambling.

Women accumulated money for merchant activities through a lending and gambling society known as the *hui*. The manner in which the *hui* provided money for goods purchase was not described until recent village studies. In the modern *hui*, the participants bid for loans and the society lasts until each participant has acquired a loan once. The initiator of the *hui* provides a meal for the participants but gets her loan interest-free.[22]

Lending was regulated by Vietnamese law codes. The maximum rate of interest was limited to 36 per cent (3 per cent per month). (This is low when compared with rates that were charged during the colonial period.) A further stipulation was that the accumulated interest must never be allowed to exceed the amount of principal originally loaned.[23] This last provision saved the borrower from perpetual indebtedness.

Land and crops in Vietnam were pledged as security for loans and this was accomplished in a way very different from Western practice. The most frequent arrangement where a guarantee for loans was involved was the *dien co*. This gave land as a pledge but did not yield the right of permanent possession. The only right actually granted was that of using the land for a stipulated length of time.[24] Only usufruct, not ownership, could be forfeited to the lender. This type of agreement often worked in this manner:

> The land was not actually given to the creditors as security; the debtor did not actually give up his land, but merely gave the creditor the contract and his deed of property. The land was managed for the creditor either by a third party or by the debtor himself, by virtue of a renting agreement added to the original contract.[25]

The use of contracts cited here seems advanced but the extensiveness and longevity of the use of written contracts in Vietnam is questionable. Gueffier did not comment on the use of land and credit contracts in traditional Vietnam. Other authors actually have asserted that written contracts were not found consistently throughout Vietnam. It is most probable that contracts with money-lenders were most common around trading and urban centres.

The land-pledge agreements that emerged in later precolonial Vietnam were ingenious in protection of the customary rights, while they were at the same time adapted to market trading. The old village rights were protected because the contract putting the land up for security had to be certified by three village notables, representing the village interest. The traditional family rights were protected because only the right of use was pledged and the creditor could not take over the land indefinitely. At the same time the usufructuary rights to land were marketable and pledgeable as security. The holder of land forfeited as security had the obligation to keep up the property and to pay the land tax on it.

The rights of the debtor were likewise restricted. Although the land still belonged to his patrimony he was no longer allowed to dispose of it. He could not sell the land, put it up as security in another transaction, or divide it among his heirs. The debtor could not lose his land, because if the creditor was not paid by the end of the agreed period he merely kept the usufructuary rights until he was reimbursed in full. There was thus provision for credit in traditional Vietnam, but the institutions were such that credit could not lead to concentration of landholding and perpetual indebtedness for a large part of the population. These would be the problems of the colonial era.

4 The Colonial Impact

The French established control over the Vietnamese countryside in the middle-to-late-nineteenth century and proceeded to institute changes in administration and laws which opened up rural Vietnam to the forces of the world market. Markets for foreign and native products were soon developed through the sponsorship of French exporters and importers. The development of land markets was also aided by the French administrators. These administrators and legal advisers transformed Vietnamese property institutions by reinterpreting Vietnamese practices into compatibility with French conceptions of private and public property categories. The new categories were conducive to market exchange and through the market process, peasants and villages lost their rights to land and large shares of the agricultural produce. The variability of market demand and prices along with an unregulated extension of usurious moneylending resulted in rapid concentration of landed wealth in the hands of absentee landlords.

The main purpose of the French colonisation of Vietnam was the economic development of the country in ways which would benefit French capitalists. In order to develop a commercial system in which they could sell industrial goods and purchase raw materials, the French embarked on vast projects of economic improvement and institutional change. Although they made some attempt to understand the social structure they were trying to change, their understanding was never good enough to guide their policies to the hoped-for results. Their programmes reflected their efforts to achieve a capitalist market structure, but they were often frustrated when the results of their policies led them into deeper and deeper administrative problems. Frequent reorganisation and a rapid turnover of high officials led to rapidly changing laws.

DEVELOPMENT OF THE INFRASTRUCTURE AND TAX POLICIES

Transportation facilities were the first to be developed. From 1860 to 1935 the French built 15 625 miles of roads, 1570 miles of railroads and opened up several canals.[1] These new facilities served to open up the world market to the rural Vietnamese and aided in the opening up of the Vietnamese commune to commercial forces. In Cochin China particularly, agricultural production, mostly rice production, expanded because of the newly created market. That is, the area of land under crops expanded initially while traditional production methods remained largely unchanged.

A great expansion in irrigation facilities also introduced by the French provided for a greatly increased area under cultivation. In Cochin China the area of cultivation increased in the following manner:[2]

1883	675 000 hectares
1903	1 300 000 hectares
1923	1 906 000 hectares

For the southern part of Vietnam alone, exports of rice increased from virtually nothing to 1 million tonnes in 1938.[3]

These vast development projects were financed through the transformation of the traditional Vietnamese taxation and redistributive systems into a Western budget and tax system. In traditional times the emperor and his representatives, the mandarins, received a portion of the village output for their own use and they also collected an additional part of the crop in order to set up large storehouses of rice in good harvest years for distribution in poor harvest years. In contrast, the major financial concern of the French administration was to maintain a balanced colonial budget and because of their costly projects, this led directly to high taxation. The colonialists seemed to take for granted the ability of the Vietnamese to finance French development projects. Lack of concern about the conditions of the taxpayer and ignorance about traditional Vietnamese standards of equity led to arbitrary as well as oppressively heavy taxation. Instead of setting up storehouses for famine periods, the French exported rice in good years and there was none left for distribution in poor harvest years.

An elaboration of some colonial taxation measures will point out the direction of policy. The French admirals who controlled Cochin China in the 1860s raised the land tax from 5 to 10 francs per *mau* and the personal tax from 2 to 10 francs per person. Total tax receipts in Cochin China increased from half a million gold francs in the 1860s to 20 million by 1880 and 35 million by 1887.[4] Rice land was the major source of income which could be taxed. If we compare these figures on increased taxation with figures on increase of cultivated area, we can see that tax collections increased at about twice the amount of increase in cultivated area. There was no increase in productivity or other improvement to support such a heavy increase in taxes. Through heavy taxation with harsh enforcement, rice exports from Cochin China increased steadily despite some poor crop years.

The colonial taxation policies in Tonkin were even more oppressive. In this area the Vietnamese undertook armed resistance which was very costly for the French to repress. This caused a deficit in the Tonkin treasury which, according to Western economic custom, had to be extinguished by higher taxes. Taxes were doubled between 1890 and 1896 and raised 50 per cent again before 1898.[5] There was very little increase in cultivated area and no increase in productivity which could possibly justify such a heavy increase in taxes.

French colonial taxes were particularly destructive of village institutions because these taxes were collected directly from the villagers in Vietnam. Colonial administrations of other Western powers and French colonial administrations elsewhere relied mostly on indirect import and export taxes which influenced primarily the commercial sectors. The French were able to collect direct taxes from the Vietnamese because personal and land taxation had been enforced for centuries and there was an already existing administrative structure which ensured compliance. The French gained control of this administrative structure and drastically increased the traditional land and personal taxes. French policy made regional budgets in Vietnam dependent exclusively on the direct taxes collected by regional officials. Colonial budgets in all regions of Vietnam could then be balanced and remain during times of extraordinary public works projects and times of poor crops because the regional officials had a vested interest in expanding programmes and harshly enforcing tax increases to support these programmes.

VILLAGE ADMINISTRATION

Political administration followed the general policy of direct French control since there was a well-defined administrative hierarchy in Vietnam which the French could easily take over. Because of their remoteness and 'backwardness' the tribes in the hinterland of Laos and Vietnam were left to rule themselves. The Vietnamese structures, because of their political development, were easier to penetrate and rule. In all three regions of Vietnam – Cochin China, Tonkin, and

Annam – French administration was imposed on many levels of political authority. French personnel were used in local administration in Vietnam though in other colonies in Southeast Asia these positions were filled by indigenous officials. French administration often penetrated to district and village levels, especially in Cochin China which was classified as a colony.

A French colonial official, Kresser, has graphically described the French attempt to extend their control to the villages:

> As soon as the conquest was accomplished and the country pacified we sought to mix in with the organization of the village, regulate it, determine more precisely the responsibilities devolving on each member of the council, submit the administration and the budget of the commune to a strict and permanent control, and remedy abuses of all sorts as well as the oppression the notables practised with regards to those they administered.[6]

Most interference in village government was done in the name of 'reform' but few reforms had the expected results. In Cochin China, judicial and police powers were taken away from village notables and given to French policemen and judges. Tax assessment, the supervision of public works brigades or corvées, and the supervision of military draft was taken from the notables in southern Vietnam 'in order to protect the poor villagers'.

Administrative reforms were also imposed on the notables. The colonial government assigned exact duties to the notables and officially limited their numbers. Educational requirements were set up which favoured those trained in the new Franco-Annamite schools. Further reforms of 1921 and 1927 attempted a new organisation which partially returned traditional powers, but the old notables refused to participate. Finally in 1930, discouraged with reform, the French replaced traditional elections with the appointment of notables. French-appointed mandarins thenceforth named village and cantonal heads, subject to ratification by the French *Résident*.[7]

In effecting tax reform the French dropped the category of non-taxpayer. In traditional Vietnam, a person without property had less prestige and was called a non-taxpayer. In the interest of 'social equality' this category was dropped and henceforth those who did not pay taxes were violating the law. Traditionally it was non-prestigious to be poor, but according to the new system it was criminal to be poor. Pauperism, vagrancy and crime grew steadily as a result of these reforms.

The heavy burden of French taxes often led to complicated changes in village institutions. In traditional Vietnam, each taxpayer received a *khau phan* (ration) from the communal lands to help to pay his taxes and provide a ration for his family. The dual purpose of the *khau phan* was destroyed when the personal tax was increased from the traditional 10 per cent to 50 or 70 per cent of income from the communal land parcel. No longer did the *khau phan* provide a basic ration for the villager's family and no longer could the tax payment easily be met. Changes in village government and high taxes also had effects on village granaries. Storage of grain in the village decreased and merchants took over the function of storing grain, but at a high speculative profit.

Opposition to these French policies and their effects on the village emerged by the early-to-mid-twentieth century. Two opposing political forces arose among the Vietnamese leadership, the nationalist–communists on one side, and those Vietnamese who collaborated with the French, on the other. The communist opposition tried to gain control in the countryside (this is discussed in the next chapter) and the French tried to repulse them with many of the same methods that the USA was to use in a later period. In the 1930s, Paul Kresser explained the French view that the Vietnamese commune had to be reformed in order to fight the communists:

> One of the indirect results of the events which took place in Cochin China between 1930 and 1931 at the instigation of the Communist Party had been to make clear the necessity of reforming that traditional institution, the Annamite commune ... The firm and continued action of the French government alone has been able to quell the feeling of fear that has shown itself in the communal authorities.[8]

This was the French version of the later US 'Pacification Campaign' and 'the other war'.

LAND CONCESSIONS

When the French first occupied Cochin China in the 1860s there were lands 'belonging to the public domain' which they wished to convert to private property. Gueffier states that the French government had acquired this land from the Annamite government by virtue of the conquest.[9] The colonialists made a study of Annamite land law but

interpretations were difficult. The equitable interpretation of traditional rights to fit into the French categories of private and public land
was impossible. Some properties which were disposed of as if they
belonged to the public domain were later 'recognised' as 'private
properties'. Much of the land which was auctioned off as part of the
public domain was probably *cong dien* (communal land), *tu dien*
(family land), or some other category of land over which the
community formerly held rights.

The French colonialists made concessions 'legal' by forcing the
emperor to cede to the French Governor General his rights to dispose
of land. In doing so, the French misinterpreted the emperor's right of
disposition. The traditional concessions for opening up new lands were
not hereditary, but were a lifetime right or merely a right to collect
taxes. They could not be considered a concession of ownership. The
French concessions included all the Western property rights pertaining
to private ownership.

The best way of describing the French policy on concessions is to say
it was inconsistent but had a definite bias toward Western property
rights. The following is an example of policy changes:

> the land in and around Saigon was at first sold in lots by public
> auction (decrees of February 20, 1862) – or by private contract
> (decree of June 17, 1862); in 1864 (decree of February 25) the land
> was sold at a fixed price, or rented out with the promise that it would
> be sold later to the renter. In 1871 (decree of December 29), it was
> decided to go back to the system of auctions.[10]

The concessions of rural land in Cochin China also followed rapidly
changing laws. According to an 1864 decree, a system was inaugurated
whereby land was sold for a fixed price with a minimum of 10 francs per
hectare and free concessions could be made to reward cooperative
public servants. By a decree of 1874, concessions were to be free to
those who would agree to cultivate all the lands within a period of ten
years. In 1878, taxes on concessioned land were postponed for the first
four years after which taxes and a payment of 10 francs per hectare had
to be paid. In 1882, all lands classified as uncultivated new lands were
to be given in concession without charge. Then in 1886 the maximum
amount of rural land granted without charge was set at 10 hectares. In
1889, this was changed to 500 hectares and in 1890 the maximum limit
was abolished. In 1889 the period allowed with no cultivation was also
brought down from ten to five years.[11] These laws, which were drafted

to extend cultivation, were not consistent with each other and also did not consider traditional tenure rights.

After the French had pushed north and conquered Tonkin at the end of the nineteenth century, they found large sections of cultivable land which had been abandoned temporarily because of the war. The colonial government disposed of these lands by making concession grants or by selling the land at low cost to Frenchmen and cooperative Vietnamese mandarins. The small farmers, on returning to their fields to plant crops, found they had to make rental agreements with share payments amounting to about half their crops.

Some of these formerly cultivated lands in Tonkin and other lands which had never been cultivated were given in extensive grants – 'latifundia of 8500, 10 000, 11 000, 13 500, 14 500 and 21 000 hectares were granted to isolated individuals'.[12] Before 1810, 223 000 hectares of land were given in 337 grants. Many of these immense grants remained uncultivated. When the Europeans were able to find labourers to clear the land, these peasants would often become attached to the land after a while and would try to drive out the European 'owner'.

By the twentieth century France had conquered all Vietnam, Laos, and Cambodia, and land laws applied to the whole area, now called French Indochina.[13] According to a decree issued in December 1913, new lands were to be sold if possible but up to 300 hectares could be given free. Land was supposed to be sold at a public auction except for grants which were made by public officials. The Governor General could make grants of over 1000 hectares and lesser grants could be made by lower officials. At this time also, the French began to put some limits on property rights to ensure the development of granted land. The person receiving the property would not be given a final deed until final payment for the property was received and the land was cultivated. A stipulation was also made that the individual receiving the grant was not to disturb graves or pagodas which might be on his property and he was required to permit access to them. (This designation again brings up the question of whether the grants were really of previously unused land.) Further to encourage the development of granted land, a decree of September 1926 specified that cultivation had to begin the year after purchase.

Encouragement of large landholding through concessions was deliberate. Although land was given away or sold at low prices, only people who understood the continually changing system of concessions had a chance of obtaining land. These persons were the French colonials (*colons*) and cooperating Vietnamese mandarins. Small Vietnamese farmers did not have a chance of obtaining land on the frontier under the concession system. Under this new system, the peasant cleared land for a fixed fee paid by the owner, and not for a future interest in the cultivatable land as was true in the traditional system.

The new system for the development of land increased the total cultivated area by 8 per cent (if we assume that all concessions were undeveloped previously – we know this is not true for some lands; therefore 8 per cent is a generous estimate). It is not unreasonable to suppose that opening up new land through migration could have produced an increase of 8 per cent in fifty to eighty years. Only a little over a third of the area concessioned was cultivated in the French period. The rest was 'owned' so that it could not be brought into cultivation in the traditional manner through group migrations and settlements.

The laws of the French, although inconsistent, incorporated most of the usual Western property rights. Individuals could hold most rights to land without the restraints of community or state. Individuals could own land without cultivating it; that is, untilled land could 'belong' to someone other than those who first cleared and tilled it. The innovation of selling land at auction was introduced, as was land speculation. In general, Western institutions involving landed property were adopted by the French in Vietnam to deal with concessions.

This was done purposely because the French initially set up a dual set of property laws, one set for the French concessions, and another for the Vietnamese. The Vietnamese would be ruled with the traditional Vietnamese laws (by French interpretation). Of course, Vietnamese renters of French concessioned land were effectively living under French property law.

The policy of concessioning was developed for the purpose of promoting economic progress through the private enterprise system. We have seen that the policy was not very successful in developing new land, while it inhibited the traditional system of land development. It was also not successful in the development of new production methods on the land which was cultivated. Rice was cultivated in concession areas with traditional techniques of intensive cultivation. The French concessionaire was not a capitalist entrepreneur; he did not administer an estate. The concessionaire in rice areas was only a landlord who collected rents from small peasant producers who provided their own inputs and guided their own production. There were rubber, coffee and tea plantations set up on some concessioned land. These were managed by their owners but production techniques were not advanced.

The concessionaires were not the only landlords to arise under the colonial system. The concentration of landholding, with the adjunct of usurious moneylending, was dependent on many additional factors. In Table 4.1, we can see that in Cochin China about 12.5 per cent of the cultivated land was owned by French concessionaires. Vietnamese concessionaires owned a somewhat higher amount, so that 25–33 per cent of the cultivated land was held by concessionaires. By the time the French left Vietnam, however, 80 per cent of the Cochin-Chinese peasants were tenants and about 75 per cent of the land was owned by landlords. Most land was concentrated by other means.[14]

Table 4.1 French concessions 1931[a]

	Total cultivated land (in thousands of hectares)	Concessions (in thousands of hectares)	Actually cultivated concessions (in thousands of hectares)
Tonkin	1200	120	30
Annam	1000	170	25
Cochin China	2400	600	300

[a]Joseph Buttinger, *Vietnam: A Dragon Embattled*, p. 598.

THE CREATION OF A LAND MARKET

In traditional Vietnam concentration of property was not very extensive because the laws and customs of the community and the central government were hostile to it. When the French arrived in Vietnam with their desire for marketable property, they proceeded to institute land and credit markets. In the interest of creating effective markets, they suppressed traditional laws which had prevented large landholding and they instituted laws and policies which led to concentration.

The Survey and Land Register

The colonialists were first concerned with finding landowners. 'At the time of the occupation, the first task which the administration set out to accomplish was to find out who were the landowners.[15] The colonial government thought that it must survey the land and find the real owners. Their survey ran into trouble. Gourou stated, 'It is impossible even for officials of the cadaster to discover the real owner of a parcel.'[16] Where the usufruct of land had been pledged or given for some reason, officials would credit the usufructuary as owner. The French officials thought that property would be more secure if it were in a clear official status rather that under private agreement which was merely acknowledged within the village. Putting everything in 'clear official status' involved the imposition of French property rights.

The colonial officials effected a transition of the *dia bo* (traditional land taxation list) into a definitive land register in Cochin China.[17] In May 1863 the French ruled that all traditional deeds and titles to land in Cochin China should be turned in for new deeds and titles. This measure could not be implemented. In 1865 they declared that all land transactions must be registered. In 1871 they ordered the villages to draw up current books analogous to the *dia bo* and after 1877 an abstract from this land book had to be included with the deed in any transaction involving a piece of property. The book then acquired probative power and was declared a definitive land book by administrative officers, but it did not have absolute authority in court. Next came perhaps the most decisive decree in diverting the *dia bo* from its original purpose and creating a generalised Western land registration system. This was the decree of 1891 which transferred the job of keeping the *dia bo* from the community and gave it to the French administration. Each government administrator was charged with keeping the records of property in his district and the villages were merely given a copy of the land book.

In Tonkin and Annam the assault on traditional property rights was not so great nor so direct. French-controlled land registration systems were not set up as they were in Cochin China. Property laws and court decrees succeeded in changing property rights enough to disrupt land redistribution patterns and to cause concentration of land but this was not on the same scale as in Cochin China. Table 4.2 shows a representation of the concentration of land in the three areas. In Cochin China where the land registration system was placed in French hands, Le Than Khoi found considerably greater concentration of landholding. In Tonkin 180 large landlords owned 20 per cent of the land, in Annam fifty large landlords owned 10 per cent of the land and in Cochin China 45 per cent of the land was owned by 6300 large landholders.[18]

Table 4.2   Concentration of land in Vietnam under French occupation[a]

	Tonkin		Annam		Cochin China	
	Number	%	Number	%	Number	%
Partition of Landholders						
Small						
0–5 ha.	946 500	98.2	646 700	98.5	183 000	71.7
0–12.4 acres						
Medium						
5–50 ha.	17 500	1.8	8900	1.35	65 750	25.8
12.4–124 acres						
Large						
over 50 ha.	180	0.02	50	0.008	6300	2.5
Partition of Land						
Small						
0–5 ha.	480 000	40.0	400 000	50.0	345 000	15.0
0–12.5 acres						
Medium						
5–50 ha.	240 000	20.0	120 000	15.0	850 000	37.0
12.5–124 acres						
Large						
over 50 ha.	240 000	20.0	800 000	10.0	1 035 000	45.0
over 124 acres						
Communal Land	240 000	20.0	200 000	25.0	70 000	3.0
Total	1 200 000	100.0	800 000	100.0	2 300 000	100.0

[a]Le Than Khoi, *Histoire du Viet-nam*, p. 422.

French Land Law and the French Courts

There were fundamental differences between French law and traditional Vietnamese law. The French had pledged to abide by Vietnamese customs and they first tried to set up two systems of land law. French law was to apply for the French, and French-interpreted Vietnamese law was to apply for the Vietnamese. The two systems were in conflict because the most fundamental principle of French law was the protection of individual rights, and the most fundamental principles of Vietnamese law was the protection of family, commune, and state rights. As conflicts arose between the two systems, the French system took the upper hand and collective rights were sacrificed to individual rights.

Problems arose when transactions were made between natives and Europeans. Such transactions were made on forms prescribed by French law and without participation of village notables in the agreement, thereby village rights in land were sacrificed. Where there were conflicting contracts involving the same parcel of land, French law would also predominate.[19]

In practice even *native* litigation in Cochin China was subject to French law and French judges. 'It was French or principally French jurisprudence which governed native litigation even in Annam and Tonkin – always in Cochin China.'[20] French judges were mostly ignorant of Vietnamese customs and language and had to rely on interpreters.

The decrees passed by the colonial administration showed a trend toward destruction of native property rights in favour of an individual ownership system. The usufructuary market had to be destroyed as the ownership market was established. One important step in this procedure was the decree of the Governor General of 5th September 1882. This decree stated that legal action against property could be taken in Annam: that is, property could be sold by court order. In precolonial Vietnam custom forbade the seizure of property when the usufruct of land had been given as security. The traditional contract, *dien co*, merely involved the loss of usufruct until the loan was paid. Permanent control of the land could not be sacrificed as the result of a loan.

There was disagreement between Philastre the official interpreter of the Vietnamese law code, and other French writers on traditional contracts and the rights they encompassed. Philastre thought that the lands put up for security belonged to the creditor. Consistent with this interpretation, French law required that creditors be listed in the *dia bo*. Gueffier disagreed with this interpretation and stated that creditors never had greater than usufructuary rights, even in the event of non-payment of debt.[21] Usufructuary rights simply continued until the debt was paid. Under these conditions when the *dia bo* was changed from a tax register to a land register, rights were taken away from the debtor. He lost the right to pay back the debt and in so doing to free his land.

The French enforced another law which tended to reduce the significance of *dien co* contracts. They decreed that if the creditor had possession of property for more that thirty years he became the legal owner by virtue of his uninterrupted tenure. Gueffier contended that this law was taken from the traditional law which prescribed that after thirty years, repurchase was not authorised.[22] The nineteenth-century precolonial law had referred to the *mai-lai-thuc* (option to repurchase) contract and not the more frequent *dien co*.

Initially, breaking communal barriers was not easy, for in traditional Vietnam the commune would not allow any outsider to control its land. Even as late as the 1930s, Gourou found that it was difficult for anyone to buy land in a commune other than that in which he was born.[23] The villagers banded together to prevent the dispossession of one of their fellow-villagers. They resorted to destruction of the new owner's crops if necessary or would try to allocate a large share of taxes to the outsider. The large landowning buyer was expected to take the seller as his tenant and he would find no other tenant if he wanted to make a change.

This hostility of the villagers could not always successfully oppose large landowning. In the disjunctive new villages in the south intrusion was easy. Even in northern villages large landowners could gain control if they had the mandarin's support.

Not only were village rights in family patrimony abrogated by French laws, but also village rights to communal land were ignored. A decree of the *Résident Supérior* in 1903 attempted to renounce the policy of privileges of the village notables.[24] This decree took away from the village its judicial power and legal authority. After this decree, the village could neither take a case to court nor make a contract without special authorisation of the *Résident* who was chief of the province. When the contract involved more than 500 piasters, the village had to get the authorisation of the *Résident Supérieur*.

French laws also attacked communal land directly. The 1903 decree permitted the alienation of *cong dien* if authorised by the *Résident Supérieur*. This decree was directly antithetical to traditional laws which had consistently tried to preserve *cong dien* from alienation. According to a decree of 1923, all communal lands which had been occupied for at least twenty years would be granted to the occupier in full ownership.[25] Here prescription (the acquiring of rights through long-term use) was made lawful; this again was antithetical to traditional law. All communal lands first occupied during the French takeover would come within the twenty-year requirement for full ownership. For lands occupied for less than twenty years, a claim of occupation might be difficult to disprove. Traditional laws over hundreds of years had consistently declared the inalienability and non-prescriptibility of communal land; within fifty years the French had reversed both these fundamental principles.

It took the colonial administration a long while to realise the value of periodically redistributed communal land. It was not until 1930 that measures were taken to protect communal land still in existence.[26] A decree of October 1935 ordered all provinicial heads to require the villages placed under their authority to proceed regularly and periodically with the distribution of the communal lands among their inscribed members.[27]

The French decrees and court decisions regarding land law succeeded in weakening several classes of traditional rights. Rights of family heads with respect to their patrimony were abrogated by the decrees which destroyed the usufructuary market and created an ownership market. The village's control over communal land was limited by laws which allowed alienation and prescription of communal land and rulings which curtailed the power of village officials. This restructuring of land rights was the first step in the transition to land concentration. The next step was to entrap the peasant in indebtedness.

MONEY-LENDING

The French-colonial courts introduced change as much through the non-enforcement of traditional laws as by purposive change in law. According to traditional law, the maximum legal rate of interest which money-lenders could charge was 3 per cent per month, or 36 per cent per year. Outstanding interest could never exceed the principal of the loan. During colonial times interest reached 10 per cent per month and over.There was from 50 to 100 per cent interest on a six-month advance of rice.[28] No limit was set on the relation of interest to principal so that when peasants were not able to make payments on loans, perpetual indebtedness at high rates resulted. Where the money-lenders were able to bring foreclosure on loans, money-lending was the vehicle for the transition to large landholding and tenancy.

A form of usury was practised before the French arrived in Vietnam. The longevity of the precolonial institution of money-lending is an open question, but it certainly took on a different form in traditional Vietnam. Money-lending was a local institution involving Vietnamese and Chinese merchants and lenders. The outcome of taking a loan was not foreclosure on the peasant's land.

French colonials blamed the high interest rates of their era on the imperfect markets for land and credit. Gueffier stated that if the creditor had more security, rates of interest would be lower.[29] We have studied the process of transfer of rights from debtors to creditors throughout the period of French rule, yet the interest rates *did not drop*. There are two principal reasons for this – the great political and economic power of the money-lenders which allowed high rates to be charged, and the Vietnamese peasants' unfamiliarity with the credit market.

Those who lent money held certain political, economic and social positions which gave them power over their debtors. The Chinese merchant-intermediaries had been in Vietnam in precolonial times, when there was some merchant trade between the good rice-producing areas in the south, and the handicrafts areas in the north. International trade in rice was legally restricted at that time. When the country was opened up to international trade in colonial times, the Chinese intermediaries expanded their activities. As a class they monopolised merchant activities in Cochin China. They speculated in rice by buying at harvest-time and selling back to the peasant at twice the price later in the year. If the peasant ran short of funds the merchant also became his money-lender, increasing his power *vis-à-vis* the peasant. Although the merchant Chinese were a relatively permanent population, the amount of repatriation of profits was approximately VN\$ 5 000 000 annually. This compares with VN\$ 40 000 000 for the French (both government and private) and VN\$1 240 000 a year for the Indian money-lenders.[30]

Indian money-lenders, called *chetties*, made most of their profits through usury and accumulation of land rather than through merchant activities. *Chetties* received the protection of French laws because, in most cases, they were French or British subjects. *Chetties* were able to gain a foothold in Cochin China during the bad harvests of 1905, 1906 and 1907.[31] They lent money or rice to hungry peasants in return for an interest in their land. In the thirty years that followed, they gained control of 25 per cent of the rice land in Cochin China and with the extension of the market, began to move into other parts of Vietnam. The French and collaborating Vietnamese were also engaged in money-lending activities in addition to their major occupation of landowning on a large scale. The Vietnamese constituted the largest landlord group. They bought land from other groups who had acquired it through usury or they conducted their own money-lending activities.

There was solidarity among the various nationality groups in their monopolistic shares of the markets. The Chinese predominantly controlled and divided the merchant market and engaged in money-lending. The Indians controlled and divided the most speculative sector of the non-institutional lending market. Wealthy Vietnamese and French had predominant control of the land market. The peasant's choice of buyers, landlords and money-lenders was further reduced by the dual roles of some groups as money-lender–buyer and landlord–money-lender. Changing landlords or buyers was not very easy when the peasant owed money to his current landlord or buyer.

The French attempted to create an institutional credit system which they expected would solve the money-lending and usury problems. The private credit institutions which had been attempted and had relied on native savings failed because the Vietnamese seemed to have a lack of confidence in the institutions and an aversion to individual saving. This was a natural reaction to a foreign institution because traditional savings were organised through communal government and other communal associations.

The government-controlled lending institutions started with the creation of *Caisse de Prevoyance* in 1907.[32] Not until after 1923 did the government institutions reach anything but the upper and middle-class farmers, however. Thompson contended that, after 1923, these institutions did reach the market that was formerly the preserve of the *chetty* and succeeded in reducing the rate of interest.[33]

One reason why the French institutions had trouble penetrating the exclusive markets of money-lenders is the inflexibility of institutional-ised credit. European contracts provided for a specific period of time in which the loan had to be paid off. The harvest was unpredictable but the loan payment was fixed and constant. The repayment period was also often not long enough. The money-lenders were more likely to make longer-term loans which were more easily renewable.

The failure of the credit market was due in part to the peasants' unfamiliarity with market methods of distribution and allocation of resources. The Vietnamese peasant family used loans mainly for types of consumption purposes. First, the peasant borrowed for contingency expenses such as marriages, burials and bad harvests. These needs had been primarily taken care of by associations and the village when the traditional redistributive system of exchange was in force. Second, conditions were so bad in terms of high taxes and rents in some areas that even a normal harvest could not be made to last until the next harvest season and the peasant had to borrow for normal consumption expenditures. The peasants could have borrowed for productive investment but evidently this was not typical. Productive improvements carried out by individuals or families was not part of the traditional system. In precolonial times large productive improvements were community or central government activities, that is, it was beyond the means of the individual to improve the irrigation system.

Another factor which caused the development of usury rather than an effective credit market was the absence of any traditions about the payment of debts. Gourou mentioned that the peasant would borrow with the more or less conscious hope of not repaying his debt.[34] He also stated that the Vietnamese was a good taxpayer because this would bring him prestige in the village, but he was a very poor debtor because of the lack of established traditions against non-payment of debt.[35]

The concentration of power on the part of the creditor groups, and the lack of traditions of individual entrepreneurship by the debtor groups, led to the failure of the credit market. The course which the credit market took – usury – led also to the concentration of land with little accompanying technical advance. Nevertheless, the failure of credit and the land market to bring about development did not prevent the destruction of the old systems of distribution and exchange in the villages.

LABOUR MARKET

The establishment of a labour market in Vietnam was a consequence of the functioning of the land and produce-markets. Peasants in the village usually turned to renting the land which they had previously held, and they usually also became part-time paid labourers on larger holdings owned by others. About 10 per cent of the village population became paid agricultural labourers who neither rented nor owned land.

In addition to paid labour in the village, an industrial labour market developed. The dispossession of the peasants' holdings in the countryside provided the poor conditions which made labour available for French plantations, mines and industries in Vietnam. In the southern regions, peasants who could not find enough work in the village to feed themselves had to work on the plantations, which they called 'hell on earth'. Working conditions were poor and food was inadequate. When workers under contract tried to run away, they were tortured or hanged. Conditions were so miserable that even according to rubber companies' records, the mortality rate was 30 per cent.[36]

Plantations, mines and industries, however, never grew to a very large part of the total economy in Indochina during the colonial period. Official statistics showed 220 000 industrial and plantation workers by 1929 but these statistics are considered to be low because they measured registered workers and often more that one Vietnamese used one official workers' card.[37] At its largest, this working class included between 5 and 10 per cent of the Vietnamese population of working age.

RESULTS OF COLONIALISM

The colonial impact brought most of the changes which usually accompany the introduction of markets and capitalist property relations. The French colonialists developed transportation and communications which opened up parts of Vietnam to the world market. Peasants increased their production of commodities, particularly rice, which could be sold in the world market. Production was increased through an increase in the area cultivated rather than a change in production techniques and this increased production was exported. Meanwhile, the introduction of Western medicine and public health accelerated population increases.

Production of rice did not increase very much in Tonkin and Annam during the entire French period, but over time, less of it stayed in the village for consumption. Statistics for the whole of French Indochina show that rice production rose from 4.3 million tonnes in 1900 to 6.3 million tonnes in 1937.[38] The greatest part of this increase was in Cochin China. As is shown in Table 4.3, yields in the three areas of Vietnam are similar, although only Cochin China produced for the export market.

Exports of rice increased rapidly when the French took the harbour of Saigon in 1860. Increases in rice exports were as follows:[39]

Year	Tonnes of rice
1860	57 000
1877	320 000
1937	1 548 000

About 70 per cent of the value of Vietnamese exports was in rice and the only other important export was rubber. 50 per cent of rice exports went

Table 4.3   Rice: acreage, yields, production average, 1935/6 to 1939/40[a]

Country	Acreage	Yield per acre	Production	Production per capita
	1000 acres	*lbs.*	*1000 m.t.*	*lbs.*
China	48 853	2 259	50 064	270
Japan	7 862	3 408	12 153	384
French Indochina	14 306	1 0006	6 530	620
Tonkin	3 674	1 129	1 882	418
Annam	2 337	928	984	354
Cochin China	5 690	1 232	3 179	1 298

[a]US Department of Agriculture, *Agriculture in French Indochina* (Washington, DC: Government Printing Office, 1950) p. 24.

to China, and this factor was significant because of the fluctuations of the Chinese silver market.[40] In addition to the usual vagaries of the world market for agricultural produce, Vietnamese peasant producers had to deal with the price fluctuations of their rice market brought about by the fluctuations of the Chinese silver market.

There remain two important questions concerning the colonial impact. First, who received the benefits from the increase in production resulting from opening-up trade in world markets, and second, how much did the population increase negate the effects of production increase? As indicated in previous sections on money-lenders and landowners, foreign groups received a large part of the benefits. Regarding the distribution of income within the country: in 1931, 49 per cent of imports were absorbed by the rich who constituted less than 10 per cent of the population.[41] The shifts in income distribution brought about with the establishment of markets become clear when we realise that for the whole of Indochina the most highly-paid 10 per cent of the population earned 37 per cent of all income, but in the more 'developed' Cochin China the highest paid 10 per cent earned 57 per cent income.[42]

While the greatest benefit from trade was to the landlord and merchant classes, population increases more than offset any initial benefit to the peasants. Buttinger sums up the situation by stating that whereas production of rice for the whole of Indochina increased by *24 per cent* in the period 1900 through 1937, population increased by *80 per cent*. *Per capita* domestic availability of rice fell from 232 kilos in 1900 to 182 kilos in 1937 because production lagged behind population and too much of what was produced was shipped abroad.[43]

5 The Nationalist-Communist Resistance

The *Viet Minh*, which led the successful anticolonial movement, came from a tradition of anticolonial activism which was continuous throughout the period of French rule. Although it did not gain a forceful cohesiveness until after 1930, the anticolonial movement ceaselessly carried on the Vietnamese tradition of nationalistic action against foreign domination. The early resistance of the peasants took the form of revolts against high taxes and lack of food and non-participation in French governing institutions at the village level. The most long-lasting violent resistance to French takeover was on the part of a peasant insurrection movement in the northern part of Vietnam which was led by De Tham. This movement actually held out until 1916, nineteen years after the scholar-gentry's resistance to the imposition of colonialism had been destroyed.[1]

The early resistance among the scholar-gentry took the form of non-participation in government official positions at a level higher that the village, written protest against colonial abuses and isolated acts of violent activism against the colonisers. The initial response of part of the scholar gentry was to form a 'Loyalty to the King'(*Can Vuong*) movement. This was crushed by 1897, some years after the king had been captured and his followers beheaded.

A large segment of the confucian scholar-gentry did not resist, but instead collaborated with the French colonialists and provided administrative help which contributed greatly to the French colonialists' ability to conquer and run the country. The king's brother was enthroned by the French as their puppet king to give them an appearance of legitimacy. They were able to use this ploy to attract the services of much of the traditional Vietnamese élite.

There were some among the initially collaborating group whose nationalism eventually got them in trouble. Ho Chi Minh's father, for example, was relieved of his post for his nationalist sympathies and because he was one of the mandarins who refused to learn French. The passively noncooperating mandarins with nationalist sympathies were often reduced to the level of village teachers or wandering scribes because of their attitudes.

Soon after the turn of the century, there arose a group of resistance mandarins who began to use Western ideas and Western technology to support their anticolonialism. Western intellectual ideas were introduced to the Vietnamese, not by the French, but by these nationalistic Confucian scholars.[2] Chinese translations of the works of the French enlightenment reached Vietnam and were absorbed by these intellectuals. The power and importance of modern technical advances for Asian peoples was made clear to these scholars by the Japanese victory over Russia in 1905. These resistance mandarins learned about the new social concepts of individualism, democracy and social contract from Western thinkers but they also paid attention to the importance of technical progress, capitalism, industrialisation and markets. The result of contact between Confucian resistance mandarins and Western ideas and institutions was a resistance movement which emphasised the training of young Vietnamese in Western sciences and social concepts and which actually set up capitalist enterprises for the benefit of the anticolonialist movement.

Pham Boi Chau was perhaps the most important leader in this group of anticolonial mandarins. He passed the mandarin exams with highest honours and carried the respect that this honour gave him in Vietnamese society. He supported a pretender to the throne, Cuong De, as a means of attracting followers to his anticolonial cause, although he is reported to have believed in republican democracy as an ideal form of government. Chau believed in armed resistance against the French and therefore supported local uprisings and violent attacks. He contacted the Chinese anticolonial leader, Sun Yat Sen, for support for an attack on the French, but the two disagreed on strategy and particularly on which country should be liberated first, Sun of course preferred China, and Chau chose Vietnam. Chau also formed the 'go East' study movement which sent young Vietnamese students to Japan to learn about the Japanese success in independent development.[3]

Another important leader, Pham Chu Trinh, was also a mandarin with highest honours who promoted popular education and modern learning for the Vietnamese. He felt that modern learning would awaken the Vietnamese so that they could take charge of their own independence. He did not support violent attacks on the French, but instead pressed them for reforms. Trinh disapproved of monarchy and the mandarinate form of government and instead, promoted Western forms of republicanism and democracy.[4]

Trinh, in his work, emphasised the priority of setting up modern schools and commercial firms in Vietnam. For example, he helped to initiate a school in Phan Thiet for modern learning and a corporation producing dried fish and fish sauce. In Hanoi, in 1907, he set up the Eastern Capital Free Tuition School which was attended by about four or five hundred students. The instruction emphasised science and mathematics and languages and made use of the Romanised script (*quoc ngu*) of the Vietnamese language.[5]

The French reacted to these attempts by Chau and Trinh to educate the Vietnamese, by suppressing their programmes and instituting limited reform of the French education system for Vietnamese. Trinh's school in Hanoi was shut down and the French formed an agreement with the Japanese which made it difficult for Vietnamese to travel to Japan on Chau's programme. Meanwhile, the French Governor General Beau set up a University in Hanoi for Vietnamese students, but this institution took in less that half the number of students that Trinh's school could accommodate. The General also promoted the idea of sending some Vietnamese students to France.[6]

Schools were not the only means of communication used by Chau and Trinh. They both travelled throughout Vietnam on lecture tours promoting anticolonialism and learning from the West. Many of their ideas were popularised by easily memorised songs and poems designed for recitation. They also wrote books which were circulated among the literate Vietnamese. The impact of these men and others like them on the Vietnamese people was extensive. Although they did not succeed in their anticolonial objectives, they set up some of the preconditions for this by educating young Vietnamese in Western Science and economics and by undercutting the influence of the collaborating mandarins by their examples.

In 1908 there were peasant demonstrations against French taxes and corvées in Central Vietnam. Because of their propaganda effort, the anticolonialist scholar-gentry were blamed for this unrest among the peasantry. Those resistance scholars who could be caught were rounded up and sent to jail, whether or not they had participated in the protests.[7] The demonstrations were brutally suppressed by the French. Since the French linked the efforts of Vietnamese scholars with the dissension in the countryside, they decided to cancel their limited educational reforms and they closed the University and the Directorate of Public Education.

Any link between the dissident scholar-gentry and the peasantry could be a potentially dangerous one for the French. Many times in

Vietnamese traditional history, this kind of link had been utilised to build up military strength to throw off foreign oppressors (as with the Chinese or the Mongols) or to overthrow a weak and decadent Vietnamese dynasty. The forces in 1908, however, were neither organisationally nor militarily strong enough to attempt to overthrow a technologically advanced Western military power like the French.

COMMUNISM AND NATIONALISM IN THE 1920s

The early communist movement in Vietnam was intimately interconnected with the life of Ho Chi Minh. His attraction to communism was, in addition, representative of his contemporaries and therefore a brief summary of his early life is important for understanding the resistance movement. Ho was a connecting link between the reform movements of the past and the Vietnamese communist future. His father had connections with the resistance mandarin, Phan Boi Chau, and Ho was influenced by Chau in his early years. In his youth Ho listened to Chau quoting nationalistic poetry and throughout his life he never forgot Chau's message. Ho also attended the school which was set up by Pham Chu Trinh. He learned French and learned about Western philosophy and science in this school, and he became a teacher for a short period when he finished his studies there.

Attracted by ideals of freedom and democracy in French writing, Ho was interested in going to France. He signed on as a galley assistant on a ship and worked his passage. Upon his arrival in France he was struck by the difference between the French colonisers in Vietnam and the masses of French people. 'So,' he thought,'France was not exclusively a nation of policemen and customs officials. There were also the masses – the vast working class – warm, sentimental, poor'.[8] He became a photo-retoucher in France and began working with Pham Chu Trinh who was in France at the time petitioning for reforms.

Ho's brief encounter with reformist politics was disappointing. He and Trinh sent an eight-point petition entitled 'The Rights of the Nations' to the Versailles Peace Conference. This petition asked for legal rights, representation in Parliament and basic freedoms of press and assembly for the Vietnamese. The request was not even considered by the Conference and when Ho tried to argue the case with Woodrow Wilson, he was shown the door. Ho took this as a lesson that petitioning for reforms was a dead-end strategy.[9]

Next Ho Chi Minh became involved in socialist politics. In 1920 he became a founding member of the French Communist Party. His reasons for involvement were nationalist and, in particular, a reaction of strong support for Lenin's 'Thesis on the National and Colonial Question'. Reading that paper was a turning point in Ho's life: 'What emotion, enthusiasm, clear-sightedness and confidence it instilled in me'.[10] Ho supported Lenin's positions among his political friends and allies and gradually learned more about other aspects of communist theory through study and practice in his involvement in the French left.

At first, patriotism, not yet Communism, led me to have confidence in Lenin, in the Third International. Step by step, along the struggle, by studying Marxist–Leninism parallel with participation in practical activities, I gradually came upon the fact that only Socialism and Communism can liberate the oppressed nations and the working people throughout the world from slavery.[11]

In 1923 Ho left France for the Soviet Union where he attended a conference of the Peasants International. He studied there and associated with and gained the respect of people in the Comintern (Communist International) for the next year and a half. Then, in late 1924, he went to Canton to assist Borodin, the Comintern's envoy to the Chinese revolutionary government. Pham Boi Chau's exile in this city had attracted a sizeable group of young Vietnamese anticolonialists and Ho immediately began organising among these exiles.[12]

Within this community, Ho formed the first Marxist Vietnamese organisation, The Vietnam Revolutionary Youth Association (*Thanh Nien*). This was essentially a study group in which Ho taught other Vietnamese what he had learned in France and the Soviet Union. He summed up Marxist–Leninism in the Vietnamese context and presented this group and the modern patriotic movement with the following new principles:

1. Revolution is the work of the worker and peasant masses and not of some heroes, hence the necessity of organising them and leading them into struggle.
2. In order to triumph, the revolution must be lead by a Marxist-–Leninist party, hence the necessity of setting up a new type of party.

3. The national revolution must be integrated into the world revolution, the Vietnamese people must act in concert with the world proletariat, hence the necessity of conforming to the policy of the Third International.[13]

Thanh Nien published a regular underground newspaper and built communication among underground elements in China, Siam and Vietnam. This network was greatly strengthened by the nationalist upsurge in Vietnam in 1925–6, when Chau was condemned to death by a French court, and also by the death of Trinh a year later. Many of the student groups involved in the protest demonstrations developed contacts with the *Thanh Nien* and recruitment of a wider base among students in the country was possible in this period. Leaders of worker-groups which participated in these demonstrations were also brought into contact with *Than Nien*.[14] The network was further strengthened by an alliance with and later a merger with the *Tan Viet*, a group of students and released political prisoners.

Consistent with its strategy of organising the masses *Thanh Nien* directed its members to work in factories, plantations and mines and to organise peasants, students and small traders. This was the group's 'proletarisation' drive which started in 1928–9. Nguyen Khae Vien later reported that the cadres going into these work situations still knew little about Marxism and had little practical experience, but that they were nevertheless partially successful.[15]

The competitors with the *Thanh Nien* for leadership of the Vietnamese anticolonial movement in the 1920s were the Nationalist Party and the Constitutionalist Party. The constituents of the Nationalist Party were not very different from those of the *Thanh Nien* in its early stages – mostly students and young intellectuals of the modern rather than the mandarin tradition. The Nationalists aimed part of their recruiting campaign at the army, and therefore included more soldiers than did *Thanh Nien*. The Constitutionalists represented the interests of the large landlords and the emerging national capitalist class so that there was a higher proportion of this class among the Constitutional membership than among the *Thanh Nien* or the Nationalists.

The Nationalists were heavily influenced by the Chinese *Kuomintang* and their programme was aimed at achieving national independence and setting up a democratic government. The Nationalist party tried to win over Vietnamese soldiers from the French armed forces in order to prepare for their struggle against the French. This was the main difference in tactics between the Communists and the Nationalists. The Communists stressed recruitment from within mass organisations but the Nationalists stressed recruitment from within the military.[16] In 1929, the Nationalist party was responsible for the assassination of a French plantation recruiter. When the French police closed in on the group following this incident, the party stepped up plans for armed insurrection. On 9 February 1930, Vietnamese soldiers at the Yen Bai garrison in Tonkin killed some French officers. This was coordinated with similar actions in neighbouring provinces. The French put down this uprising quickly and completely and the Party lost its entire leadership. After Yen Bai the younger followers turned to other political groups and the Nationalists essentially dropped out of the arena of Vietnamese politics.[17]

The Constitutionalist Party got much of its direction and its politics from the formation of the national capitalist class in Vietnam. During the First World War native industry had been built up in Vietnam using Western technology because imported goods were so difficult to obtain. Soap, carpet, textile, brickmaking, ironwork, pottery, and silk industries prospered. Vietnamese businessmen's associations were formed in 1919 with an interest in preserving and extending the market for these native, as opposed to Chinese and French, goods.[18] In 1923, many of these Vietnamese capitalists and landlords who were living in Saigon opposed the granting of a monopoly to export and import goods through the Port of Saigon to a French company. The Constitutionalist Party developed around this opposition. The movement had the support of Chinese merchants, leftist parliamentary representatives in France and a large part of the population of Saigon. With this widespread support the Constitutionalist Party was able to defeat the monopoly project.

The Constitutionalist Party, however, was as transitory as the Nationalist Party. Its leader, Bui Quang Chieu, travelled to France to petition the French government on behalf of his Nationalist–Republican constituency in Saigon. When he returned he proclaimed, 'I aspire to devote myself to Franco-Vietnamese harmony.' This was not exactly what the Saigonese had in mind for political leadership and consequently the Constitutionalist Party lost much of its popular backing. Then, after the upsurge of the worker peasant movements in the depression years of 1929–31, the native capitalist and landlord classes consolidated their political alliance with the French and they never again led the nationalist struggle.[19]

The 1930s – Formation of the Communist Party and the Nghe Tinh Soviets

The political influence of the *Thanh Nien* had grown during the period of the late 1920s. There were cells in all three regions of Vietnam by 1930. Cadres in *Thanh Nien* organised among factory workers, rickshaw drivers and the peasant population. They often organised peasants by becoming teachers in rural areas.

At a meeting of the *Thanh Nien* in May of 1929 while Ho Chi Minh was out of the area, some members introduced the idea of forming a party. The majority of the delegates thought that the idea was premature, but several delegates from Tonkin left the proceedings and initiated their own party, called the Indochinese Communist Party. Delegates from Annam in October 1929 and the *Tan Viet* created the League of Indochinese Communists.[20]

When Ho returned to Hong Kong in 1930, he was able to effect a unification of the two splinter groups of the *Thanh Nien*, the Tonkin and Central Vietnam groups. He then instructed these groups to join the *Tan Viet* group. In October, 1930 delegates of the newly-formed party met in Hong Kong and the name, Indochinese Communist Party, was chosen for the larger group. This title was in keeping with the Internationalist tone of Comintern policy at that time. The policies adopted by the newly-formed party also followed Comintern guidelines. These policies took a left position on rural class relations, as is evident particularly from point 5 of their ten-point programme:

1. To overthrow French imperialism, feudalism and the reactionary Vietnamese capitalist class.
2. To make Indochina completely independent.
3. To establish a government composed of workers, peasants and soldiers.
4. To confiscate the banks and other enterprises belonging to the imperialists.
5. To confiscate all plantations and property belonging to the imperialists and the Vietnamese reactionary capitalist class and distribute them to poor peasants.
6. To implement the eight-hour working day.
7. To abolish public loans and poll tax. To wave unjust taxes hitting the poor people.
8. To bring back all freedoms to the masses.
9. To carry out universal education.
10. To implement equality between men and women.[21]

Some of these policies had almost immediate application in a significant rebellion in two provinces of Vietnam, Nghe An and Ha Tinh.

The world-wide depression had an important impact on Vietnam as the price of rice and other export goods dropped and the French maintained and even raised, the taxes that the peasants had to pay. The peasants throughout Vietnam were squeezed between lower incomes and steady or increasing outlays for taxes in this period. The impact of the crisis was particularly hard in Nghe An and Ha Tinh since in these two provinces there were also poor harvests.[22] Funds for loans were practically non-existent and peasants had their backs to the wall. Nghe An–Ha Tinh was a geographical area with a tradition of resistance and an area where the newly formed Communist Party had connections and cadres working among the workers in the towns and the peasants in the countryside. On 1 May 1930, 1200 workers and peasants from the countryside paraded in the streets of Ben Tuy city in Nghe An. The Communists also planned a march of 3000 peasants on the same day demonstrating against a land concession to a Vietnamese collaborator. Thus, in these two provinces there began the first skirmishes of the Vietnamese revolution which would take forty-five years, to the day, to complete.

There is debate about the extent of Communist influence on the uprisings which became known as the *Nghe Tinh* Soviet movement. There were frequent demonstrations in the area in the next four months – mostly petitions for tax relief. Then violence increased by September as French aeroplanes bombed peasant demonstrators and peasants attacked mandarins and notables who tried to collect taxes which the peasants considered unjust. Government officials vacated the area and the peasants set up their own organisations in the villages which were liberated for several months from French control. The uprising seemed to be a combination of Communist initiative and spontaneous peasant activity. The Party organised the poor peasants in sacking stores of rice belonging to the rich Vietnamese. Many of the other tactics seemed to be more spontaneous, however. For example, the sacking of government offices and destruction of tax records and land registers was not pre-planned. The Soviets took the landlords' land and divided it among the peasants, although that had not been authorised by Party directive.[23] In addition to the leadership offered by the Communists, the peasantry had a long tradition of uprising and revolution and it was from this history (outlined in Chapter 2) that they found patterns to follow.

The French finally defeated the insurgents and took back the two provinces through the use of force and inside information provided by rich Vietnamese whose rice had been taken by the insurgents. After experiencing the disastrous effects of turning rich Vietnamese to the side of the French, the Communist Party, in subsequent famines, authorised the appropriation of French stocks of rice, but not those in the hands of rich Vietnamese.[24] The occurrences of 1930-31 taught the Party cadres some valuable lessons about peasant rebellion.

The French official reaction to the *Nghe Tinh* Soviets was to assert that the Communists were to blame for the uprising and subsequently to arrest and imprison all the Communists that they could round up. This had some immediate negative effects for the Communist movement, as many good cadres were behind bars, but it had an interesting long-run effect which the French did no foresee – the Communist Party was subsequently linked with peasant and anticolonial causes in the minds of most Vietnamese.

THE POPULAR FRONT

The Seventh World Conference of the Comintern developed policies which were to have great effects – both short-term and long-term – on Vietnam. The 'popular front' policies for Euopean countries meant alliances with non-Communist parties in an attempt to form a united front against the threat of Hitler's Germany. The Communist parties in colonial countries were to form alliances with landlord and bourgeois classes and their parties and to cease pressing their demand for national independence because the immediate aim was to defeat Fascism. This latter policy was dropped when the war against Fascism ended, but the policy of forming united fronts with other classes continued throughout the post-war period in Vietnam and elsewhere. Basically, the united-front policy meant that there would be a stage in the revolutionary process when the workers and peasants would be in the leadership, but would ally with other classes to bring about a bourgeois–democratic revolution. The second and later (Socialist) stage would be revolution of the working class.

The Popular Front policy in France led quickly to a change in government. The French Popular Front government came to power in 1936 and changed some of the most repressive and undemocratic aspects of the colonial system in Vietnam with respect to political activity. Strikes among the working class of Vietnam were made legal and the Indochinese Communist Party was made legal. After a period of relative inactivity after 1930–1, the Communist Party sprang into action on an above-ground basis as well as continuing to build a strong underground organisation.

In June of the following year, at a national conference, the Party decided to put aside temporarily the slogans 'Overthrow French Imperialism' and 'Confiscate the landlowners' land and distribution to the tillers'.[24] However, they decided to organise an Indochinese Anti-imperialist Popular Front which indicates that they were not entirely willing to give up the anti-imperialist fight. Their policy was supposed to unite all Indochinese against Fascism and Imperialism. Later, in 1938, the name of the united front organisation was changed to Indochinese Democratic Front and the enemy was then defined as French fascist and reactionary colonialists – not all French imperialists. All progressive and democratic forces were henceforth to be united in a popular front organisation.[25]

Changing the previous call for 'land to the tillers' was an important policy reversal which had to be explained and this was one of the reasons why party intellectuals, Truong Chinh and Vo Nguyen Giap wrote *The Peasant Question* in 1937–8.[26] The two Trotskyist groups which had developed considerable strength in Cochin China were continuing to call for confiscation of landlords' property. Their difference in position with the ICP was definitely in the Trotskyists' favour in Cochin China, where most peasants had lost their land to large landlords. The Trotskyists, however, were pinning most of their hopes for revolutionary action on the urban working class which they were busy organising during this period. *The Peasant Question* was also, in part, an answer to this Trotskyist working-class strategy and a justification of the ICP's position of seeing the peasantry as a revolutionary force. Many political moderates thought that the reforms being carried out by the Popular Front government in the countryside of Vietnam were really helping the peasants and this delusion also had to be set straight.

Chinh and Giap showed that the problems of the peasantry were many and complex, there was landlord oppression, seizure of land by officials, high taxes and usury. In addition to this, the peasants had to bear the burden of high prices charged by French salt and alcohol monopolies. In order to combat these problems, the French Popular Front government had offered a programme of low-interest loans, irrigation, migration and agricultural cooperatives. Giap and Chinh found this programme inadequate to deal with the problems of the peasantry. They pointed out that although the Popular Front government had constructed a programme to deal with the real problems of peasants in France, they were not doing the same for peasants in Indochina.[27]

Chinh and Giap analysed the condition of the peasantry *vis-à-vis* the working class and socialism. They found that generally, except for the landless labourers, the peasants were members of the rural petty bourgeoisie. Their class position was between that of the bourgeoisie and the proletariat. There were several strata of peasants, however. There were tenants or poor peasants who did not own enough land to support themselves. There were the middle peasants who did own enough land to support themselves. There were also the rich peasants who farmed their own land and also rented out land and hired labourers. The poor peasants' political interests were clearly with the proletariat. The middle peasants were a strata which was less reliable for support; their support could go either to the workers or the capitalists. Since the rich peasants' interests were essentially the same as those of the bourgeoisie, they could not be relied on to support the working class.[28]

This analysis differs from the study done by Mao Tse-Tung on the Chinese peasants in 1926. Mao suggested a new class category–that of semi-proletariat. He thought that poor peasants and semi-owner peasants were in this category. The middle peasants were the only agricultural petty bourgeoisie according to Mao's analysis. The rich peasants fitted into the middle bourgeoisie stratum of the capitalists' class.[29] Although the class analysis differs, the political conclusions of the Chinese and the Vietnamese analyses are virtually the same. In both cases, the poor peasants could be relied on politically, the middle peasants were tenuous and the rich peasants had interests which would push them to support the bourgeoisie.

Chinh and Giap proposed a set of programmes for solving the peasants' problems. Their suggested programmes fell short of land-to-the-tiller and therefore adhered to popular front policies. They called for redistribution of the communal land which had been usurped by officials, scientific methods for better flood control, improved health and education in the countryside and a new system of rural elections so that progressives could participate in politics. They thus differentiated themselves from the French Popular Front government policies, yet they followed Comintern guidelines.

DIVERGENT POLITICS IN THE SOUTH (COCHIN CHINA)

Opening up Vietnam to the world capitalist economy produced a differential impact on the economic structures of the Southern Region (Cochin China), and Tonkin and Annam. As we have seen in the last chapter, in Cochin China the traditional communal village was destroyed by the force of capitalist intervention. Large absentee landlords gained control of most of the soil and the peasants lost a lot of power over their land and control of their output. There was a political reaction to the intense exploitation and rapid changes which occurred in the South which made the Southern resistance movement qualitatively different from the movement in Annam and Tonkin.

In Annam and Tonkin, traditional communal ideals could be remembered and the ICP could easily link up their collective ideals with the peasants' and workers' knowledge of the traditional mode. The new mode of production had not made as much headway in destroying the old in these areas. Production in these areas was semi-socialised as there was interdependence and collective work along with individual labour in the Annamese and Tonkinese villages.

In the South, on the other hand, private property relations reigned in the countryside and production was socialised – that is, hired labourers were interdependent and worked collectively. Labour in agriculture had moved from being semi-socialised under the traditional mode of production where there was some private and some collective property holding to becoming socialised labour under a capitalist private property system. There was a vast majority of agricultural labourers and tenants in the South and according to the analysis of Chinh and Giap, these would be the groups which would identify most with the urban working class. They would have the most to lose from continuing under the capitalist mode of production. Chinh and Giap explicitly recognised the advanced role of the peasants of Cochin China, 'There is a huge gap between the standard of living of landlord and tenants. This is why peasants in Cochin China have more class-consciousness than peasants in other areas of Indochina and are the vanguard of the present peasant struggle movement'.[30] Here, they link the advanced political position of peasants in the South with a difference in standard of living which is the result of changed property relations. They do not explicitly bring up mode of production differences in the South, but they do clearly recognise the advanced and more radical character of the struggle in the South. The difference between the type of struggle and pace of struggle in the different parts of Vietnam brought problems within the revolutionary movement.

After the French authorities suppressed the communist movement following the *Nghe-Tinh* uprisings in 1930–1, the movement was in disarray. The southern groups were the first to recover, but there was considerable dissatisfaction with ICP leadership among these groups. The beginning of a significant Trotskyist movement emerged as part of this dissatisfaction with ICP leadership. Vietnamese studying in Paris had developed contacts with French Trotskyists. They set up two Trotskyist groups in 1931, the Communist League (*Lien Doan Cong San*) and the Left Opposition (*Ta Doi Lap*). The Trotskyists differed from the ICP on many points and they recommended changes in ICP policy. They wanted the ICP to put the proletariat at the head of the party and not at the tail where they seemed to think it was following the *Nghe-Tinh* Soviets. They wanted to reorganise the party 'on the base of factory cells and not that of street cells and peasant cells'.[31] They were interested in building a party which would lead directly toward dictatorship of the proletariat and socialism and wanted to dissolve the Anti-Imperialist League because they saw it as a way for non-revolutionary nationalists to enter the Party[32]

The ICP, which was slowly rebuilding itself, did not agree with all the Trotskyist criticisms, but it did see the need for proletarianising the party. Therefore, some basis existed for cooperation of the ICP and the Trotskyist groups and they formed a united front organsation called *La Lutte* in Cochin China in 1933. The group which also included unaffiliated revolutionaries, published the *La Lutte* newspaper.[33]

In this early period there was considerable conflict between the Comintern and the newly rising ICP in the South. The ICP was more concerned than the Comintern about the preponderance of non-proletarian elements in the party. The Comintern also stressed the importance of alliance with the national bourgeoisie and the ICP was reticent on this point. There was a difference on the question of working with Trotskyists at this time. The Comintern saw the Trotskyists as 'counter-revolutionary' and 'social-fascists' and the ICP members, who were regularly working with Trotskyists in *La Lutte*, took a much softer line. The ICP, therefore, came under sharp criticism from other parties within the Comintern. The French Communists reminded it of the principle of democratic centralism whereby the ICP must submit to and carry out the resolutions of the Comintern. The Central Committee of the Communist Party of China also wrote a letter to the ICP stressing this theme.[34]

During the Popular Front period, the ICP in Cochin China continued to play a very important political role. This was at least partly because more legal reforms were instituted in Cochin China than in the other parts of Vietnam. Both the ICP and the two Trotskyist Parties, now called the Struggle Group (*La Lutte*) and the October Group, became very active in electoral politics. At first the ICP continued to work with one of the Trotskyist groups in *La Luttte*, but as the ICP began to accept the Comintern line on alliance with the national bourgeoisie, this association became more and more tenuous. The ICP, as we have seen, changed its line on fighting French imperialism beginning in 1936. At that time it moderated its position toward the Constitutionalists and also toward the colonial administration. By May 1937, the ICP in Cochin China started to publish its own paper called *L'Avant Garde* and attacked the Trotskyists as 'professional agitators'.[35]

The ICP, which had to follow the Comintern's Stalinist line, was at a disadvantage in Vietnam and particularly so in Cochin China. The Trotkyists had been very active in the Indochinese Congresses which were held jointly by the two groups to formulate demands for a Commission of Inquiry coming from France at the beginning of the Popular Front period. There were 600 committees of inquiry set up by the Congresses in the Saigon–Cholon area and throughout Cochin China. The Trotskyists were very effective in these committees. When it later became clear that the colonial administration would not carry through an extensive set of reforms, the Trotskyist groups criticised the administration and also criticised the ICP. In their view, the ICP was betraying the Vietnamese people in order to please the French Communists. The Trotskyists stepped up their demands and the strikes they led increased while the ICP decreased its militance. The Trotskyist Party membership increased to 3000 and these groups built considerable support among the general population of Cochin China. In 1939, the most prominent Trotskyist leader, Ta Thu Thau, and two other candidates received 80 per cent of the votes in an election for the Colonial Council for Cochin China, defeating the ICP candidates and others.[36]

Meanwhile, the ICP was organising, unchallenged, in the other parts of Vietnam. However, its Democratic United Front ran into internal conflicts even in these areas. As the ICP decreased its militance because of the Comintern Popular Front policy, its popularity waned.

Leadership in the Party was taken by intellectuals like Vo Nguyen Giap and by worker organisers like Ton Duc Thang (who was later to become the second president of the Democratic Republic of Vietnam).

There was a strong working-class movement in Vietnam which had gained its knowledge about trade unionism and socialism mostly from France. During the First World War, 100 000 Vietnamese had been sent to France to be used in the army as support troops, and trained in the use of modern machinery and upon their return after the war they became workers in French industry in Indochina. These workers learned about the Socialist Workers Movement and trade unionism in France and they applied that knowledge upon their return to Vietnam.[37] They transformed workers' societies and mutual aid associations, set up on the traditional peasant model, into Western-type trade unions which led strikes and demanded negotiations with employers. Many leaders among these working-class organisers also became leaders in the Communist Party organisation.

The working class of Vietnam was not large, making up about 5 per cent of the total population, but the impact of the working class was larger than this statistic would indicate because of the rapid turnover of workers.[38] Only a small percentage of workers became permanently working-class and most were peasant workers who spent a short period of time in industry and then returned to their villages. If at all possible, peasants would also commute to their jobs from their villages. The peasants' familiarity with working conditions in the factories and mines and the workers' ties with the peasantry aided the peasant–worker alliance which was needed to fight colonialism. This was a unique situation in colonial countries. It came from Vietnamese traditions about maintaining ties with one's native villages and the condition of high turnover in the labour market.

The period of the Popular Front government was one of active labour organising. There were thousands of strikes and the Party was internally involved in this labour activity. The Party called a public meeting in Hanoi – notably on 1 May 1938 – which was attended by tens of thousands of workers,[39] who demanded that the Popular Front government should legalise labour unions. After this demand was granted, many legal unions were set up.

The direct effects of the change in the Comintern's programme on the Indochinese Communist Party policies were slower in coming than the indirect effects caused by the French Popular Front. In the absence of Ho Chi Minh, the ICP held its first congress in March 1935. The policies coming out of that conference were very different from Comintern policies. The ICP determined that circumstances were strongly in favour of revolution and that 'class struggle must be organised and carried on with heroism and resolution'.[40] There was considerable conflict between Ho, (then residing in the Soviet Union) and the party leadership on this line, but in his absence the Party continued its more militant class line.

JAPANESE POWER AND THE AUGUST REVOLUTION

The Popular Front government fell in France in 1939 and as a result repression fell upon Vietnamese Communists. Progressive newspapers were closed down in Vietnam and Left organisations were dissolved. The French also arrested Vietnamese Communists and rounded them up in detention centres. Nevertheless, the Indochinese Communist Party was prepared for the end of the Popular Front. It had an underground apparatus, so it moved underground and transferred most of its activities to the countryside where the colonial police apparatus was weaker.

Indochina in 1939 was already feeling the tensions of the impending world war. The Japanese showed their power in the area by occupying an island close to Vietnam. As a result of the Japanese threat, the French intensified their corvées in Vietnam, building more roads and airfields and setting up munitions factories. They also increased taxes and made requisitions on the local population in order to send increased foodstuffs to France. In addition to the hardships of the Vietnamese in the country, tens of thousands of Vietnamese workers were sent to France to aid in France's war preparations.[41]

In the next period, the international alliances of the ICP ceased to be a hindrance and began to be a considerable aid to them in organising within the country. No longer constrained by the Popular Front, the ICP immediately started condemning the French (and British) policy of compromise with the Fascists.[42] In November 1939, the Party central committee substituted the call to form a 'Democratic Republican government' with a call to form a worker–peasant government. The Central Committee also made clear the new policy of *national liberation being the primary objective*. The essential task of the Vietnamese revolution was to overthrow imperialism and there was no longer a constraining Popular Front policy. The land problem in the period, however, was to be subordinated to the struggle against imperialism. A United Front would have to be formed which would include patriotic landlords.

When the French were overrun by the Germans in June 1940, France was completely cut off from her colonies and Indochina was open to Japanese aggression. Japan, however, manoeuvered patiently to gain the collaboration of the French in Indochina rather that launch an immediate attack. The Japanese wanted the use of Indochina as a base for their greater military projects and they wanted to acquire food and raw materials like coal and rubber from Indochina. They also wanted to be sure to cut off Indochinese aid to China. All these aims could be gained most effectively if the French could be persuaded to continue to maintain order in Indochina. Under the threat of war, the Japanese convinced the French to accept their terms which included a limited occupation of part of the country.[43]

When the Vichy government was organised in France, it chose Admiral Decoux as its leader in Indochina. Governor Decoux eliminated whatever democratic councils existed in the governing structure. He also followed instructions of the Japanese on the compulsory sale of rice to Japan and the forced planting of jute on former rice land. (The Japanese evidently had a need for jute bags.) Rice shortages were naturally the result of these forced conversions and sales. Discontent among the people in the countryside increased considerably as a result of the double burden of French and Japanese oppression.

In September 1940, the Japanese landed 6000 troops near Haiphong. French troops withdrew from the area along the Bac Son road. The local ICP asked the people of the Bac Son area to disarm the withdrawing French troops in order to equip themselves to fight Japanese imperialism.

Meanwhile, in the south, the Japanese were ordering the French to organise Vietnamese troops to go to Cambodia in order to help Japan's ally, Thailand, in a war there. There was considerable resistance among the soldiers about being sent to the front and South Vietnam was on the verge of insurrection. At this juncture, the Central Committee of the Communist Party met. In this Seventh Plenum of the Central Committee, in November 1940, decisions were made (i) to maintain the troops from the Bac Son insurrection, (ii) to set up guerilla units and to progress toward general insurrection and seizing power in the whole country. They decided, however, that the time was not ripe for general insurrection in the south. Such an insurrection should be coordinated with uprisings in other regions at some future time. When the Party representative returned to South Vietnam, however, the order for insurrrection had already been given. The uprising was brutally repressed by the French. Villages were burned down and tens of thousands of people were killed.[44]

THE VIET MINH

Early in 1941, Ho Chi Minh returned from the Soviet Union and China and assumed leadership of the Party. Ho and his compatriots worked out a new strategy which took concrete form in the establishment of a new United Front organisation, the *Viet Minh* (*Viet Nam Doc Lap Dong Minh* or Vietnamese Independence League). National liberation was the primary focus of this group and preparation for insurrection was its primary task. Class and regional interests were subordinated to national interest in this period. To emphasise nationalism and to make clear the new focus, mass organisations were renamed. For example, workers' organisations were called 'Workers' Association for National Salvation' and women's organisations were named 'Women's Association for National Salvation', etc.

Elements in the Party were still very concerned with class struggle. The same party plenum which created the *Viet Minh* was apprehensive about a deficiency in worker-organisation. They wanted especially to increase proletarian elements in the party. Ever since the party had relied on rural areas for bases and had shifted most of its activities to rural areas for security reasons, there had been uneven rural/urban development in the struggle. Regardless of its tactical move to rural areas, the Party wanted the workers' movement to be at the vanguard of other movements. Despite party directives aimed at change, the problem continued. The unsatisfactory development of the workers' movement was again mentioned two years later at a meeting of the Standing Committee of the Central Committee of the Party in February 1943.[45]

On the other hand, the Party and the *Viet Minh* organisations were experiencing very rapid growth in the countryside, In the Central Lowlands and the North there were struggles around the redistribution of communal land, forced cultivation of jute instead of rice and the requisitioning of paddy. Revolutionary military bases were established by the *Viet Minh* in the highlands of Vietnam and in the North. Eventually, as support grew, several bases in the North were tied together and a liberated zone was created. The Standing Committee of the Central Committee was able to establish itself on the outskirts of Hanoi.

Although support was also growing for the *Viet Minh* in the South, diverse political movements continued to cut into its strength. Many Vietnamese youth were convinced by Japanese propaganda that the way to fight European power was to line up with a strong Asian power. Some of the rhetoric used to support this Japanese doctrine of a 'Greater Asia' were 'a community of culture and race' and the creation of a 'co-prosperity zone'. The Constitutionalist Party became pro-Japanese and received financial and political support from the Japanese.

The Trotskyist movement enjoyed a revival in the South around this time. The Trotskyists published material which was critical of the *Viet Minh*-style nationalism which ignored class differentiations. In the South, where absentee landlordism predominated, the *Viet Minh* was particularly vulnerable on this point. Southern peasants tended not to feel a community of interest with their landlords on nationalist struggles, especially if those landlords lived in Saigon.

The religious sects were, numerically, the most important arena of political diversity competing with the *Viet Minh*. Two sects developed considerable support in this region, the *Cao Dai*, an ecumenical religion, and the *Hoa Hao*, a reformed Buddhism. Both sects had elements of nationalism in their ideologies. The *Cao Dai* had become receptive to Japanese propaganda even before the war. Because of this, it was under attack by the French before Japanese control in Indochina was established. The *Hoa Hao* had been in trouble with the French for different reasons. Its mass gatherings threatened to turn into anti-French demonstrations. The Japanese were interested in supporting conservative religious–nationalist tendencies. Since the Japanese had left French nationals in charge of administration, however, there was not much they could do directly to help these religions. They ended up supporting the *Cao Dai* and the *Hoa Hao* politically and financially through their espionage activities.

Despite the diversity of its adversaries, the international connections of the ICP and the leadership training that its officials received from the Soviet Union and the Chinese Communists, proved to be very important in its rise to power. Most significant was the international perspective which the ICP leaders gained and their ability to predict international events. The ICP was prepared for the Japanese entrance into Indochina, its struggle with the French and its later takeover of the government apparatus. Ho Chi Minh understood that the correct moment to take power would be after the Japanese defeat and before allied troops could enter Vietnam in large numbers. Ho's many years of observing international events paid off when he was able to lead the *Viet Minh* in the August Revolution. In August 1945, the *Viet Minh* was successful in taking power in the whole country.

ANTI-COLONIAL WAR: 1945–54

Diverse political elements continued to weaken *Viet Minh* claims to country-wide leadership in the next period. By the time of Japanese withdrawal, a United National Front which included the Trotskyists, the *Cao Dai* group, the *Hoa Hao* and the pro-Japanese parties, was formed in the South.

The *Viet Minh*, seeing the end of the war and the return of French colonialism as imminent, instituted a policy of broad coalition with other nationalist groups. Early in September 1945, the *Viet Minh* formed an alliance with the United National Front. This alliance, however, did not prevent fairly rapid French takeover. In mid-September the British arrived and within days they reinstalled the local French in power in the southern cities.

In the North, the Chinese Nationalists entered Vietnam and brought with them members of the Vietnam Revolutionary League and the Vietnam Nationalist Party who had been in exile in southern China. Ho Chi Minh 'bought' toleration from the new army of occupation by feeding them – at huge cost to the rice-hungry North. The Nationalist Parties were very concerned about the ICP control of the *Viet Minh*. Therefore, in a conciliatory manner the ICP decided to dissolve itself on 11 November (it actually went underground). In March 1946, a new coalition government was formed between the *Viet Minh* and representatives of the Vietnam Revolutionary League and the Vietnam Nationalist Party.

The coalition government was successful in negotiating with the French an agreement which became known as the March Sixth Agreement. The Agreement permitted French troops to re-enter North Vietnam, but the French government recognised the Democratic Republic of Vietnam as a free state which had its own government, parliament, army and treasury. This agreement bought time for the *Viet Minh* to prove itself an effective government of most of Vietnam.

The *Viet Minh* was energetic and very successful in carrying out its programme in the countryside. There was a great push for agricultural production and public works were organised to ensure full utilisation of the soil. For workers, freedom for trade unions was proclaimed and the eight-hour day and minimum wages were introduced.[46]

Politics in the countryside were transformed as 'peoples' committees' replaced the old 'councils of notables'. Some hated landlords were killed in this period, but many former notables were elected to the new village committees. The rival upper strata could not be replaced at this early stage since the rural poor lacked literary and leadership skills. In order to attack this problem, the *Viet Minh* instituted a literacy campaign in the countryside. 80 000 teachers taught basic literacy to 2.5 million people in this campaign.[47]

Land reform was not an important part of the *Viet Minh* programme at this time. Redistribution of commercial land was the most widespread reform. The land of former colonialists was not distributed and villages rented out this land instead. A 25 per cent rent reduction was legislated, but this remained largely unenforced. The poor peasants received considerable immediate economic benefit from the new government, however, since the land tax was cancelled.[48]

Negotiations for Vietnamese independence broke down over application of the March Sixth Agreement in the South. The French financial interests were particularly interested in holding onto the South and the French held military and political control over most of the South. After March, France refused to recognise Cochin China as an integral part of the Democratic Republic of Vietnam (DRV). They put off holding the referendum provided for in the agreements and on 1 June the French Admiral proclaimed the Republic of Cochin China. The *Viet Minh* southern resistance was then set up in the Plain of Reeds and the Cape of Ca-Mau.

By November 1946, the government of the DRV had to face the impossibility of reaching agreement with the French. The government had introduced its own currency and tariffs on imported cottons. French industrialists protested against this action, but 10 000 Vietnamese workers went out on strike to support the government's measures.[49] By 1947, the French were militarily on the offensive. With their material superiority in military hardware, they were able to take over the large cities and the coal area in North Vietnam. The DRV was on the defensive, but it was able to move government operations, machinery and material to its countryside bases. The period from December 1946 until June 1949 continued to be one of defensive action, for the *Viet Minh*, combined with attempts to negotiate with the French.

Starting in mid 1946, the *Viet Minh* strategy changed. The *Viet Minh* decided that revolution in the countryside was necessary in order to convince the peasants – who were also the soldiers of the resistance – to fight hard enough to win against the French. The first step in this countryside revolution involved changes in the land reform programme. In 1949, laws were passed to make the 25 per cent rent reduction policy an official law. The distribution of land belonging to colonials and Vietnamese who supported the French also became official policy.

Because there were so many absentee landlords who supported the French in South Vietnam, 89 per cent of the land which could be distributed under this law was in Cochin China, where 500 000 peasants received land. In North Vietnam, the rural revolution was harder because it was at the expense of landlords living in the village.

In 1950 there were changes in the international sphere which led to further changes in Vietnamese policy. The USA started to enter the picture in support of French Imperialism. The USA advised the French to set up a rival government headed by the former emperor, Bao Dai. This rival government was immediately recognised by the USA and other Western countries. At this point Ho Chi Minh turned to the Communist countries for recognition and aid. The *Viet Minh* received aid from the Soviet Union and from the Chinese Communists, who had just taken power in China.

In the next year, the leadership of the Vietnamese revolution was restructured in order to provide tighter leadership for the difficult tasks ahead. The Communist Party became an official entity again, adopting the name of *Lao Dong* or Workers' Party. While the Party had been 'unofficial', it had grown tremendously, from around 5000 members in 1945 to more that 500 000 in 1951. The growth developed with the growth in support of the revolution and the incorporation of most of the *Viet Minh* into the Party. In this period of rapid political change, there were many converts to Marxist–Leninism. At this point also, the *Viet Lien* was set up as the United Front group. Those people who identified with the cause of the *Viet Minh* but did not join the Party were incorporated into this wide-ranging group which included peasants' associations, student associations, etc.

In 1950, the party stopped its recruitment and started to reform itself, expelling members from the exploiting classes in rectification campaigns over the period 1950–2. This was the build-up for revolution in the countryside which was justified by Ho Chi Minh: 'Nearly 90 per cent of our population are peasants. More than 90 per cent of soldiers in National Defence Army, local guards, militiamen and guerillas are of peasant stock.'[50] The full support of the peasantry had to be developed by bringing revolution to the countryside *from above*, from the ranks of the most trusted party cadre. The basic method was to bypass the local *Viet Minh* leadership by sending in politically reliable cadres who were not natives of the village to contact poor villagers. The first programme undertaken was enforcement of the rent reduction and preparation for the Land-to-the-Tiller Programme. The following steps in a trial wave of revolutionary change in the countryside demonstrate the technique:[51]

1. A cadre enters the village and finds a poor peasant or landless labourer and lives with him and helps him with his work. The cadre practises the 'three togethers' policy, eating together, living together, working together.
2. The cadre asks about poverty and hardship and he explains the exploitation of the landlords.
3. The first peasant contacted by the cadre will talk to others.
4. A cell of poor and landless peasants is set up.
5. The cadre starts to talk to middle peasants.
6. A Congress of Peasant Representatives is convened and this group forms a Peasant Association and sets up an Executive Committee for this Association.
7. This Executive Committee leads the rent-reduction campaign.
8. There is a confrontation with landlords accused of criminal offences such as beating to death, rape and acting against the revolution.
9. Landlords are expelled from the Party and all village organisations. Rich peasants are expelled from the Party.

This *Viet Minh* revolution in the countryside followed the traditional more than the Marxist revolutionary pattern. In precolonial times, new dynasties would change local leaders and distribute among the poor land belonging to the losing dynasty. The *Viet Minh* took land from those who had prospered during the French and Japanese occupations, and gave it to the poor peasants, many of whom had family members in the *Viet Minh* armed forces. This is far from the Marxist concept of revolution by urban and rural workers organising in their own interest. This rural revolution was very effective, however, in organising support for a *Viet Minh* victory.

When the Land-to-the-Tiller campaign was instituted in 1953, there were widespread informational campaigns in the army to show the poor peasant soldiers that they had property to look forward to when they defeated the French. Appeals were also made to the non-peasant sectors so as not to create too much disruption while winning the peasants over. The generosity of patriotic landlords was appealed to in traditional terms. This policy was very successful and the French were soundly defeated at Dien Bien Phu.

6 The Post-Colonial Village

A comparative study of the traditional village with post-colonial villages can show the effects of the development of capitalist markets in Central and South Vietnam. This chapter, therefore, describes typical southern and central villages in the 1950s and contrasts these with the traditional village. This technique reveals the fundamental economic changes in production and distribution in the villages during the colonial era. The effects of the extension of the market on methods of production and the production infrastructure are shown. It becomes apparent that the market affected the lives of the people of the village, the organisation of their labour, the returns they received, and also the distribution of wealth among the village population.

A major problem with this method in determining the total impact of the market on rural Vietnam is that the *Viet Minh* had reversed the colonial trend toward concentration of landholding during their control of most of the countryside in the period 1945–54. Even in areas which were not directly controlled by the *Viet Minh*, absentee landlords lost power because of the general *Viet Minh* influence in the countryside. The *Viet Minh* reforms were later stopped and to some extent reversed, in the South, by President Diem and his party, the National Revolutionary Movement. In the late 1950s and early 1960s, when the village studies which are relied on here were being completed, a resistance to Diem was forming – this was the eve of the formation of the National Liberation Front. Despite the beginnings of changes in power relationships caused by these political developments, the major changes in rural economy brought about by the establishment of markets remain evident. The impact and effects of the *Viet Minh* and the rising new movement can be partially assessed as we proceed in the description of the post-colonial village.

THE VILLAGES

In the 1950s, the Mekong Delta contained about 50 per cent of the rural population of South Vietnam (it was the predominant part of the former state of Cochin China). The Delta region is particularly interesting to study because change in the colonial period in Cochin China was an exaggeration or a magnification of the process which

111

occurred elsewhere in Vietnam. As we have seen earlier, the effects of colonialism on Cochin China were intensified because (i) the area was a frontier which accepted change more rapidly and (ii) the French pursued change in Cochin China with a vengence and it was considered a 'colony' rather than a 'protectorate' like the other four regions of French Indochina.

An argument which could be advanced against comparison of a post-colonial southern village with a generalised traditional village is that villages on the frontier were different even in precolonial times. These villages had little communal land and were somewhat dispersed. Communal land in traditional Vietnam, however, tended to become more extensive as population became more dense. We have no reason to doubt that without colonisation, communal lands would have developed in the normal manner in the south. It is, therefore, valid to make the comparison between the southern and the traditional village and to consider differences to have been largely induced by colonial intervention.

The field work for the three villages used most extensively in this analysis was done in the late 1950s and early 1960s, before the intensification of the Vietnam war.[1] Thirty years ago, at the time of these studies, the nation's population was at least 80 per cent rural. After that time, Vietnam experienced a rural revolution because of the increasing power of the NLF. Massive bombing and military operations by the USA also resulted in major population shifts. The population in the South by the early 1970s was only 60 per cent rural and some rural areas had been almost completely depopulated.

The formal administrative structure of the two southern villages studied, My Thuan and Khanh Hau, was very similar. The administrative structure had some of the same basic units as the traditional Vietnamese village: (i) the village council consisting of the chief and other administrators with specific functions; (ii) the hamlets with their chiefs and the neighbourhood groups, or five family groups. The problem with this formal administrative set-up was that it did not have much relevance to, or influence on, the social and economic realities of the village. In My Thuan there were actually eleven hamlets and the administrative division imposed from above forming three *aps* (large hamlets) was not recognised, even by the appointed village and hamlet chiefs. All officers, right down to the heads of the five family group, were appointed in My Thuan and their main function was security – they watched the movements of villagers in their groups.[2] In Khanh Hau leaders of the five family groups were selected by the group but their functions were similar.[3] The five family groups were an administrative device, imposed in South Vietnam in 1956 and 1957 and they had no relation to neighbourhood mutual assistance work groups.

Ever since the French imposed appointed officials on the villages in southern Vietnam in 1904, religious and political matters were separated. Cult committees were unofficially formed in every village for the venerables who continued their participation in ceremonies and continued to win the respect and veneration of their fellow-villagers. This respect was not generally given to council members appointed by the Saigon government.

In central Vietnam, the appointment of officials was not begun by the French until 1945, and from then until 1954, many areas were under *Viet Minh* control. The Saigon government had problems with finding candidates for the appointed positions in the Central Lowlands which were similar to the problems faced by the French in the South at an earlier period. Only the less qualified were willing to do the job and then those appointed used their power in corrupt ways. Once appointed, the officials in the central village had considerable power and responsibility because of the tight-knit nature of the village and the economic necessities of the complex system of water control and communal land distribution. These officials could easily misuse that power.

The administrative structure of My Xa Hamlet in the Central Lowlands, resembles the traditional village structure, more that the hamlet structure. This is particularly true with respect to the distribution of communal land in My Xa. At the time of the *Viet Minh* administration of the Central Lowlands area, many small villages were combined into communes with many hamlets. The status of My Xa as a hamlet and not a village is evidently the result of such a change. For the purposes of this study we can consider it as a representative village.

LAND

Southern Village

The typical southern village in the 1950s had little communal land (about 3 per cent) and all other land was in private ownership units. A substantial amount of land was owned by absentee landlords (55.8 per cent in Khanh Hau before the land reform). About 75 per cent of the peasants in the whole of Cochin China were tenant-farmers. In Khanh

Hau 70 per cent of the land was rented and in My Thuan about 70 per cent of farmers were tenants.

In the village of Khanh Hau, the 6 per cent of land which was communal seems insignificant when compared with the 94 per cent of private land, but it was still a standard by which villagers assessed communal wealth.[4] The communal land was not distributed primarily to the poor villagers. Instead, the privilege of renting the communal land was periodically auctioned off to the highest bidder and revenues were used by the village administration. The rent of communal lands comprised the major local source of revenue for village administration in Khanh Hau. In My Thuan the major source of revenue came from the market taxes (since My Thuan had one hamlet which was a market centre) and rents of communal property amounted to 3–6 per cent of revenues.

Of the 31 hectares of land owned by the village of Khanh Hau in 1958, 17 were classified as *cong dien*. There seemed to be a feeling that the *cong dien* should be parcelled out mostly to poorer villagers. Those in Khanh Hau who were landowners (except those who were also officials) did not generally attend the auction; they left the bidding to those in greater need. Two officials, however – the police agent and the village clerk – were among the renters of *cong dien* although they were landowners. There were, in addition, 4 hectares of communal land set aside in small garden plots for renting to poor villagers. The vestiges of the traditions that *cong dien* provides a ration for needy villagers, and that officials should be allotted a plot of *cong dien*, were apparent in the disposition of *cong dien* in Khanh Hau.

Some communal land was delineated for religious purposes. In Khanh Hau 2.5 hectares was pagoda land. A Buddhist monk rented this land and used the revenue to support the pagoda. There were also 1.5 hectares of *dinh* land which were cultivated by the guardian of the *dinh*.

The land held in private ownership in Khanh Hau did not change hands freely. Most land was transferred through inheritance.[5] Land was sold on few occasions and when it was, those in a position to buy were usually already landowners and tenants had little chance of acquiring land. Sellers were usually small owners who were selling a portion of their land in order to make payment on a debt. Thus, under the *Diem* government, there was a continuation of the process of concentration started during the colonial era.

The institution of *huong hoa*, or family land used to support the ancestor cult, was still found in the modern southern village. The majority of male villagers in Khanh Hau had a great ambition to buy a small plot of land, not as an investment, but as a religious patrimony to ensure themselves a respectable place in the ancestor cult. Patrilineages which had *huong hoa* were more likely to have cooperative celebrations and frequent gatherings. In Vietnamese culture, where filial piety is greatly admired, they achieved high status.

With the exception of the *huong hoa* holdings, there was no special significance in holding land in private ownership. The tenant who rented and cultivated a large amount of land was as greatly respected in the village as the owner who farmed a large amount of his own land.[6] The tenant would, of course, have a more difficult time meeting expenses, especially during years of poor harvest or low prices on the market.

Prior to 1958, in the village of Khanh Hau, 35 per cent of the land was owned by one absentee landowner,[7] and only 17 per cent of village households owned any land in the village. 75 per cent of all landowners owned only 20 per cent of the rice land, that is, most landowners held very small shares. Aside from the largest owner who held 324 hectares, there were also several large ownership units which ranged around 20 hectares.

The rental share which a tenant paid varied throughout South Vietnam, in this period, mainly according to the amount of rebel influence in the area. During the French colonial period, rental shares had averaged around 50 per cent. The Saigon government land reform set a legal limit of 25 per cent, but in Khanh Hau rents averaged 33 per cent of the crop. In My Thuan, a less 'secure' area, rents averaged around 10 per cent. Landlords and their representatives were harrassed by area rebels when they visited the village to collect rents. Village officials appointed by the Diem government were involved, there, in collecting rents for absentee landlords.[8]

The system of rent collection was different in Khanh Hau. Representatives of absentee landlords lived in the village and collected rents from other villagers. One man who had grown wealthy in this pursuit was considered an outlander and did not participate in village affairs.[9] Another man who was a venerable at the time had some resentment held against him because of his former position as landlord's representative, but he continued to function as an insider in the village.[10]

The Saigon government instituted a land redistribution programme in 1955. The programme was designed to affect less than 10 per cent of tenant farmers in the whole of South Vietnam. It limited landownership to 100 hectares plus family worship property and this high limit was the cause of the small impact.

In Khanh Hau the land reform which took effect in 1958 benefited 20 per cent of tenants, and doubled the number of landowners. The programme was more effective in this village than in the average Saigon-government-controlled area, partly because it was more fully administered here. The land was distributed to those tenants who had rented the particular plots before the transfer programme. The average plot distributed was about 2 hectares (5 acres), and this was about equal to the average area rented in the village. The peasants were supposed to pay for the land in five years and yearly payments were approximately equal to former rent payments. There was thus no immediate benefit to peasants involved, but Hendrey found there was little resistance to paying for the land in this village.[11] In other areas of South Vietnam where the *Viet Minh* had previously distributed land, peasants resisted paying for land they thought they already owned. In Khanh Hau, however, most criticisms of the land reform came from the remaining tenants and landless labourers who still comprised the majority of the village population and who were not affected by the reform.

In traditional times land confiscated by a new regime was given to villages for the use of all village families through the institution of *cong dien* and the periodic redistribution of this land. The concept of social justice inherent in this earlier Vietnamese institution caused the villagers to be dissatisfied with the unequal reforms carried out by the Diem government. There was also a great disparity between traditional retention limits and those imposed by the government. The limit was 10 *mau* during the Le period, or 9 acres. The Diem limit was 100 hectares plus religious lands of 15 hectares or a total of 284 acres – making a very unequal 'redistribution'.

Central Village

Absentee landowning was not a common feature in the central village economy in the late 1950s and early 1960s. This was true, both because market capitalism had not penetrated the economy of the Central Lowlands to nearly the same extent as in the southern region, and because the *Viet Minh*, with their policy of expropriating absentee landlords, had been very strong in this area. There were some large local landowners, but we must redefine 'large' landowner to suit the conditions of the central village. The area farmed by the average family was less than half the size of the southern region but over 85 per cent of rice land was double-cropped in the central region. Therefore, a large holding in the region was less than half the size of a large holding in the southern region. Holdings of 10 hectares and up were considered large holdings in this context but there were only a few of these.

Tenancy, the correlative to large landholding, was not as extensive in the Central Lowlands either. The 1960 Census of Agriculture showed only 20 per cent tenancy for the central region.[12] Rentals which did exist were sometimes for convenience, such as rentals of holdings in a family's native village when the family had moved to another or the rental of an old person's holding. The amount of rent in this period was 50 per cent of the main crop if the landlord furnished seed and fertiliser (a common arrangement in the Central Lowlands) or 25–30 per cent of the main crop if these items were furnished by the tenants.[13] With a two-crop economy, these rents were low in comparison with the southern region and the reasons were, again, the absence of large-scale production for the market and absentee landlords and the *Viet Minh* resistance movement in the area. Landlords were local and were constrained by the stronger village institutions and by a history of *Viet Minh* activism against high rents.

Communal land was still extensive in the Central Lowlands in this period. Tables 6.1 and 6.2 show communal land for Thua Thien in 1959 and estimates of percentages of communal land for five of the ten provinces in the central lowlands which were computed in 1970 from responses of village officials. These statistics compiled from village officials seem to be more accurate than official South Vietnamese government sources which vary widely depending on the compiler's definition of what constitutes community lands.

25 per cent of the communal land in My Xa was set aside for communal expenses and the rest was distributed in shares to the residents of the hamlet. This finding is consistent with a 1970 study of communal land in the Central Lowlands which found that an average of 20 per cent of communal land was set aside for the expenses of the village.[14] The communal expense land was rented, in most cases, and the revenues were used for particular village expenses.

As in the traditional village, the budget was actually the division of the land, and the amount of money available for a particular public purpose depended on the harvest. Many of the traditional categories were in evidence, even in 1970:

Table 6.1   Distribution of public land and private land in selected areas, 1959

Classification	Thua Thien Province (*ha.*)	Quang Quien District (*ha.*)	Quang Loc Commune (*ha.*)	My Xa hamlet (*ha.*)
Public agricultural land	22 681	4 208	1 261	125
Private agricultural land	17 149	1 738	209	8
Other public land	33 916	1 661	503	1
Other private land	14 686	1 084		9

Source: Nicholaas Luykx, *Some Comparative Aspects of Rural Public Institutions in Thailand, the Philippines and Viet Nam*, p. 707.

Table 6.2   Percentage of communal land in villages according to village officials

Quang Tri	62
Thua Thien	64
Quang Nam	50
Quang Tin	10
Quang Ngai	28

Source: Edward Fitzgerald and Henry Bush, *Village Use of Communal Rice Land*, p. 10.

There is 'open land' (*but dien*) used to buy supplies for the village council. There is 'riceland for supplying food' (*phan dien*) used to pay honoraria to Village Council members. There is 'school land' (*hoc dien*) used to support village schools ... There are 'riceland for the worship of the village guardian spirit' and 'riceland for the worship of Buddha' (*ruong than tu* and *ruong phat tu*) used for religious ceremonies and to maintain pagodas, temples and shrines.[15]

The *cong dien* and *cong tho* was still distributed in equal shares to all villagers in the Central Lowlands, either all people born in the village or all people currently residing in the village, depending on local custom. In some villages men and women both received shares, and in some villages only males received shares. The inclusion of women in the distribution was most likely an innovation of the *Viet Minh* since 'males only' had been prescribed by the law codes in Vietnam since the Le Dynasty and there is no mention of the inclusion of women in descriptions of the precolonial and colonial village. In areas such as Quang Tin and Quang Ngai, where villages had too little communal land to distribute reasonable portions to all villagers, distributions were to the needy in the villages (See Table 6.2).

In My Xa the distribution was equal in every respect imaginable and the institutuions were designed specifically to achieve this result. The village lists had disappeared and in its place there was a lottery system and a system of grading lands of differing fertility so that as much equality as possible would be the result. The distribution was carried out every three years. There was first a general meeting where a thirty-person committee was established to grade the land. They considered the amount of fertiliser used and the quality of the stand of rice in their grading process and yields were measured using a box designed for that purpose when the harvest came in. The size of the share of land distributed was determined by the expected yield. That is, first quality land was given out in smaller shares than second quality land, and third quality land had the largest plot sizes. The shares were also computed so that the yields of the poorer quality land were slightly larger than the yields of better quality land in order to compensate for the greater cost of fertilisation of the lower quality land.[16]

After this grading procedure which divided the land into three 'qualities', priorities in the distribution were determined by lottery in order to make random the remaining differences. People who were residing elsewhere but were born in the village were allowed to choose residents to draw for them. This was a considerable number of people in My Xa, nearly half the eligible recipients, and was most likely the result of the proximity of the village to the city of Hue. Most of the eligible non-residents were non-farmers whose share was passed to relatives who were farmers in the village. Table 6.3 shows the distribution between residents and non-residents, men and women. Although there were 905 eligible people, there were only about 300 drawings because families tended to draw as a unit for all their members, including those who were non-resident.[17] Since families

Table 6.3   Distribution of land between residents and non-residents by sex, My Xa Hamlet, 1960

Residence category	Men	Women	Total
Resident	191	265	456
Non-resident	220	229	449
TOTAL	411	494	905

Source: Nicholaas Luykx, 'Some Comparative Aspects of Rural Public Institutions in Thailand, the Philippines, and Viet Nam', p.708.

members, including those who were non-resident.[17] Since families were patriarchal, this custom undercut the official equality between men and women in the distribution.

My Xa was not the typical central village in that practically all land was communal. Using other descriptions and studies of communal land in addition to the My Xa study, however, we can affirm our impression of the continued importance of communal land in the central village. This continued importance of communal land is a strong indication of the difference in central and southern Vietnam in the penetration of market forces. It is also clear, however, that the mid-twentieth-century central village did not distribute its land in the traditional manner. Changes occurred with the penetration of the capitalist economy and the reaction against that incursion which was mainly socialist – the *Viet Minh*. The colonialists were probably responsible for the introduction of the lottery which replaced the village lists. The *Viet Minh*, in line with socialist politics and the participation of women in the anticolonial struggle, were probably responsible for the inclusion of women in the distribution.

LABOUR

The division of labour in the Mekong Delta village did not become more specialised with the expansion of markets. With the entrance of capitalism the peasants simply expended more labour in expanding their rice production for sale on the market and this expansion stopped with the limitation of available rice land. There was no increased production of agricultural goods other that rice in the southern village and there was less handicraft production than in the traditional Vietnamese village.

There was an important increase in paid labour which accompanied the increase in numbers of people who neither owned nor rented their own land. Landless labourers and smallholders hiring out their labour was the natural correlation to concentration of landholding. The rich and middle-level farmers – that is, the landowners who stayed in the village – were the users of hired labour. The absentee landlords merely rented out their lands rather than hiring labour to farm them.

As in the traditional village, there was a definite seasonal limitation in the work of rice cultivation, with the transplanting and harvesting season being peak work periods. Agricultural activities did not take more that half the year in Khanh Hau. According to Hendrey, there were at least six months of the year during which the large majority of employable labour in the village did not work except sporadically on large maintenance tasks.[18] Secondary productive occupations in Khanh Hau were carpentry, involving thirty villagers, implement-making by two or three villagers, and basket-weaving by most mature females in the village. There were also a few rice millers who had set up operations in the late 1950s (rice milling used to be done by using hand-mills) tailors and seamstresses. Vietnamese handicraft items and some imported goods were purchased from outside the village and sold by women merchants. Because of a lack of direction at the village level to extend the canal system and double- cropping through public works, there was a lack of productive opportunities when compared with the traditional village. There, second crops, handcrafts and public works had kept the population working the entire year.

Reciprocal labour exchange continued in South Vietnam in this period, with villagers working in each others' fields, expecting no payment between members of the group. 75 per cent of the villagers were included in the economic level where reciprocal assistance remained important in labour supply. According to one study, 'Farmers of this level rely a great deal on mutual aid in preparing the fields, transplanting, irrigating and harvesting.'[19] Mutual assistance extended also to work activities such as construction and repair of the thatch-roofed houses used by the great majority of people in the village.

Middle-level and well-to-do farmers hired work teams for various tasks such as transplanting and harvesting. 66–75 per cent of adult villagers worked on these teams at some time during the year. The work teams were organised and managed by 'labour contractors' (*trum cay*) who were appointed by the village council from those who applied for the job. There were approximately forty to sixty men and women in each group. The standard pay in 1958 was VN$30 (90US cents) for each man and VN$20 (60 US cents) for each woman, plus two meals a day.[20] Groups were open to all villagers, but labourers tended to come from the same neighbourhoods and remained in the same groups from year to year. This composition of work groups mirrors the traditional reciprocal labour exchange relationships.

Important divisions of labour continued between the sexes in the modern Vietnamese village. According to Hendrey, there were fourteen occupations exclusively for men and eleven occupations exclusively for women. The area of overlap was less, with seven occupations being joint male and female tasks. Men continued to prepare the fields and the seedlings; women continued to handle the transplanting. Both men and women were involved in harvesting: men usually doing the threshing but women occasionally handling this. Although women continued to be mainly responsible for cooking, gardening and peddling, some participation in these activities by men was noted by Hendrey. The traditional division of labour in agriculture was continued and it was clearly not a division according to physical strength because women performed most tasks which involved heavy carrying. Men handled the important beginning (ploughing and harrowing) and ending (threshing) parts of the rice-production cycle.

In the Central Lowlands, traditional patterns of labour exchange continued, for the most part. Most peasants maintained a certain amount of independence because of their communal shares and although many worked for hire occasionally, there was only a small group of peasants who earned their living predominantly as hired labourers. Along with their share of land, the peasants had an obligation to donate a certain amount of labour days for public works in the village. This averaged ten days per year in the area studied.[21] Non-residents who received communal land made a cash donation in lieu of a direct contribution of labour and the more wealthy villagers also made cash contributions which were used to buy materials for the public works projects.

WATER

Part of the water needed for wet rice cultivation in South Vietnam is accumulated from rainfall which is trapped in the fields by dikes. River water is used for irrigation in most places to supplement this rain water.

The most efficient technique of irrigation is to irrigate only the high fields, and then let the water drain into the lower adjoining fields. Sometimes the fields closest to the water supply are irrigated first and then the dikes are breached and the water flows into the next field. Trenches can be formed by moulding temporary dikes close to permanent ones. The water can be pumped or spilled into the trench and carried to distant fields. In Khanh Hau coordination of efforts for this type of irrigation did not function smoothly. The owners of fields which were closest to the water source were sometimes opposed to having dikes built in their fields.[22]

There were two principal methods of transporting water from low to high ground in Khanh Hau, the scoop or basket lift and the waterwheel. Mutual assistance groups divided the task of irrigating. They took turns pedalling the water wheels and measured time by burning joss sticks. There was one mechanical pump in the village which was rented but most villagers found this method too expensive.

Cooperation in the distribution of water was a difficult problem in the delta village under Diem. In Khanh Hau there were many water disputes each year which the village council attempted to arbitrate.[23] Cooperation, which is essential to efficient techniques of water distribution in South Vietnam, was restricted because of the importance of the private property rights which had been established in South Vietnam.

In My Thuan there was little irrigation other than that naturally occurring when the river seasonally overflowed its banks. Farmers diked the fields when the water reached the desired level. There was an extensive 'dry' area in the village and there was no double-cropping because of lack of irrigation. Donoghue attributed this situation to lack of village cooperation and lack of 'incentives' for high production.[24]

In the Central Lowlands, by contrast, distribution of water was still a function of the hamlet and village, and upkeep of the water-control system involved many levels of government. In a commune studied by Luykx, Quang Loc, there was one long dike built as a retaining wall for brackish water. There were also four dams, eight weirs and a number of canals. Although the retaining wall built in 1957 would aid only two of the twelve hamlets in the commune, all twelve hamlets contributed labour. There was district and commune representation in the supervision of the project which took eighteen months to complete and measured a mile and a half in length.[25]

Upkeep of the water-control facilities was a continuous responsibility of the commune. The responsible member of the commune administrative committee made inspection trips of all the water control facilities of the commune every 2 weeks. He inspected damage reported by all the chiefs of hamlets. If repairs were necessary, a meeting between the hamlet chief and the commune administrative committee would decide material and labour requirements. Authorisation was required from the district headquarters for the repair project and the provincial-level administration had to be informed. This procedure did not seem to inhibit the process of completing a project since about three such projects a year were undertaken per commune. Essentially the commune administrative committee organised the labour contribution to the project and the economic member supervised the labour contribution. Only when material aid was involved from the district would that level become more heavily involved.

There was a strong contrast between the southern and central villages of the mid-twentieth century regarding centralism in water control. There was little cooperation on even the hamlet and village levels in the southern region because of the development of private, individual property rights. In the central village, on the other hand, many levels were involved in water control and there were labour contributions from hamlets which would not even be affected by a particular project. Water control was a serious and continuing responsibility of the commune in the central region, and in this respect also, the central village much more closely resembled the traditional village than did the southern village.

VILLAGE AUTHORITY AND CONTROL OF PRODUCTION

In the south since the French period the appointed village officials had lost much of their political and economic power in the village. With little communal land and few water-control facitilities, the role of the officials in production decisions was unimportant. Public-utility projects were not initiated by village officials and large-scale projects encompassing many villages, such as those accomplished in traditional Vietnam, were not carried out. In the village of Khanh Hau, there was only one public works project attempted in the 1950s and that was initiated at an official level above that of the village. This project was not complete because of the opposition of property owners in the village. It was Hendrey's opinion that the majority sentiment of the village definitely favoured more canals, but the village administration was not strong enough to push these projects through.[26]

Village authority was still a male sphere in the villages studied, since the Saigon government had appointed only male officials. Nevertheless, one of the functionaries, a kindergarten teacher, was a woman. This was a particularly interesting difference because of the restrictions on the education of women in the traditional period. In the early 1970s, this author observed a woman Saigon government official at the provincial level, indicating that the traditional restriction against women officials was not long to be maintained either.[27]

In the central lowlands, in contrast, traditional patriarchal control in the village was intact and heads of families and neighbourhood groups in the central village were involved in coordinating production, and hamlet and village officials were involved in production. The constant involvement in water-control facilities and their construction and maintenance was important in this regard. The chief of a hamlet would select and assemble labour for repair tasks, would take his group to the work site and supervise, if it were an individual hamlet project. The responsible member of the commune committee would oversee repair and maintenance of commune projects. As we have seen, the district chiefs also became directly involved in new construction at the commune level.

The different degrees of responsibility at the village level can be seen through the southern and central village budgets. In Khanh Hau, with budgets in the range of $60 000 to $90 000 in 1956, 1957 and 1958, a single proposed expense in 1958 for public works in maintaining the village office ($2000) was not spent.[28] There were expenditures of only $3000 for health and education for personnel and equipment for all three years together. In Quang Loc commune in the Central Lowlands, on the other hand, expenditures of the commune (excluding returns to hamlets and assessments to intercommunal equalisation fund) were approximately $1 900 000 and $1 500 000 in 1958 and 1959. Expenditures on public works and health and education were $880 000 and $650 000, or 40–45 per cent of the budget. Expenditures on equipment for maintaining dams, dikes and canals were $223 000 in one year and $72 000 in the next.[29] The large amount of labour used in public works was not evaluated but would have added considerably to the total communal expenditure.

BREAKDOWN OF THE TRADITIONAL PATRIARCHY –
PEASANT WOMEN'S STATUS IN THE SOUTH

With the introduction of capitalism the peasant patriarch was dealt
severe blows – he was dispossessed of land ownership, a share of the
communal land and political power in the village. Without property
and power, however, the male peasant was more on a level with his
wife than he had been under the Confucian system. Under tenancy,
the male family head still played the dominant role in coordinating
production and distributing the produce, but his rights were tenuous.
He was no longer supported by a strong village patriarchal control and
the tight network of the extended family.

The patriarchal extended families dissolved into nuclear families
under the impact of the new system. The dissolution of the traditional
pattern in Khanh Hau took the form of sons remaining in the family for
only a short time after their marriage and then setting up a separate
household. The youngest son stayed in the family home and cared for
the mother and father in their old age. Under this new system, the
family member in charge of ancestor worship was chosen by adult
males and females instead of this honour automatically going to the
eldest male.[30] Typically most families did not own any patrimony to be
divided among the siblings so there was no inheritance reason for
remaining in the extended-family household. Most families did not
even possess a small plot of *houng hoa*, which could be used to defray
expenses of family gatherings, rituals and feasts and this lack
weakened the extended-family system considerably.

Nuclear families were usually headed by males in the southern
village, but widows and separated women were also heads of
households. These women heads of household made up 7 per cent of
households in Khanh Hau.[31] Women were heads of households in
this time and not the earlier period because of the breakdown of
extended-family networks. In the modern period when a woman lost
her husband, she was no longer expected to move back to her
parent's or her brother's home. Women as heads of households could
manage property in their own right. Women could hire people to do
certain male tasks, such as ploughing, or, more rarely, she could
handle this task herself. This was not the usual household arrangement since the male was always head of household when present. But
the actuality of some females controlling production was a
breakthrough.

Marriages continued to be usually arranged by the parents in the southern village in the 1950s. Where the parents did not have prior arrangements and there was some choice by the couple, the parents always had to approve. Deference was expected of a daughter-in-law toward her mother-in-law even though she did not usually have to live with her mother-in-law, except for a short period after her marriage.

In the 1950s polygamy was more common in the southern village than in the traditional village. Nevertheless, it was only the rich élite of the village who participated.[32] The increased inequality of wealth and income which accompanied colonialism encouraged the extension of this institution among the more affluent. While the poor could barely afford, or could not afford, to keep their household together, the élite male of the village could extend his household by taking a second wife to share the work with the first. Second wives were the only alternative to paid domestic labour in this period. A new type of polygamy which was practised in the modern village was the man's maintenance of two separate households. This practice of maintaining separate households was the preferred arrangement of the élite in Khanh Hau.[33] The pattern of smaller households being maintained in polygamous marriage fits into the general tendency towards smaller households in this capitalist period.

The most important transition for women was the shift from unpaid labour to wage labour. The work teams for transplanting and harvesting rice were now paid work teams, and the woman in her home village could earn income independently of her husband or father. Athough she was paid only 66 per cent the wage rate of a man, the importance of her new position was that she could earn income for agricultural labour. In the former system, the only women with independent income were those merchants who were widows or wives of officials. With paid agricultural labour, the ordinary peasant woman could earn her own wages. Other sources of income for women were domestic work, seamstress work, and sales of home-made items such as rice cakes, woven mats or baskets. Women could sell these items to merchants or peddle them themselves.

The distribution of power within the average peasant family was changed greatly with the introduction of wage labour. With the new system, the control of productive resources that peasant males possessed in the old society had decreased significantly, and the income-earning ability of women increased substantially. Because the woman continued to be manager of the household budget, the woman who participated in wage labour could take her earnings directly into the household without her wages going through the hands of her husband. For the rich peasant élite, however, the situation was very different. The peasant men who were more powerful in the village, because of the resources they had accumulated through market transactions or appointed government office, were able to maintain a powerful position within the family. Few of the wives of these rich peasants and small landowners worked for a wage. Their wives were kept busy with many household responsibilities which involved elaborate cooking and entertaining - part of the expected behaviour of women in this class.[34]

PRODUCE MARKETS, MONEY AND CREDIT

The market for rice was very important to the contemporary southern village. In Khanh Hau 66 per cent of the rice crop was sold for cash. Some villagers sold high-quality rice and bought low-quality rice for consumption purposes. The price of rice was an important determinant of village well-being and entered into crop-planning decisions. Hickey stated that the expected market price of rice was probably the factor most often discussed by farmers during the dry season.[35]

The market for produce was not fully competitive even though there were many sellers and many buyers of rice. The rice-buyers had access to better information about the latest prices in Cholon, the rice-export centre of Vietnam. They could take advantage of this knowledge by buying quickly at the old price when the price went up. Although the price of rice was of great importance, villagers did not normally sell rice only on the basis of price considerations. The necessity of selling quickly to meet rent, and interest payments to money-lenders, was a major consideration.[36] Small producers sold to local merchants who sold to Cholon city merchants, large producers benefited by selling directly to Cholon merchants.

There were market-places in nearby villages and towns where villagers bought meats, fish and other consumer items. There were also some pedlars, usually women, among the villagers themselves and a few village stores. Villagers bought both traditional goods and Western consumer goods. For example, traditional medicine was combined with Western medicine and some families bought beer and soft drinks but rice wine was still an important item.

Most economic transactions in the southern village were monetary. Labour, when hired, and the services of artisans, were paid for in coin. Even 'brideprice', or the payment which compensated the bride's family for the loss of her labour, and gifts at weddings and funerals were sometimes in cash.[37] Some rents were paid in cash, some in kind.

In the Central Lowlands, rice was not produced for the export market. Small amounts, like other goods, were exchanged in local market-places, but mostly the rice crop was eaten in the village and transferred directly to relatives in the city who still held shares of *cong dien* in the village. As long as city-dwellers retained one foot in the village through reciprocal exchange relationships with relatives there, it was difficult for the market to take over the distribution of produce. Relatives in the city gave the villagers rights to cultivate their shares of *cong dien* in exchange for a share of the harvest. Market exchange, even in the mid-twentieth century, was not the dominant mechanism by which villagers moved to the city and maintained their food subsistence.

In the rural markets, little money changed hands, except on the rare occasion when a buffalo was sold. Mostly fruits and vegetables, eggs, chickens and an occasional piglet were sold.[38] Peasants then used their proceeds to purchase their necessities. In My Xa the market met for three hours a day and the commune market met daily.[39] This is in contrast to traditional Vietnam where the markets were not usually allowed within the confines of the village.

The My Thuan Khanh Hau, and My Xa village studies are poor sources for any accurate desciption of the part money-lending played in the conversion to large landholding. Since the first Indochinese war, the security situation in the countryside and the relatively insecure power position of large landlords had discouraged certain types of money-lending. Large landowners no longer lent money to tenant-farmers although they did lend these monies within the memory of those in Khanh Hau village. At the time of these studies in the south, the Indian and Chinese money-lenders restricted their activities to towns and did not engage in agricultural money-lending. In the Central Lowlands the money-lenders virtually disappeared.

The village studies, however, can show general trends regarding who borrows and the use of funds. 66 per cent of the southern villagers had debts.[40] The incidence of debts was much greater among the lower income group and among this group there were some who wanted credit, but were unable to get it for lack of collateral. Collateral most often used was land or 'futures' on the next year's harvest. Collateral was not used in loans from friends or relatives, which was the major source of loans since the war.

Interest rates were extremely variable. 54 per cent of loans made by relatives were interest-free. Other rates varied according to length of term, size of loan, and source, but there was some clustering around the 30 per cent rate and the 100 per cent rate.[41]

Sources, other than friends and relatives, were 'mutual aid societies' or *hui* and storekeepers and fertiliser-pedlars. The mutual aid society in the modern southern village was a social and gambling as well as lending society and was used most commonly by women merchants with regular income. It was a way of acquiring capital for a stock of goods.[42]

In Khanh Hau, at the time of the study, people borrowed money for fertiliser and other farm expenses as often as for consumption purposes. This is the order of reasons for borrowing that Hendrey gives: (i) in order to buy food and other necessities, chiefly during the period between harvests; (ii) to buy fertiliser; (iii) to pay medical expenses; (iv) to pay ceremonial expenses; and (v) to cover farming costs.[43] It seems probable that fertiliser is so high on the list because the fertiliser dealers were willing to extend credit, and there were then few sources of credit in the village. When the households with higher income borrowed money it was usually to buy land or for investment in businesses such as rice mills or speculation in paddy.

The way indebtedness passed to tenancy for small villagers is described by Hendrey:

> There have been very few instances in which a creditor had foreclosed on a mortgage. Instead, it is more common practice for a debtor, finding his debt mounting because of his inability to meet interest payments, to sell some portion of this land and use these sales proceeds to pay his debts.[44]

In the Central Lowlands, credit was organised in a different way. Short-term credit was usually available for peasant households experiencing a bad harvest from within the hamlet. Rice would be borrowed at 20 per cent interest to last until the next harvest, five or eight months later. Some families in My Xa, however, would instead send their children into domestic service in Hue City.[45]

In the case of a disaster such as a flood which would wipe out the crop for the entire area, families would try to borrow from people they knew in the cities. In My Xa, this was evidently not a problem because all families knew people in Hue City. At the time of a large flood, they had all acquired loans, half from relatives and half from businessmen. The amount borrowed was $1000–$4000 ($35–140 US). The loans from relatives were free of interest and the loans from businessmen carried a 3 per cent interest rate. Generally, credit extended from the city to the countryside was only between persons who were personally acquainted and trusted one another. In My Xa no security was put up for loans, no futures on crops and no land, since the land was almost all communal.[46] Evidently, loans were paid back under these circumstances without disputes. When the peasant families were not able to pay on time, extensions were granted.

Credit was difficult to obtain for villages not near cities and for peasants without contacts in cities. These were important probems of the system. On the other hand, there was not the danger of loss of land that there was in the credit systems in the southern area. The traditional mechanism under the emperor of storing rice from good harvest in order to prepare for possible poor harvests was preferable to both modern systems in the case of hardship loans – at least the store of rice would be distributed more equally and not depend on connections as did credit. In the case of investment loans, the modern systems under Diem seem preferable to the emperor's system because they made possible the use of technical innovations such as fertiliser and new seed varieties. As we will see in the chapters on the NLF, however, state- and village-controlled investment led to increased output without increased inequality.

ACCUMULATION OF CAPITAL AND TECHNOLOGICAL CHANGE

There was considerable difference between the traditional village and the southern villages of the late 1950s. This difference was in the presence of markets and changed production relationships; there was, however, little improvement in production methods. The modern commercial economy initially increased production for the world market but did not facilitate mechanisation of rice production. The introduction of the market did not increase labour productivity since there was merely a one-step increase in the number of hours worked as area under crops initially increased. Labour input per worker decreased again as population grew and the area under crops did not increase. Private ownership meanwhile produced concentration in landholding which destroyed the strength of the village, thereby preventing the construction of a network of canals which would have facilitated double-cropping and increased production as population grew.

Table 6.4 shows the population density and percentage of double-cropping by province in Central and Southern Vietnam. The southern area which was developed for exports of rice, shows no correlation between double-cropping and population growth, while the Central Lowlands, producing for home consumption, shows a high correlation (91 per cent). The development of private property in the south prevented the traditional mechanism of increasing production with population growth.

One technological advance which was adopted in the 1950s in some delta villages was the use of chemical fertilisers. In Khanh Hau one man reputed to be wise started its use in the village and it caught on quickly. There was little understanding of how to use fertiliser although there was some general idea that the more fertiliser was used, the better the crop would be. There was no differentiation between kinds of fertiliser for various types of soils. In My Thuan no chemical fertiliser was used. Fertiliser was something the villagers knew about but they did not know how to use it or where to get it and they considered their soil fertile enough.[47]

Some pesticides were used in Khanh Hau by the rich farmers. In the 1950s one villager bought a gasoline pump but all other irrigation was done by traditional methods. Large rice mills had been constructed in the delta since 1950 and in Khanh Hau few farmers still milled their own rice. With these exceptions, production techniques were much the same as before the French impact; most equipment consisted of age-old implements and there was no knowledge of alternative agricultural techniques.

There were some fairly profound changes in the commercial economy of the village of Khanh Hau in the decade of the 1950s, but there seemed to be no similar changes in My Thuan. A major change was considered by both Hendrey and Hickey to be an increase in 'entrepreneurial' activity. There were investments by wealthy villagers in rice milling and rice merchandising. These were activities which were left mainly to the Chinese before 1950 but Chinese merchants were no longer numerous in rural Vietnam. There had recently been some small business activity unrelated to rice. Two brothers attempted a lumber business which failed and the village chief bought a gas station in a nearby town.

In general, the rich Vietnamese did well in their new undertakings,

Table 6.4 Double-cropping in Cochin China in contrast to the central lowlands

Province (no.)	Central Lowlands population density on rice holdings per hectare	% of riceland double-cropped	Cochin China population density on rice holdings per hectare	% of riceland double-cropped	Province (no.)
(1)	13.4	87	8.1	0.1	(1)
(2)	11.8	84	6.9	2.0	(2)
(3)	11.7	75	4.7	0.1	(3)
(4)	10.9	66	4.3	5.0	(4)
(5)	10.0	85	3.8	10.0	(5)
(6)	8.4	67	3.3	16.0	(6)
(7)	4.6	49	3.3	0.0	(7)
(8)	4.4	27	3.2	0.0	(8)
(9)	2.5	39	3.2	0.0	(9)
			3.0	0.0	(10)

Source: Republic of Vietnam, Department of Rural Affairs, *Report on the Agriculture Census of Vietnam*, pp. 48–50.

although there seemed to be some moral inhibitions. For example, one rice farmer in Khanh Hau got out of rice merchandising because he believed the merchant had to be a 'teller of lies'.[48] There was little stigma remaining against commerce although the occupation remained less prestigious than government service or farming. The 90 per cent of the population who were not rich were not part of this new commercial economy because these peasants did not have the necessary capital to become involved. They tried to get along under difficult constraints and they accomplished what was realistically attainable within limits set by their environment.

In the central village there were also some changes in techniques and 'entrepreneurial' activity. Commercial fertiliser was used on poorer grades of land, but the less-costly pig manure was preferred for land which would respond to natural fertilisation. The institution of communal land and the cohesive nature of the village did not prevent the adoption of this technical innovation of commercial fertiliser, but older methods, where applicable, were also used. In the southern village, on the other hand, only commercial fertiliser was used.

There were also commercial activities such as rice milling in the central village. In the Central Lowlands, however, politics entered the picture and the rice millers had to be approved by the chief of the province. Shopkeepers in the hamlet applied for authorisation also, but only the informal approval of the hamlet chief was necessary.[49] In this manner, there were direct political controls on business activity in the village. These controls did not seem to inhibit small businesses, but it seems unlikely that businesses would have been able to accumulate a large amount of capital and become large-scale in the collective environment which existed in the central village, even under the Diem government. The central village would react negatively to the inequality necessary for large-scale business. The modern southern village, on the other hand, had no controls over such activity.

CONTRASTS

In a broad comparison of the post-colonial delta village with the central and the traditional village, the most striking contrast is the change in land tenure. From institutions of small-scale holdings combined with communal lands, there emerged a system of large-scale landlordism and widespread tenancy in the south. These changes were accompanied by a loss of cohesiveness in the village unit to the extent that the village lost control over irrigation rights and the right to build new canals. The commercial economy entered the village, but this event had no permanent positive effect on the peoples' living standards, since the technical capabilities of the people were not increased.

With the capitalist transition, most Vietnamese patriarchs lost their base of power in the village and, to a lesser extent, their base of power in the family also. With tenancy, the family head held usufruct rights to a certain small area of land with the agreement that he would pay a large rental share. Other men became landless labourers and, along with their wives, they merely worked for a wage. Women's options for independence, meanwhile, increased with the introduction of wage-labour opportunities in agriculture in their home villages and industrial work outside the village. Women could control productive resources as head of household after transition, but this was not the usual situation. Of course, a woman's position decreased, along with that of her husband, if she were in a tenant- or landless family.

The southern rural society was engaged in the transition to capitalism. Markets for produce were established and markets for land, labour and credit were at least partially established. In a competitive market system, factors of production are supposed to find their most productive uses through exchange. This was not a purpose of the exchange of land in the southern village. Land was sold in order to pay debts or was passed on in inheritance. Land was bought for the purpose of accumulating rent payments, and it was not put to a more productive use by the new owner; most often it was rented out to a tenant who farmed the land in exactly the same manner as the former owner, and in fact in many cases the tenant was the former owner.

Labour and credit were exchanged in markets, but these markets also did not function like those in a developed capitalist economy. There was a dual labour system in the village, most peasants working for a wage from people with larger holdings for part of the time, and working in mutual-exchange teams part of the time. Credit was used by people with higher income in the village for business purposes and was also often used by average farmers to purchase fertiliser. At least half the time, however, credit to the average farmer was for subsistence and not for investment purposes.

The market system had an impact on the villages of the Central Lowlands also, but by the 1950s markets were still peripheral to the functioning of the rural economy. Redistribution of land and reciprocal labour exchange were still the predominant modes of exchange in the villages and exchange between cities and the countryside was often also reciprocal. That is, people would make exchanges of money, produce and children's labour with relatives in the city.

7 Socialism in the North

In 1954, the government of the Democratic Republic of Vietnam needed the support of the poor peasant majority in the countryside in order to carry out its programmes. Although many of the richest landlords had been removed in the process of the previous struggle, the village oligarchies were either still intact or they could reconstitute themselves. Social change in the countryside depended on support of the government by the poor peasants. This was a lesson which had been learned from the Rent Reduction Campaign and its positive impact on soldiers at Dien Bien Phu.

The northern village, in 1954, looked very much like the Central Lowlands village just studied. It too, was tight-knit and depended on an administrative hierarchy which was in charge of water control and other public works as well as communal land. Socialist land reform and collectivisation policies revolutionised the countryside. They were successful, in the 1950s and early 1960s, in changing the local power structure as well as promoting the development of agriculture and the growth of output. It was two years after the signing of the Geneva Accords, however, before a class-conscious policy could be carried out in the countryside. In 1954, the North Vietnamese assumed that the elections promised in the Geneva Accords would be carried out in two years. The post-Geneva strategy was therefore to welcome village notables who had formerly sided with the French in an anti-American united front in order to prepare for the coming elections. For this front to be successful, the leadership had to decrease the extent of class struggle developing in the countryside after the Rent Reduction Campaign and the victory at Dien Bien Phu. To this end, a number of policy changes were developed which included a more formalised method of bringing 'cruel landlord notables' to trial. Another new policy concerned the requisitioning of property of ordinary landlords. It was determined that compensation should be paid or that landlords should be allowed to show their good faith by donating property to the village for redistribution.

Within six months of the implementation of this united front strategy, it became obvious that the USA did not intend to follow through with the promised elections, but was attempting to undercut government control in the North through various subversive activities. It also seemed, at the time, that the USA was trying to start a war with

Communist China which would surely involve the Democratic Republic of Vietnam (DRV). In light of these factors, on 3 March 1955, the Fifth Plenum of the Workers Party decided that the policy of lenience toward landlords should be reversed. They determined that the major task for the DRV was to consolidate the North by accelerating land reform, by repressing counter-revolutionaries and by restoring the northern economy.[1] The policy pendulum swung in the direction of class struggle and cadres in the countryside were criticised for not publicising the land reform more widely.

LAND REFORM

Decisions about the forthcoming land reform programme were made at the top party levels. The idea was not only to change production relations among the rural population but also to change the structure of the Party in rural areas. In all subdivisions of the country, including zones, provinces, districts and villages, a land-reform hierarchy was set up which was separate from the existing administration and party committees. The basic land-reform hierarchy was recruited from the most committed party members. Their numbers were supplemented by party members from the recently demobilised military and from the urban working class. Although many of these committed cadres were from petty-bourgeois backgrounds and had relatives in the countryside, they were not specifically assigned to the areas from which they came.[2]

In the period when the Workers Party had emphasised a united front policy against the French and later the Americans, many landlords had joined the *Viet Minh* and some had joined the Party. Some of these landlords were using their positions in the *Viet Minh* and in the Party to maintain control over their tenants and their dominance over local government. Land reform cadres were instructed to remove these elements from the Party and from all positions of authority in the village. The land-reform cadres were taught to be wary of the official party hierarchy existing in the countryside and they were even given the impression that the existing organisations might be 'organizations of the enemy'.[3]

The process by which the land reform was carried out in the villages was very similar to the process of carrying out rent reduction. The cadres were supposed to find poor peasants and practise the 'three togethers', 'living together, eating together and working together'.

The individual cadre was to locate and train a poor peasant and make him a leader. It was the poor peasant who was actually supposed to carry out the land reform.

In practice, the leadership training was often not as effective as planned and the cadres were often impatient. Many cadres did not wait for the poor peasants to make decisions. Instead, they told the peasants what to do or made decisions for them.[4] In addition, practising the 'three togethers' did not really put the cadres on the same level as the poor peasants. There was still considerable social distance because the cadres' food and clothing was provided by the government. Even if the cadre was from a poor background, he had many more resources than the poor peasant he was recruiting and if he was not from a poor backgound, the social distance was immense.

The object of the land reform was to create a rural revolution in which the country and the Party would be rid of landlords and rich peasants. The land reform was to be carried out by poor peasants, with the Party's help, and the poor peasants were to make an alliance with the middle peasants. The existing majority of party members in the countryside were from middle-peasant backgrounds and, except for mistakes in classification, care was taken by the land-reform cadres not to alienate the middle-peasant class. While landlords were treated harshly, middle peasants were given preferential treatment. Out of respect for them, the average amount of land that they were allowed to keep was higher than the amount given to poor peasants.[5] The anger of the poor peasants was directed, by the cadre, toward the landlords and away from the middle peasants. What were later to be considered errors in need of rectification, were actions against rich peasants, landlords and sometimes wrongly classified middle peasants.

Reformed village political organisations were set up in the midst of the land-reform campaign. Open meetings of local party branches were held where poor peasants and landless labourers could bring evidence. This process led to the expulsion of rich peasants and landlords from the Party and often poor peasants were recruited to village administration to replace those deposed. These poor peasants were promoted rapidly and they often did not have adequate experience for the jobs they were supposed to handle.[6]

There has been considerable publicity about the approximately 5000 landlords killed in this period.[7] Landlords were brought to trial and imprisoned or killed during the land-reform campaign for a mixture of reasons. Some landlords were active supporters of the French and some had been responsible for the deaths of supporters of the revolution. In addition, there was class hatred towards many landlords because of their cruelty and acts of beating or rape. Vengeance for previous acts was certainly part of the reaction of peasants to landlords during the 'trials of landlords' in the land-reform campaign.

In theory, the structure of the land reform was supposed to leave the landlords with about as much land as their former tenants plus their houses and most other goods. In practice, the landlords were typically left with less land than anyone else in the village and they often lost their houses, too. The vengeance of former tenants seems to have taken on its own momentum in this period and the land-reform hierarchy, at least to some extent, lost control of the situation. Many landlords were beaten or killed for past sins against their tenants. Some rich peasants and landlords who were loyal to the *Viet Minh*, and even experienced cadres, were taken before land-reform committees. These resistance landlords were stripped of their former positions and they were often also imprisoned.

Party leaders reacted to the extent of disruption in the countryside, and the trials of cadres, by instituting a 'Rectification of Errors' campaign. The errors which the party was interested in rectifying were: (i) the tendency not to discriminate between patriotic and non-patriotic landlords; (ii) the tendency not to consider the families of landlords who had worked with the revolution and those who had children who had served as soldiers; (iii) the tendency not to discriminate in the treatment of the landlords' children; (iv) the unjust treatment of innocent and wrongly classified people, and (v) the use of excessive violence.[8] During the Rectification of Errors, many members of the resistance who had been labelled as rich peasants and landlords, were reclassified as middle peasants and they resumed their former positions in the Party and in the village administrative hierarchy.

Christine White believes that patriarchal behaviour was the reason for some of the mistaken categorisation during the land-reform campaign. The class categories used in the land reform did not recognise the existence of patriarchy. Those who engaged in 'feudal' behaviour such as wife-beating and gambling were sometimes wrongly classified as 'feudal landlords'.[9]

The land reform had important and mostly unintentional effects on women in the patriarchal family structure and in the village. Men and women were all divided into the same class categories: landlord, rich peasant, middle peasant and poor peasant. Women officially had a share in the land distribution although land usually went to families with male family heads. Women were active in the land-reform trials because crimes of 'cruel landlord notables' had often been against women. Women were not among the ruling élite, since they had been excluded from village administration. They were not, therefore, likely to be targets of the land-reform reorganisation. Women nevertherless suffered the economic restrictions doled out to patriarchs on whom they were dependent.

There were few women cadres involved in carrying out the land reform in its early stages because of the policy of recruiting land-reform cadres from the military. In the process of the land reform, however, women who had been active in village self-defence often became land-reform activists. Women were groomed by land-reform cadres into lower-level administrative positions by waves three, four and five of the land reform. By wave four, 30 per cent of the land reform activists were women.[10]

INDUSTRY

Meanwhile, socialist development in the rest of the North Vietnamese economy was proceeding apace. Although changes in social relations of production pre-dated changes in production forces (technology) in the agricultural sector, Vietnamese planners of the industrial sector, including Le Duan, were very firm in their belief that productive forces were the key to the development of socialism: 'The changes in the productive forces bring about changes in the relations of production and in consequence the political and intellectual life of the society also changes.'[11]

Recovery in the industrial sector in North Vietnam was very rapid after 1954. The North Vietnamese quickly embarked on a programme of reconstruction and they successfully set a foundation for independent development. They used foreign aid from several socialist countries, with large contributions coming from the Soviet Union and China. Although aid in the North in the 1950s was about the same amount as US aid in the South, its purposes were very different. The North was laying the foundation for industrialisation by extending electrification and setting up machine-tools, cement and steel factories. Meanwhile, in the South, US development funds were used in supporting a weak and unpopular administration and in building a few light manufacturing plants which were tied to the foreign trade sector.

The industries which already existed in Vietnam in 1954 were processing industries – preparing raw materials for export – and a few consumer goods industries: textiles, tobacco, vegetable oil, matches, paper and china. The French, upon leaving Indochina, took a lot of their machinery, raw materials and expertise with them. Spare parts were also not available to the Vietnamese. Consequently, industry was almost at a standstill at the end of the war.

In the period 1955–7, priority in economic planning was given to restoring the output of the economy to its 1939 level. Industry was brought under collective or state direction for the purpose of pursuing this end. The former French-owned industrial and commercial establishments and public utilities were easily nationalised, since the French had left the country. Industries owned by patriotic Vietnamese were left in private hands but in most cases, the state either bought the output produced by the enterprise or supplied the raw materials. The state also fixed prices so that a 'reasonable' level of profit was maintained.

Light manufacturing, which provided between 10 and 20 per cent of consumers' needs, was reconstructed by 1957. A few new industries were established, such as cigarette-making, liquor manufacture and new varieties of cloth and pharmaceuticals. Some heavy industries, however, such as coal, cement and tin, had not reached their 1939 output levels by 1957.

Handicraft industries, practised in the countryside, still provided the bulk of peoples' needs for non-agricultural goods. There was no attempt to direct these industries but the socialist state did influence them by eliminating the competition of foreign industrial goods. Credit was also extended to the artisans and tax breaks were given to new handicraft producers.

The main task of the next three-year plan, 1958–60, was to complete the socialist transformation of production relations. In this period, handicraft industries were brought into collectives and agricultural collectives were formed in the countryside. Private industry was transformed into state or state–private industry also in this period. Many enterprises became joint state–private, which meant that capital became state property and production and distribution came under the direction of the state plan. The former owners received a fixed rate of interest on their capital of from 6 to 8 per cent.

The state organised industry into two categories, state-controlled and regional industry. State-controlled industry included all large-scale enterprises and most heavy industry. These industries were part of the central plan. Regional industries were small in scale and included all small machine-tool enterprises and small consumer-goods enterprises. These regional industries and handicraft cooperatives were integrated into regional plans and came under regional administration.

By 1960 the value of industrial production in North Vietnam had grown to 1.5 billion *dong*, from 0.3 billion in 1955 (1959 prices) – a fivefold increase. Amost 40 per cent of consumer goods were provided by industry, as opposed to handicrafts, and this was double the percentage in 1954. About 33 per cent of production was in the heavy industry category and the central administration controlled 40 per cent of industrial production. Perhaps most importantly, for purposes of development strategy, investment as a percentage of national income had risen from under 10 per cent in 1955 to almost 20 per cent in 1959.[12]

Starting with the first five-year plan (1961–5), the basic direction of Vietnamese planning was to emphasise socialist construction. Economic rehabilitation and reorganisation of production relations along socialist lines had been completed and it was time to emphasise heavy industry in building the foundation for socialist industrialisation. The goal was to develop electric power one step ahead of other industries like metallurgy and machine-building. By 1965, 80 per cent of state investment was going toward heavy industry and 43 per cent of industrial production was in heavy industry. The value of industrial production had doubled by 1965, rising to approximately half of total output.[13]

North Vietnam relied on foreign assistance considerably for the financing of their industrial development. Although the Soviet Union contributed only 40 per cent of these foreign development funds and China contributed 50 per cent, for ideological reasons the Soviet Union got most credit from the Vietnamese. Leading Party members were more sympathetic toward the Soviet Union and there seemed to be a pro-Soviet bias even in this early period. Eastern Europe contributed the remaining 10 per cent of foreign assistance funds. Funds were often for specific industrial projects and technical assistance came along with money and machinery. Over 40 per cent of state investment in this period was from foreign sources and this investment plus foreign technical assistance made a huge impact on the local economy.[14] Bernard Fall gives us a view of some of the changes in North Vietnam's economy resulting from foreign assistance:

To see the difference one need only visit a short stretch of Road #6 from Hanoi to Ha-Dong, a town ten miles away. When I saw it first, in 1953, no man's land began with the last French bunker of the Hanoi perimeter. In 1962, one spanking new factory or school after another lined Road #6 from Hanoi almost up to the city of Ha-Dong; the big Soviet machine-tool factory and its housing blocks, the Ministry of Agricultural Hydraulics, a rubber factory, a textile plant, and the Minorities Institute were among the most conspicuous additions.[15]

The Vietnamese relied on internal accumulation in the industrial sector for most of their non-foreign-assistance investment funds. To a certain extent, at least, this was intentional. Large surpluses from agriculture could not be expected without agricultural mechanisation. After 1960, however, the stagnating agricultural sector began to affect the industrial sector negatively. As seen in Table 7.1 investment funds increased until 1960 and then levelled off. As a consequence of the poor harvests of the early 1960s, the North Vietnamese increased their already significant contribution to agricultural development by expanding production of fertilisers and semi-mechanised machinery. Large-scale hydraulic works were also extended. It would be reasonable for Vietnamese planners to expect some return from this increased investment in agriculture, which could contribute to the economic development of the country as a whole. Unfortunately, for reasons we will discuss in the next section, production in the agricultural collectives did not increase as a result of these measures.

Table 7.1   Investment and consumption shares in national income

	1957	1958	1959	1960	1961	1962	1963 (est.)
Investment	11.0	14.5	19.2	18.4	18.4	17.3	17.0
Consumption	89.0	85.5	80.8	81.6	81.6	82.7	83.0

Source: Irene Norlund, 'Industry in Vietnam's Development Strategy'.

By the mid 1960s the war in the south was becoming increasingly expensive in terms of North Vietnamese labour and capital inputs. There was no second five-year plan until after the end of the war in 1975. The US bombing of the North caused massive destruction of the industrial structure which had been set up. Arms factories, however, were dismantled and taken to the countryside. Investment in the period 1965–75 concentrated on replacing destroyed production facilities and most investment was in the rural areas, in order to minimise the risk of American bombing. Industrial production decreased from 1965 to 1968, but only by 0.3 billion *dong*. Then, output turned around after the bombing was limited in 1969 and increased over 1 billion *dong*, up to 3.7 billion by 1973.

Because of American intervention and its impact, the underlying problems facing collective agriculture and its effects on industry could not be seriously dealt with in the 1960s. These problems could not even be considered until after the war and after a period of recovery from the war.

AGRICULTURAL COLLECTIVISATION

There were many reasons why the North Vietnamese began thinking of building cooperatives in the countryside in the period immediately after land reform. Socialist ideology, especially the ideology coming from China before the China–Soviet split, favoured collectivisation. Before the Central Committee of the Workers Party was ready to move on these issues, pro-Mao cadres in the rural areas pushed for cooperatives, and then later for 'high level' cooperatives (collectives). There was a debate in the Party which mirrored early Soviet collectivisation debates. The pro-Mao cadres argued for the building of cooperatives on the Chinese Model (collectivisation). Other cadres maintained that price incentives should be used to increase production in the countryside, relying on the peasant family economy to respond to these price increases.

There had been a hold-up in taking the issue of cooperatives seriously because the North Vietnamese leaders judged that the integration of the country with the elections promised in the Geneva Accords was still a possibility. By 1958, when it was clear that the USA had taken complete political control in the South, the goal of integration with the South was put off indefinitely. Cooperatives were then brought forward as an issue.

The most frequent argument in favour of cooperatives mentioned in the North Vietnamese literature is that the rural class structure was reasserting itself through the contingencies of the market. Poor peasants, after a bad crop year, were selling their land or parts of their land to 'middle' peasants. (There were supposedly no 'rich' peasants left, so the euphemism for rich peasants was 'upper middle' peasants). The 'upper middle' peasants were doing very well in acquiring land in the North after land reform.

Collectivisation of the Soviet type which would modernise agriculture was not possible in underdeveloped North Vietnam. Nevertheless, there were other possible positive effects of collectivisation on productivity. Hydraulic advances could more easily be made, especially at the village level, if there were no objections to new canals being built because of private property rights. Channels could be built straighter and fields could be larger, maximising the usefulness of available cultivable land. Cooperative labour could also be more easily organised for construction projects.

Not the least important reason for collectivisation was the gaining of control of any agricultural surplus (no matter how small) for the purpose of financing industrialisation of the country. The price of rice for feeding city-dwellers and workers in the new industries could be kept low if deliveries (requisitions) to the state were made by collectives instead of individual farmers. Individual peasants would tend to eat much of their own surplus rather that sell to the state at a low price. The collective had no choice about whether to sell or not sell.

There were other reasons for collectivisation put forward by the North Vietnamese which seem more tenuous. The Vietnamese expected economies of scale from more specialisation in the division of labour. Cooperative work teams were set up for the cultivation of green manure (*azolla*) and for water-control projects. It is hard to see any great advantage in specialisation in these endeavors since they involved mostly unskilled labour. Another rationale was that cooperativisation was supposed to prepare the way for future modernisation. This is a weak argument because of the extended time period before mechanisation of agriculture would be possible. It is also argued that medium-level technical advances would be more possible through extension service and demonstration plots in the village, if there were cooperatives. This is a difficult position to argue since extension service has been so successful in other countries, such as the USA, where private farming is the rule.

Politically, the collectivisation campaign was seen by the more radical cadres as means of continuing class struggle in the countryside. Collectivisation would benefit poor-peasant households more than middle-peasant households and political control of the collective could theoretically be put in the hands of the poor-peasant class by regulations which favoured this class for leadership positions.

Mutual aid teams, in the traditional pattern, had been set up throughout North Vietnam prior to the cooperative movement. It is not totally clear how much of the initiative for these teams came from the Party. Most likely much of the impetus for their establishment came from the tendency for peasants to carry on with traditional institutions essential to production. It seems that the Party and the State tried to change the functioning of the neighbourhood mutual-aid teams by making them more permanent and by adding the function of teaching new techniques to the leaders of the teams.

There was a three-year period, 1958–60, in which cooperatives were first developed and in which the cooperative debate continued. The movement to form lower-level cooperatives took place fairly rapidly, once it was underway. In 1959, 45 per cent of peasant families joined cooperatives and in 1960 another 41 per cent joined.[16] The already formed mutual-aid teams were transformed, wherever possible, into production cooperatives. Credit cooperatives and sales and purchase cooperatives were formed simultaneously in the villages.

Cadres recruited the poor peasants for early participation and then later turned to the middle peasants. Membership was supposed to be voluntary, although ideological and political pressure must have been put on peasants to get them to volunteer for membership so quickly. There was a peaceful transition, however, with little vehement opposition. The rental payments that middle peasants received for their land, water buffalo and implements certainly must have alleviated some bad feelings about the movement.

The second stage, or the movement of lower-level cooperatives to the upper lever, was another hotly debated issue. Because of this second debate, the total collectivisation period was very drawn out in North Vietnam as compared with the Soviet Union or China. There were actually two periods of active conversion to high level coopera- tives, 1960–1 and 1964–5. Alec Gordon claims that there was very little progress toward full collectivisation in the period 1962–3 because of reactive or conservative forces in the party, including Le Duan, gaining control of policy. This conservative group claimed that the socialist revolution in the countryside was complete. Troung Chinh, on the other hand, pushed for a continuance of the collectivisation process and his more radical policy eventually prevailed.[17]

FAMILY ECONOMY

Unlike collectivisation in China, the North Vietnamese collectivised economy was not designed to supplant the peasant family economy at any time in the foreseeable future. The collective sphere did not provide more than half, and it often provided less than half, of the family's resources.[18] In China, the collectives were in a stronger position *vis-à-vis* the family economy because the collective provided 90 per cent of the family's resources and extensive collective child-care facilities were established. There were even experiments with collective eating arrangements.[19]

There were two rationales for the preservation of the family economy in North Vietnam and both were indicative of the limits of socialist planning in the Northern countryside. In the first place, the collective economy did not have the capacity to provide many of the basic necessities for cooperative members. A sub-economy, run by the family patriarch, was deemed necessary for the provision of these necessities. Second, the family economy was needed to harness 'surplus labour' which the collective economy was unable to absorb. The State saw that the family patriarch was able to organise the labour of old people, young people and women for productive pursuits in the home and on the family plot.[20] A minimum of 5 per cent of the cultivable land available per capita was allocated to cooperative members, but is was controlled by the family patriarch, and the State took advantage of this patriarchal family structure. This land was used to grow vegetables, some rice and other high-value crops. In addition to this source of income, families raised pigs and chickens for the market and they made handicraft articles.

The basic subsistence food, rice, was mostly produced by the collective in this period as were other staples such as corn and potatoes. These staples were considered the central production activity. The family economy was judged to be 'supplementary' even when most income came from the family economy!

During the collectivisation campaign, a number of cadres were concerned that the family economy would be the seed of renewed capitalism in the countryside. These people were cautioned against this 'leftist' deviation in the Party's theoretical journal, Hoc Tap, 'the contradiction between the supplementary (family) economy and the cooperative and the government is a minor one, not antagonistic in nature'.[21] Since work was not preformed by hired labour, but by household labour, the party argued that exploitation was not taking place. Some cadres were so concerned that capitalism would rear its head, despite these arguments, that they did not distribute private plots in villages for which they were responsible.

SUCCESSES

Throughout the period of land reform and in the first part of collectivisation there were significant increases in agricultural production in North Vietnam. There was a 47 per cent increase in the production of staple crops (rice, potatoes and corn) in the period 1955–9 (see Table 7.2). Using the very unusually high 1959 production figure for staple crops of 5.8 million tonnes, however exaggerates production increases in the 1950s. Weather conditions that year were particularly good. It took the North Vietnamese until 1972 to reattain the high output rates achieved for staple crops in 1959, and until 1974 to pass this production mark.[22]

There are readily apparent reasons for the lack of staple-crop-production increases for the Vietnamese in the 1960s, apart from any possible good or bad effects from collectivisation. There were some very bad weather conditions in the early 1960s, especially in 1960 and 1963. The effects of wartime on the agricultural labour force and the bombing of the dike system had a large impact on production for the rest of the decade. With the vagaries of weather and its profound effects on production and additional wartime effects, generalisations about the effects of collectivisation and land reform on production seem tenuous.

A more relevant statistical comparison can be made between agricultural production in the South and the North. There were production increases in the late 1950s in South Vietnam also, but Southern rice production barely reached the level of output achieved in the late 1930s, while the North doubled the rice production of the late 1930s. The South produced the same 5.3 million tonnes of rice in 1959 as in 1939, while the North increased their production from 2.4 million tonnes in the late 1930s to 5.1 million tonnes in 1959 (see Table 7.3).

Production increases in the North in the 1950s were achieved mainly through small-scale water-control projects. The argument of the Northern Communists is that without changes in the relations of production, these projects would not have been possible. Getting rid of landlordism and the private property rights which interfered with

Table 7.2   Production of staple crops in
North Vietnam

Year	Production of Staples* (metric tonnes)
1955	3.94
1956	4.79
1957	4.39
1958	4.96
1959	5.79
1960	4.70
1961	5.20
1962	5.17
1963	5.01
1964	5.52
1965	5.56
1966	5.10
1967	5.40
1968	4.63
1969	4.71
1970	5.28
1971	4.92
1972	5.74
1973	5.19
1974	6.28
1975	5.49

* Staples include rice paddy, maize, manioc and potatoes. Secondary crops are calculated in paddy rice equivalents.
Source: Adam J. Fforde, 'Problems of Agricultural Development in North Vietnam', p. 318; and Andrew Wickerman, 'Collectivization in the Democratic Republic of Vietnam', p. 486.

canal building was imperative. Land reform and cooperativisation not only achieved collective property rights over the land in question, but also cooperative labour was more easily organised for water-control projects because of these programmes.[23]

Table 7.3   Rice production

	North Vietnam	South Vietnam
1938		5.30
1939	2.45	
1954	2.60	2.57
1955	3.60	2.84
1956	4.24	3.41
1957	3.89	3.19
1958	4.58	4.00
1959	5.11	5.31

Source: Bernard Fall, *The Two Vietnams*,
pp. 163 and 294.

In the late 1950s and early 1960s the North Vietnamese built and repaired thirty-eight large irrigation projects and thousands of medium and small projects. They also built seventy power stations for electrification. 100 pumping stations were built and 3000 pumps of various varieties were delivered to cooperatives. These water-control projects guaranteed a steady supply of water for 47 per cent of the cultivated area, permitting double- and triple-cropping in these areas. In addition, there was more seasonal control for the rest of the land.[24]

North Vietnam was not able to leap into mechanisation of agriculture in this period, but they did make some medium-term changes which they called semi-mechanisation. 98 per cent of the land was still ploughed by water buffalo instead of tractors in the early 1960s, but the ploughs themselves were improved. In addition, wheelbarrows were produced in Vietnam which 'liberated peoples' shoulders'.

The North Vietnamese government pushed for an increase in diversified crops in areas not suitable for growing rice. Production of potatoes, for example, grew by about 75 per cent between the early- and mid-1960s, and manioc and sesame production increased.

With increases in the production of staple crops in the late 1950s and the continued growth in production for market of vegetables, pigs poultry, and handicrafts in the 1960s, many formerly poor families were able to accumulate surpluses. There was a resulting housing construction boom throughout the countryside. Kilns were built and families collected bricks until they could build themselves substantial new houses to replace their mud huts.

Allowing for some heightening of the contrast for effect, the following Vietnamese source gives us a picture of changes in the countryside in North Vietnam in this period:

> The recent changes in the appearance of the rural areas is full of promise. The spectacle of desolate, muddy villages with a few ancient tile palaces of lords interspersed with rows of obscure thatch and mud houses and clusters of flimsy, twisted huts exists no longer. In its place is the spectacle of well lighted, attractive new brick houses belonging to the agricultural cooperative workers.[25]

CONTINUING PROBLEMS

The North Vietnamese dilemma which has been called the 'middle-peasant problem' persisted in Vietnam despite considerable attention by the government and the Party. After the land reform, and at the beginning of the collectivisation movement, it was clear that middle peasants were tending to dominate lower-level government positions. In the structure of cooperative leadership, therefore, there was a one-third limit put on middle peasants. In addition to this, a one-third lower limit was put on the participation of women in cooperative management. These limits were not always maintained, however, especially after the slowdown in cooperative organising in 1961. Party politics tended to shift to the right and toward greater acceptance of the middle peasants as part of a 'homogeneous' collectivised peasantry.

A problem of middle-peasant domination also manifested itself in the Party. A party member in Bac Ninh Province reported at the end of 1962:

> we failed to hold fast to the class policy of the party in the countryside, the ratio of party members coming from the middle peasant class greatly increased ... party members coming from the poor peasant class were gradually eliminated.[26]

The middle peasants initially showed less interest in collectivisation than did the poor peasants but the middle peasants were eventually able to work within the new structure in ways which tended to preserve their positions and status. If they achieved positions of leadership in the collective, they received extra shares of collective returns and they could best preserve their family economy interest by being aware of collective policies and the 'contracting out' of some collective responsibilities such as rice-drying.

The contradiction of the 'non-socialist family economy' and the 'middle-peasant problem' are not linked together in North Vietnamese sources. Both the family economy and the problem of continued class division in the countryside are seen as relics of a Feudal past which will be gradually overcome, but they are seen as separate problems. The Vietnamese leadership does not recognise patriarchy and therefore it does not seem to see how economic differences can be preserved and encouraged through the family economy.

A patriarch with a larger family and more enterprising or skilled family members was in a good position for economic betterment in the collective village in the 1960s. If he could also earn extra shares of the cooperative's product through participation in management, this would further benefit his position. If he had more children of working age, his position was better and this situation was not limited by biology since it could be altered by adoption. If the patriarch had a number of older male children, he could do particularly well in the cooperative work-point distribution, since male cooperative jobs, like ploughing, often earned more work points that the female cooperative jobs, like transplanting. In the patriarchal family economy, on the other hand, older relatives, younger children and females could be put to work raising vegetables on the 5 per cent land or raising pigs and chickens. They worked on sewing, weaving and handicraft items as well and they sold these items on the private market. With all these variables present, there was considerable likelihood of variations in the standard of living of households. This inequality could be preserved and increased over time. There was no mechanism in the rural economy for these differences to decrease without an increase in collective responsibility *vis-à-vis* the patriarchal family economy.

Cooperatives had internal contradictions related to a patriarchal system of production being re-established in the collectivised village. Many of these resulting problems were never truly solved:

1. Cooperative members tried to keep the number of work-days expected of each member down in order to keep the ratio of labour to payment up because they knew that more workdays would mean less payment per day.

2. More fertiliser and more concentrated effort was often devoted to the 5 per cent land than to the cooperative land.
3. Many cooperatives were not planned well or organised well, as many cooperative managers operated in devious ways *vis-à-vis* the state.

In precolonial times, what happened in the village (now called a production brigade or a cooperative) did not always correspond to what the high echelons prescribed in their regulations. The modern cooperative officials often continued to act like the village oligarchy of patriarchs in the past by considering the state plans to be mere formalities, 'many times the plan became a show for the approval of the superior level only but in reality another plan was followed or work was performed without a plan'.[27] A foundation for the continuation of traditional ways of doing things was most certainly that very 'family economy' that the Party officials thought of as 'supplementary' and not a danger to the cooperative system. The partriarchs who controlled their own family economies could not fail to have self-interest in mind when dealing with the cooperative and since they did control their family economies, they could hardly be expected to act in egalitarian ways in their roles as cooperative managers.

In order to try to solve some of the cooperative's problems, the government embarked on a campaign to train cooperative managers in 1962. This started as a six-month campaign but it lasted three years. 1400 cooperative leaders were trained in planning and accounting. These leaders were encouraged to create more jobs in the collective and increase the number of collective work-days. They were taught to plan the labour of cooperative members carefully by requesting members to register the number of work-days they could commit ahead of time. They were also encouraged to be aware of new techniques and new crops. Cooperative planning seems to have been improved and made more consistent through this effort, although problems remained.

Despite the Workers' Party's attempts – through land reform, through collectivisation and through the training of cooperative managers – to revolutionise the Vietnamese village, a lot of very traditional attitudes remained. Traditional attitudes about women and youth, for example, often prevented technical cadres from carrying out their missions in the countryside. When they returned from technical agricultural training, women were assigned to be kindergarten and elementary school teachers. Young men were given jobs in the village office or in the police section. Neither were allowed to teach villagers or to carry out experiments with new varieties of crops.[28] Although collectives were required to have some women leaders, women often had opportunities for more responsibilities closed off to them or women were appointed after careless training or no training.[29]

The basis of traditional attitudes in the patriarchal family and the traditional family economy was not fundamentally changed by the land reform, the collectivisation movement or the campaign to train cooperative leadership. A levelling of income was possible as was a move forward in water control and productivity. Through these movements, also, a more even distribution of power, especially among males, was accomplished. Ironically, it was the war with the USA in the next period which challenged traditional attitudes and allowed for more female leadership than was possible in the collectivisation period. Women were then the dominant labour force and they became leaders when men were sent to the front in the South.

Collectivised agriculture in North Vietnam fed the war effort by providing a stable quantity of rice and other staple foods at a time when many, perhaps 25 per cent, in the male labour force were taken off to war. Although certainly aware of the lack of growth in production of staple foods in the collectives, the North Vietnamese leadership was not able to deal with the situation during the process of fighting the war. Instead, they relied on imports of rice from China. Only in the late 1970s would the Vietnamese leadership be forced to come to terms with contraditions within the collectives.

In order to describe in detail the process by which collective ideals had to change when faced with the realities of patriarchal power in the village, we turn, once again, to a village model. The next chapter will describe the revolutionary Northern village in the early 1960s.

8 The Revolutionary Village

The microeconomy of rural North Vietnam was formed out of complex interactions between class, gender and party policies. The village-in-transition upon which the Vietnamese policy-makers were attempting social change resembled the Central Lowlands village described in Chapter 5. It was still mainly a traditional patriarchal village, but one which had suffered some of the negative and unegalitarian effects of the impact of world capitalism. Party and State policy and practice concerning land reform and collectivisation had impacts on this village-in-transition. The ideal collective structures visualised in Hanoi often looked very different at the local level and it is the purpose of this chapter to point out these differences. From village studies and interview data, a view can be reconstructed of the northern village in the 1960s and the way that collective and patriarchal family economies actually operated within it.

The traditional village oligarchy had been wiped out in the process of the land reform in the 1950s. 'Middle peasant' leadership was asserting itself in most villages in this period. The Party's policies pushed for poor-peasant leadership but these policies were never totally successful. The Party also had in mind a gradual transformation from the 'dominant' collective economy with a 'supplementary' family economy, to a totally collectivised economy. The family-economy sector was supposed to be dissolved eventually. The actual process was quite the reverse and the Party and State were forced to accept a *fait accompli* in the 1970s, since the patriarchal family economy had increasingly taken over collective responsibilities. Analysis of the village of the 1960s shows in detail the structural problems of the Vietnamese collective and the strength and gradual ascendency of the Vietnamese patriarchy.

A problem with the sources used for this study of the 'average' village is than the villages studied tended to be nearer Hanoi and to be more political that the typical village. The cooperative studied by Chaliand in Hung Yen province, for example, had forty party-members at a time when the average village had two.[1] The village studies done by the Vietnamese themselves, on the other hand, were done for the purpose of informing policy.[2] They would lack usefulness if they were done only on the 'best' cooperatives. Pham Cuong's study of the village of Nam Hong shows that one hamlet-sized cooperative in the village operated very efficiently and another one was very poor. We can get a fairly accurate view of the typical revolutionary village from the sources available, if general trends and statistics analysed in the previous chapter are kept in mind.

THE VILLAGE AND THE COLLECTIVE

Production collectives were run by the village administration in some areas of the countryside but in some villages production collectives had not grown beyond the hamlet level. In any case, the village officials administered the sales and purchase collectives and credit collectives and it was the aim of the State and the Party to form village-level production collectives as soon as the villagers were ready to accept this change.

There were three levels of administration in the northern village of the 1960s. In a sense, the General Assembly of Villagers ruled, because they selected the Administrative Committee. This committee was quite large, however. For example, in one cooperative it included sixty-five members or one-tenth of the total of the cooperative membership. The day-to-day decisions were made by a smaller group, the executive organ of the Administrative Committee, called the Management Committee. This Management Committee was made up of the collective's President and General Secretary, who were elected by the General Assembly, and the heads of production brigades, who were selected by the Administrative Committee.[3]

The Workers' Party leadership was interconnected with collective leadership at the village level. There was a controlling commission in the village which was invested with permanent overseeing responsibilities. The Workers' Party cell secretary generally headed this commission. The party cell nominated the president of the collective but this nomination had to be approved by the members of the collective in its General Assembly. The president was usually a member of the Workers' Party cell.

In the early 1960s, women were a small minority of officials of the cooperative but toward the late 1960s women's leadership increased. As more and more men from the village, including male cadres, were recruited to join the fighting on the southern front, women were recruited increasingly as workers, as cadres and as managers. Affirmative action regulations were set down to encourage women's participation. In 1967 it was ruled that in a cooperative or industrial unit where women made up 40 per cent of the unit, there must be a woman on the management committee, if women made up 50 per cent of the unit, a woman should be assistant manager and where women made up 70 per cent of the workforce, there should be a woman manager.[4] These regulations were enforced more consistently in industry than in agriculture but there were some women who became presidents and vice presidents of cooperatives. In the village studies relied on here, women made up 60 to 65 per cent of the workforce and therefore a woman president would not be required. This was probably a typical condition for a cooperative in agriculture in this period.

LAND

Although large landholding was less extensive in the North than in the South, there was significant concentration of landownership in some areas of the north and there were members of the landlord class in virtually every village. In Hung Yen province, in the 1940s for example, landowners – who formed 3 per cent of the population – owned 70 per cent of the land. Many of these landlords were French and they left the country before 1954. Some of the Vietnamese landlords sided with the Revolution and some took the side of the French. Many of the pro-French landlords went south. In Dai Lai Village, in Thai Binh Province, there were two big landlords in the area and both fled to the South with their families.[5] In Nam Hong Village, the most important landowner, who owned about half the village land, fled south in the enemy's wagons. Landlords who stayed and who had practised 'odious crimes' which had resulted in the deaths of cadres and guerillas were 'sentenced to death' by the villagers.[6] Other landlords were re-educated.

Even after the process of retaliation and re-education of pro-French landlords was completed, the situation with respect to landlord–tenant relations in the countryside was unclear. Patriotic landlords had been integrally involved with the *Viet Minh*. Some had been *Viet Minh* cadres and some of these cadres had had to keep their identification secret during the struggle with the French. There was confusion in the countryside with the peasants not knowing whether to trust these cadres. Another problem adding to the confusion was the behaviour of some cadres. An official from Hung Yen Province mentions the 'dictatorial behaviour of some of the cadres' as a factor in the confusion.[7]

It was to address these problems and confusions that the party sent cadres from outside the villages to be reformed, to conduct the land reform. In Nam Hong village, a brigade of reform cadres entered the village and lived among the poor peasants. While sharing the peasants' labour, cadres educated peasants about their interests as a class and transformed them into militants. The reformers also identified the rich peasants and the landowners before the land reform was launched. 502 hectares of land belonging to the former landlords and to the village were divided up among the villagers. All debts were cancelled and dwellings, oxen and farm animals were distributed to the poorest villagers. This process was carried out in five months, between February and June of 1955.[8]

Anti-landlord sentiment in the villages was so spurred on by cadres from outside the village, that 'mistakes' were made in some villages, according to some later North Vietnamese accounts. In Hoa Xa village, in Ha Tay Province, for example, a man named Nhuan, who was owner of six *mau*, was charged with being a landlord. His wife and children were among those who brought the charges. All of Nuan's land and his house was taken from him. He was left with only one room which he shared with the wife and children who had accused him! The so-called landlord did not protest, according to a peasant from the village, but a year later a group of party officials arrived in the village and declared that an error had been committed. Nhuan was given back two *mau* of land and his house.[9]

Nhuan's family must have been greatly relieved after the overcrowding they had had to endure along with the man that they had helped to sentence. One wonders whether they had realised at the time of accusation that they would have to share his sentence. Chaliand mentions that the family was on good terms so we can probably presume that the patriarch had changed his 'cruel landlord' behaviour since the land-reform campaign, mentioned in Chapter 7.

Just three years after the land reform in Nam Hong, poor peasants were again selling their land and usurious loans were reappearing. The Party, recognising this trend, set up pilot cooperatives in Nam Hong and in other villages in 1959. The pilot cooperative in Nam Hong guided the setting up of eight other cooperatives in the village in the following year. This system of duplicated pilots was spread throughout the countryside.

Because of voluntary membership in cooperatives, the poorest villagers and women were usually the first to join. Some peasants in Dai Lai, for example, joined because they had more labour than could be utilised on their very small plot. One woman joined so that her family would get enough to eat. Women in Nam Hong joined the collectives becaused they preferred the sociability of collective work to individualised family work. Sometimes the solution to the conflict between husband and wife when only the wife wanted to join was that the possessions were divided and each was free to join or not.[10]

Middle-peasant men feared that they would lose power and wealth through collectivisation and other peasants feared collectivisation because of inefficiency and unfairness. Those who were old or sickly were concerned about being at a disadvantage in terms of work-points. Others were concerned that they would spend large amounts of time in meetings because each member would have a different idea about how to organise production. These problems were resolved, at least partly, through the process of carrying out collectivisation. Old and disabled people were cared for by using the cooperative's social funds. Efficient collective management was a dilemma for many years but some problems were resolved by the state training elected managers.

Most peasants in the villages studied joined cooperatives after discussions, initiated by the party, about working collectively or individually. Most of the appeal was made in terms of the benefits of collectivity but there was an implied threat, which in some cases was carried out. Chaliand describes one of these cases involving a peasant reluctant to join a cooperative:

> One day he felled a tree and was unable to shift it without help. We turned a blind eye at first, but at the end of the day one of the comrades lent him a hand. 'You see', this comrade said, 'there is something to be said for collective labor.'[11]

The next moring the peasant joined the collective.

The process of passing to a high level of collectivisation meant gradually reducing rents for land and equipment and it also meant fusion of smaller units, often hamlets into a larger unit, usually the former village. This consolidation often brought arguments because the hamlets were not equal in soil fertility or in land area. Although many cooperators had enough solidarity with their neighbours to take the step of forming a small cooperative quite easily, identification with villagers who lived at a distance was much less and many arguments ensued.

> Between the hamlets, there were inequities with regard to cultivable acreage and available funds. Each one felt himself wronged when he got into a single co-op with others. Moreover, problems of

organisation and management were given rise to by the broadening of the co-op ... Faced with these difficulties, peasants asked to get out of the co-op.[12]

These arguments about unequal benefits and obligations were eventually worked out through improved management, but this was an arduous process.

The private-public division of land in the villages did not adhere to the formula of 95 per cent public and 5 per cent private land set up by the state. Nam Hong had 6.7 per cent of cultivable land in private hands, and this figure did not include kitchen gardens, orchards or fish-ponds. In Ngo Xuyen, 13.2 per cent of the land was held in private fields, private orchards and fish-ponds. Since these particular villages were being observed carefully by the state and still had more than 5 per cent of their lands in private hands, it is reasonable to assume that other villages had at least as much private land, if not more.

The most important factor concerning yields from the private and public fields was than the private fields were farmed much more intensively that the public fields. In the 1960s in Nam Hong, yields were twice as high in the private fields. The crop rotations involved two or three crops of vegetables and one or two crops of rice on these fields. A lot more labour and fertiliser were used on the private fields than on the public fields.

LABOUR

60 per cent of the labour force in the Northern villages of the late 1960s was female. Many of the men in the middle age range had lost their lives in the First Indochina War. Other men in this range and younger men were away from the village, fighting in the Second Indochina War. More than half of the men between the ages of 16 and 30 were missing from Nam Hong village. Most men missing from the villages were in the military but some were also working in the cities in government administration and in manufacturing industry.

In Nam Hong, 14 per cent of women of working age did not participate in cooperative work regularly. Women with several small children often did not participate. In addition, when these women did some cooperative work, they were given easier tasks earning fewer work points. Women who were older, in their fifties and sixties, who had many sons and daughters-in-law in their households also sometimes elected not to participate.[13]

Cooperative members were organised in production brigades of twenty to sixty people for the planting, weeding and harvesting work. There were specialised work teams for tree planting, machinery work, fish-breeding, brick-making, water control, ploughing and harrowing, etc. Men and women were often in different work teams, doing different specific tasks and accumulating different amounts of work points even when they were part of the same brigade.

Many male tasks accumulated the maximum amount of work-points per day. These jobs were ploughing, harrowing, manuring, clearing, and lifting water. Another important task earning high points, but in which women also participated, was harvesting. The female task of planting-out rice was also sometimes given the maximum daily work-points, at least in the cooperative in Hung Yen.[14]

Tasks such as weeding, hoeing, sweeping yards and making baskets, in which females usually participated, were awarded fewer work-points. Women could expect to accumulate fewer work-points than men, even if they worked the same number of hours as men for the collective. Women often did not work as many hours because of their family responsibilities. Thus their accumulation was usually lower.[15]

The late 1960s was an unusual time with respect to labour resources in North Vietnam. Many men were sent to the front and women were forced to take over male tasks in the village. Women took over jobs such as manuring and ploughing when male labour was extremely short. The usual six-man ploughing teams continued their work as much as possible, but where ploughing teams were short, strapping younger women formed teams.[16] There was, nevertheless, little chance of this temporary work assignment permanently affecting the division of labour in the countryside. When the men returned home from war and the young women married, they would be given easier tasks because of their child-bearing status.

Older people did different work from the rest of the villagers and the division of labour by gender in this group particularly reflected traditional values. Grandmothers retired to tend to the running of the household and to child-care responsibilities. These grandmothers often cared for the children, even when there were nursery schools available. In Nam Hong, for example, only 13 per cent of women over 60 worked in the cooperative although over half the men over 60 did cooperative work. Older men were assigned tasks such as planting and caring for the cooperative's fruit trees. They were also often given tasks which respected their age and status as household heads. For example, they discussed electrification with each household in the village in Nam Hong.

Children were sometimes auxiliary workers on the collective. They minded the buffalo or did other small jobs. Most of the children's labour, however, was used in the family economy.

All villagers were active in the family economy which, as we have seen, accounted for a considerable amount of production in the rural economy. Women and children especially were the most active participants in the family economy. Women did the cooking, sewing, laundry and child-rearing, and tended the kitchen garden. They had the help of older children in these tasks. Women also worked extensively on the family plot. They did collective work as well, although significantly less than men. It made more economic sense for the family to send mostly male labour into the collective because male tasks were better remunerated.

There were problems with the quality of work done on the collective *vis-à-vis* work done in the family economy. Trees planted in family orchards did well while those planted in the cooperative often did not.[17] In the early stages of collectivisation in Nam Hong, pigs in the cooperative died because of lack of care and buffalo were 'entrusted to whoever came along first each day'. Many of these particular problems were dealt with eventually in Nam Hong. The quality of labour in the fields continued to be a problem, however. The private plots yielding two to three times what the collective was able to produce speaks for itself in describing the labour quality problem in the collective.

Traditional handicrafts were encouraged by the state to take up the villagers time during agricultural off-seasons. Where traditional handicrafts were not practised, some villagers took up basketwork, carpentry and masonwork.[18]

CONTROL OF PRODUCTION

Collective

Responsibility for collective production was not actually held at the village or collective level but it was, instead, maintained at the production brigade level. Through a system of contracts with production brigades, production control responsibilities were essentially contracted out to the heads of the these brigades. The three parts of the contract between the collective and the brigade specified (i) the volume and quality of goods to be delivered to the collective; (ii) the deadlines by which these deliveries should take place, and (iii) the general expenses of the brigade in carrying out their production responsibilities. The production brigades were usually former hamlets and they were composed of anywhere from forty to seventy people

The collective management was in charge of social service and water control activities. In larger cooperatives, there were teams which specialised in water conservancy, in smaller cooperatives temporary teams were set up. In Ngo Xuyen a 'water conservancy team' was set up during each crop, comprised of a member of the management committee of the cooperative and the leaders of the production brigades. The team then saw to it that the fields were adequately irrigated or drained during the growing season of that crop.

The public works projects for improvements and upkeep of the irrigation system were closely directed by the collective management. In Ngo Xuyen village water conservancy projects to dredge the river and irrigation canals were completed in the period 1958 through 1960. In the next two years, Ngo Xuyen peasants contributed labour to a state project involving the building of raised canals running across the region. In the period following, from 1963 to 1966, Ngo Xuyen peasants dug a small channel to bring water from the raised canal to the fields. The results of this work were to give sufficient irrigation to two-thirds of the fields which had formerly suffered drought in the summer and to improve drainage on about a third of the Ngo Xuyen fields. In 1969, the cooperative switched from hand-scooping to the use of a diesel pump for moving water to higher ground.[19]

In Nam Hong, a canal was excavated in the period 1955–7, permitting water from a nearby lake to flow to the rice fields. Thirty-two ponds were dredged and deepened to serve as reservoirs. This project irrigated about one quarter of the total land under cultivation. People on work chains scooped the water from one field to another.

After the establishment of collectivisation, Nam Hong peasants worked on a large-scale project to connect the nearby lake with the Red River. A new canal was built in Nam Hong in 1964 which permitted irrigation of half the land for the tenth-month crop and smaller percentages for the other two crops. Because of the larger project, linking Nam Hong to the Red River, water levels were such that much of the land could be irrigated by gravity and the rest by using pumps.

Nam Hong also rearranged their rice fields after collectivisation. Large straight dikes were built between vast stretches of rice paddies replacing small former dikes bordering tiny parcels. This project took considerable administrative direction at the village level. The agricultural production cooperatives in Nam Hong were still at the hamlet level (meaning the hamlet still held collective property) but irrigation and drainage projects, as in traditional times, were directed from the village level.[20]

The purchase and sales cooperatives, and the credit cooperatives were organised at the village level and administered by village officials. The credit cooperatives were like village savings banks. The villagers were encouraged to save their money in the credit cooperatives and the village used the funds for collective investments. The sales and purchase cooperatives were developed to replace some private markets and also to integrate each village into a national distribution network. Village officials were directly responsible for the running of these cooperatives and for training technicians to handle their accounting and day-to-day responsibilities. Village officials were also responsible for social services such as education, health and childcare. There were primary schools, nurseries and kindergartens and health facilities in both Nam Hong and Ngo Xuyen. In Nam Hong, however, the child-care workers were paid by the production cooperatives at the hamlet level at different rates, causing problems since workers with similar village responsibilities were getting different wages.[21]

The peasants' problems in adapting to socialism in the villages were always seen by the State as problems in cooperative administration. Examples of the problems of collectivisation abound in the villages studied. The peasants even abused collective property:

> common property was not adequately taken care of. Farm tools lay about in the fields after a day's work, even during months at times. Of the 18 improved carts, there remain only a few usable ... Hence frequent and great waste ... This is one of the causes of the high cost of production and the low pay for a workday.[22]

With enough training in planning and scientific agriculture, the state believed that lack of enthusiasm for collectivisation would be eliminated and peasants would contribute more work-days to the collective.

Underemployment was a problem specifically linked to deficiencies in management by the authors of both the Ngo Xuyen and Nam Hong village studies. Pham Toan claims that Ngo Xuyen had failed to work out a judicious plan for the use of manpower. In Nam Hong, no handicrafts were practised in the off-season. Taking up such activities was recommended but the collective administration was not able to accomplish their initiation.[23]

The fact that some production cooperatives were well managed and productivity was high, and in others, management was poor and productivity low, encouraged the Workers' Party in their analysis of the problem as being poor management. Two of the production cooperatives in Nam Hong were well managed, one of these had been better managed but the efficient cadres had been promoted to higher level jobs, leaving less efficient management to take over. One of the cooperatives was poorly managed and 'conservative' and 'narrow minded' attitudes among the older cadres were seen as the reason. Nam Hong, located 20km from Hanoi, had many more party members than the average village. It can probably be accurately assumed that if there were traditional attitudes here, then they were even more abundant in the more remote areas.[24]

Patriarchal Control of Family Economy

The 'family heads', who were virtually always male, controlled the family economy and the patriarchal family was at the root of traditional attitudes which undercut the collective. Even where a woman (a daughter-in-law) was the only able-bodied full-time worker in the family in Nam Hong, the father-in-law was considered the 'head of household'. There was actually a strong competition between a collective economy and the family economy and even collective officials were sometimes not above putting family economy first:

> It is deplorable that coop members, even some brigade leaders sometimes busy themselves with more profitable jobs rather than work for the coop. At the time of *longan* harvest, for instance, they prefer going to town to sell their fruit.[25]

In the 1960s there was a tendency (which continued in the 1970s) of cooperatives contracting work out to the family patriarch instead of the production brigades. Study and criticism sessions evidently put an end to these practices in Nam Hong because they 'infringed on the very principle of collective agriculture'.[26] In a neighbouring province, however, this practice continued.

The family patriarchs differed considerably in their ability to organise their family labour force, usually composed of a wife, sons, daughters-in-law, and their children (or just wife and children, if the patriarch was young). In Pham Cuong's study of Nam Hong, he compared three family economies and found one much more efficient that the others. The most efficient family economy was headed by a former village administrator who was 'accustomed to plan his work'.[27]

Despite the large-scale hydraulic work in the villages in the 1960s there were tendencies, stemming from the conflict between the socialist and the patriarchal economy, which prevented full utilisation of increased capacities. People devoted more attention, and qualitatively better attention, to the family economy. Since the (more than) 5 per cent land yielded double what the collective land yielded, the rest of the land could presumably be brought up to nearly the level of the 5 per cent land, if given more fertiliser and better and more attention. The patriarch clearly had a firmer control over the labour force than the collective did, and this fact limited collective influence and collective production in the village of the 1960s.

TECHNOLOGICAL CHANGE

New high-yielding seed varieties were adopted in the northern villages in this period, but more for their short growing span than for their high yields. In the production conditions of North Vietnam, yields of the new seed varieties were only marginally greater than the old varieties. The shorter growing season, however, combined with better water control resulting from hydraulics work projects, made third crops possible in areas where there were formerly only two per year. The new varieties also allowed for changes in the crop mix. Very high-value crops, like vegetables, were grown as the third crop in areas near cities, replacing some staple and industrial crops.

First experiments with the new varieties in the northern villages were often disappointing. Important conditions of a precise amount of water, considerable fertiliser and great care were not always met by the cooperatives. Lessons about how to treat the new varieties were learned in time, however, and these varieties were extended to the majority of the growing area. Old varieties were nevertheless continued in areas where precise water control was more difficult:

> At present, 80 per cent of the total area of rice fields are put under these strains, while the remaining 20 per cent, comprising the fields

in the highest and lowest areas, are set aside for selected old varieties particularly adapted to the natural conditions there.[28]

Chemical fertilisers were also introduced into northern villages, although not to nearly as large an extent as in some parts of the South. Increasing the production of *azolla* and increasing use of restorative crops and pig manure was the normal pattern. Where chemical fertilisers were introduced, the peasants responded with scepticism:

> When the state supplied them (the peasants) with nitrogenous fertilizers during the first days of the cooperative, they heaped them up at the end of the field. Under the sun and rain, the fertilizers soon deteriorated or were washed away.[29]

The state had to persuade the peasants about the usefulness of chemical fertiliser but by 1970 peasants were competing for those goods in the distribution in Ngo Xuyen.

The new rice varieties and additional fertilisation increased labour inputs needed to succeed in high yields of multiple crops. Since the patriarchs seemed to have a tighter control over labour, these very intensive labour techniques were more suited to the patriarchal family economy than to the cooperative economy. New technologies could be added, despite traditional values, because the collective existed. Once accepted, on the other hand, these particular technologies advanced the family economy more readily than the collective.

There were other technical changes in the villages of North Vietnam in the areas of semi-mechanised tools and traction. Ploughs for deep tilling and improved harrows were added and there was new equipment for threshing. This equipment was produced in the new small-scale machine-tool shops in the regions. Tractors were not widely used as most cooperative members and officials found them too expensive. They were more expensive, that is, than water buffalo. From 1965 to 1970, however, the area of land ploughed by tractors increased from 5 to 14 per cent in Nam Hong. In Thanh Oai District, 30 per cent of the land was ploughed by tractors by 1970. The transition to tractors was probably hastened by the out-migration of a large part of the young male labour force in the late 1960s, because of the war.[30]

LOCAL INDUSTRY, HANDICRAFTS AND MARKETS

Handicraft industries operated in the traditional fashion, exept that they were formed into handicraft cooperatives. Handicraft villages produced their traditional wares but they were also encouraged to branch out into other handicraft areas. In Thanh Oai district, 40 per cent of the workforce made a variety of handicraft items: lace, lacquer, basket work, palm leaf hats, iron tools, silk and cotton goods, leather goods and pastry. The government decided on a policy of self-sufficiency in agriculture in the 1960s and encouraged peasants in handicraft-producing districts to pay more attention to agriculture until self-sufficiency could be reached.[31]

Local industries tended to be set up in the countryside, even before the American bombing of the cities – when this tendency increased. The local industries were under the direction of the district authorities. Managers and assistant managers were chosen by the state but a management committee was elected by the workers.

Markets set up and run by women merchants continued in socialist rural Vietnam but the socialist rural market cooperatives were set up in competition, with the express purpose of putting many of the traditional markets out of business. It was state policy that traditional markets took up too much of the peasants' time and they should therefore be discouraged.[32]

The purchase and sales cooperatives were set up on the level of the production brigade but they were directed by the collective. The head of the purchase and sales cooperative groups periodically attended meetings of the cooperative's administrative committee. The cooperative acted as an agency for the retailing of state industrial products, it acted as a purchasing agency for agricultural produce on behalf of the state and it engaged in buying and selling of local goods. Shops were set up in the various localities to replace most of the markets. In the district where Nam Hong was located, seven private markets were discontinued, leaving four. The purchase and sales cooperative thereby took over about two-thirds of the market trading. Fifty 'reformed' traders in Nam Hong returned to the land and agricultural production as a result of these changes. Since nearly all the traders were women and since many of the village officials replacing them were men, this shift from private to public trading was a shift from women's to men's work.[33]

WOMEN IN THE NORTHERN VILLAGE

From the beginning of the land reform and throughout the collectivisation campaigns, women in the North Vietnamese villages saw these socialist movements as an advance for themselves. Despite the fact that most of the socialist cadres were men, women had a strong identification with socialism. For one thing, the socialists freed women from child-marriages, concubinage, polygamy and arranged marriage. Secondly, although most women's children were still cared for by their mothers-in-law, some women in the village could take advantage of the nurseries and kindergartens that were set up. Thirdly, although women could not earn as many points in the collective as men because of women's additional household responsibilities, earning income from the collective gave women more leverage than only working directly for their fathers-in-law or their husbands.

As a patriarchal system of production re-established itself in the socialist environment of the North Vietnamese village, however, women were probably taken by surprise. What village woman would have realised that shops managed by the collective would replace their markets? The young women who were active in the land reform and collectivisation campaigns took their places in the lower levels of the village hierarchy if they did not marry and move to another village. Nevertheless, by the mid 1960s former middle-peasant men were able to establish themselves as leaders in the village hierarchy. The surpluses which were accumulated in the villages in the late 1950s and early- to mid 1960s were used almost exclusively either for socialist accumulation, such as hydraulics, or for patriarchal accumulation in the form of new brick houses. Women benefited from both kinds of accumulation since they lived in the new houses and ate some of the increased food production. But women were not usually in charge of either the socialist economy or the patriarchal economy. Women were participants in the new system and they enjoyed a better status than under the old system but this was not nearly an equal status.

Women's position in the North Vietnamese village changed again in the late 1960s but the cause of this change was predominantly the war with the USA, not the effects of socialism in the village. Women moved into village administration in North Vietnam in the late 1960s and early 1970s because so many men had been taken off to war or to higher-level administration. Women made similar political moves in the South, however, even in areas controlled by the US-sponsored regime. The women's ploughing teams, on the other hand, may have been a uniquely socialist phenomenon. This participation in high-status work, however, was temporary, since it was only for the period of a woman's young, pre-child-bearing years.

Women's participation in village administration was in a sense temporary, too. When the war was eventually over, women would be expected to resume their pre-war positions – this process will be described in Chapter eleven.

COMPARISONS

In North Vietnamese society in the 1960s, there was a political ideology of equality between the sexes which impacted on the village through the Party and the governing institutions. The official Communist ideology supported a formal equality for women and equal right to membership in the collective. In traditional times, women had not been members of the commune. Only men were allowed citizenship and only men received a share of the collective land. In the village, of the 1960s, women received a share of land but this was most often managed by a woman's husband or her father-in-law. She was paid for her work in the collective, but she usually earned less than men did. As we have seen, women's equality was more formal than real in the 1960s, but woman's status was decidedly better than in the traditional village.

Although an average of 40 per cent of the land was communal in the traditional village, a much larger segment of the land was collectivised in the northern village in the 1960s. About 80–85 per cent of the land was actually held by the collective. Collective property was also managed differently from communal land in the traditional village. Whereas in traditional times individual patriarchs were in charge of production, even of the communal fields, production brigades had responsibility for production in the 1960s.

The state intervened in production methods in the modern village much more than the emperor's government had. The communist government brought electricity and electric water pumps, fertiliser and new varieties of seed into the village. The collective village had a structure which could receive these innovations with a minimum of conflict, since each patriarch did not have to be convinced separately about the advocacy of the change. In traditional times the state worked together with and through the village in order to construct large-scale water-control facilities. The state and the village continued in their obligations with respect to public works and water control in the later village. In this respect the traditional and modern villages were very much alike.

There seemed to be much more conflict between the interests of the patriarchal family economy and the collective economy in the modern socialist village than there was between communal and private interests in the traditional village. Both communal and private plots were cultivated with considerable care in the traditional village. In contrast, the collectivised village land in the 1960s was cultivated with very different intensity and it was sometimes neglected. The traditional patriarchs were unequivocally in charge of both the collective and the family economies. In the modern economy, there was some conflict between the principles which governed the collective and the private spheres. Egalitarian principles and a modernisation ideology strongly influenced the collective sphere.

The northern socialist village and the southern capitalist village were also very significantly different from one another. The greatest differences were in the distribution of income and wealth and the centralised vs decentralised village. Because of the differential impact of colonialism, inequality was greater in the South even before the socialist institutional changes undertaken in the 1950s and early 1960s. With the communist land reform and collectivisation campaigns, great wealth and extreme poverty were eliminated. In contrast, in the South, huge differences in the distribution of wealth, income and power were common.

A lack of cohesiveness at the village level prevented effective water control in the southern village while the northern collective village was organised for efficient water control. Modern technologies such as new seeds and fertiliser were introduced in both the North and the South but with very different results. In the northern village, mechanisms existed to distribute most benefits of new technologies more or less equally, although family economies tended to benefit more than the collectives. In the southern village, on the other hand, new technologies tended to exacerbate the already unequal distribution of wealth, since good water control and sufficient fertilisers were available to the rich farmers and not the poor.

The traditional roles of women were changing throughout the colonial period and they continued to be challenged, in different ways, in both the northern and southern villages. In the North, the State challenged tradition by involving women in the land-reform distribution and in collectivisation and by encouraging women to take leadership roles. In the South, women were involved in wage labour. Because of the breakdown of extended families, women were more often heads of household. Women in the South were sometimes minor officials or schoolteachers.

The southern and northern villages both had problems and internal conflicts in this period. The conflicts in the southern village were much greater and this village was more divided than the northern village. The southern village was also much further from the traditional Vietnamese institutions and values inherited from the precolonial past. The conflict-ridden southern villages were on the verge of becoming involved in a massive struggle which would end fifteen long years later, after widespread destruction in the countryside.

9 US Intervention

After the victory of the *Viet Minh* forces at Dien Bien Phu in 1954 and the achievement of a temporary military settlement with the French at Geneva, the USA became increasingly involved in Vietnamese politics. The 17th Parallel, which had been designated in the Geneva agreement as a demilitarised zone, was turned into a border between the *Viet Minh*-controlled North and the South where a US-sponsored government was headed by Ngo Dinh Diem. The specifics of the origin of the US involvement are well documented elsewhere and we need only recall here that by 1954 the USA was providing 80 per cent of the funding for the French war in Indochina and that by January 1955 the USA had become the direct paymaster of the South Vietnamese military.[1]

To American officials, Ngo Dinh Diem seemed like a good nationalist candidate to fill the vacuum left by the withdrawal of French official administration from Saigon. After serving a term as a mandarin official under the French in Central Vietnam, Diem had resigned in protest against the French refusal to allow more Vietnamese participation in affairs of state. His anticolonialism was individualist, however, for he did not join any of the diverse political organisations formed in the 1930s and 1940s to fight colonialism. In the early 1950s Diem laid the political foundation of his later administration by travelling to the USA and winning friends such as Senator John F. Kennedy and Senator Mike Mansfield to his cause of anticommunism and anticolonialism in Vietnam. Frances Fitzgerald suggests that much of his influence was accomplished through the Roman Catholic hierarchy in the USA – Diem was a devout Roman Catholic residing in a seminary during his stay in the USA.[2]

In contrast, Diem's political base in his own country was weak, and apart from the Roman Catholics, he had few people whom he could trust as new administrative personnel. His administrative structure in Saigon, therefore, looked very much like the French administration and at least a third of his officials had been administrators under the French. In order to strengthen his political base, Diem made an alliance with large landlords by choosing as his vice president, Nguyen Ngoc Tho, one of the strongest among them. In addition, he chose large landowners to fill positions such as the head of the Ministry of Land Reform. This alliance with landlords shows further similarity with the previous French administration.[3]

174

The purpose of this chapter is to delineate the rural policies of the Saigon government and to show the interconnection of these policies with American intervention and American interests. In promoting the interests of the large landholders in Vietnam, Americans essentially filled the role the French had left behind. This strategy dovetailed with US world-wide interests which were seen as fighting communism and extending capitalist markets in the underdeveloped world.

ECONOMIC POLICIES

In the 1930s Cochin China, an area with fewer than 5 million people, produced 1.5 million tonnes of rice a year for export. This was more than any other country exported in that era and it was as much as the major rice exporters of the world – China, the USA and Thailand – exported in the 1950s and 1960s. Production of rice and agriculture in general, had declined drastically over the 1940s and early 1950s (see Tables 9.1 and 9.2). Because of its history, however, South Vietnam was judged by policy-makers to have a tremendous potential for agricultural production and export. The government of the Republic of Vietnam, therefore, established mechanisms to increase agricultural production and facilitate exports in a way which would be consistent with its political support.

The American advisers' policy in the countryside was particularly important because Vietnam had been such a large rice-exporting country. Policies would have to ensure the re-establishment of substantial rice exports within the framework of a capitalist market system. This constrained the US advisers from their more usual policy recommendations in Asian land reforms. In Japan, Taiwan, South Korea and elsewhere, the USA advised liberal land reforms with small retention limits and large-scale redistribution to former tenants. This was seen as the best way to promote stability and prevent revolution in the countryside in these nations. US policies in Vietnam were conservative in contrast and strongly supportive of landlords' interest, at least until the last years of the war when the landlords had already been dispossessed in the countryside by the National Liberation Front. (The new US-supported government reform then legitimised many of the NLF transfers.) The land reforms in Taiwan, South Korea and Japan could be more liberal because gaining control of rice for export was not important in these countries. Their economies were more focused on diversified products and they produced round rice, a

Table 9.1 South Vietnam: indices of total agricultural and total food production average 1935-39 and 1952-54 (base period), annually 1957,1958, and 1959

1952–54 = 100

	Aggregates				
	1935–9	1952–4	1957	1958	1959
Agricultural production Index	187	100	141	154	153
Per capita agricultural production index	263	100	123	132	129
Food production index	201	100	141	156	155
Per capita food production index	283	100	123	133	130
Population index (1953 = 10 800 000)	71	100	115	117	119

Source: US Department of Agriculture, Foreign Regional Analysis Division, Far East Branch.

variety with little demand in world markets. If the landlord system were not re-established in Vietnam, on the other had, the whole mechanism for exporting over 11 million tonnes of rice a year set up by the French, would be wasted since it was the landlords' share which was channelled toward the world market. Since the peasants were suffering from rapid population increases on a limited land area, they were consuming larger amounts of rice. Without production increases, or landlords, they would channel little to the world market.

At the beginning of the Diem administration, in 1956, an economic survey mission of the United Nations found little industry in South Vietnam and no heavy industry. Existing industry had lost the foreign-resident market with the exit of the French from Vietnam. The survey concluded that South Vietnam lacked the basis for a major development of heavy industry, but there were important opportunities for the establishment and subsequent expansion of a range of small and medium-sized manufacturing enterprises. These enterprises should emphasise the processing of the country's agricultural and forestry products.[4]

Although emphasing the need for South Vietnamese diversification of agricultural production, the survey pointed out the meagre amount

Table 9.2 Rice: area, production and exports, Cochin China 1934–51

| Year | Cochin China | | Exports[a] | |
	Area ha	Production MT	Milled MT	Paddy MT
1934–5	2.026	3.040	1430	318
1935–6	2.112	3.100	1539	324
1936–7	2.151	3.048	1389	140
1937–8	1.988	2.401	1016	38
1938–9	2.308	3.710	1350	322
1939–40	2.062	3.845	1526	60
1940–1	2.217	3.000	944	—
1941–2	2.372	2.975	974	—
1942–3	2.283	3.178	1017	6
1943–4	2.204	2.613	498	—
1944–5	1.987	2.214	44	—
1945–6	1.414	1.691	109	1
1946–7	1.120	1.362	90	—
1947–8	1.316	1.662	233	—
1948–9	1.103	1.330	140	—
1949–50	1.191	1.551	—	—
1950–1	1.102	1.433	272	—

[a]Exports up to 1949 are for Indochina but are virtually the same as Cochin Chinese exports since no other state exported rice during this period.
Source: US Department of Agriculture, Economic Research Service, Foreign Regional Analysis Division, Far East Branch.

of rice exports in 1956, 200 tonnes, as compared with pre-war exports. They saw no problem with population growth in the countryside since the 1930s because Vietnam was still underpopulated compared with other Asian countries. The UN even advised labour-saving mechanisation of agriculture, considering the 'lack of overcrowding' in rural areas.[5]

UN criticisms of the newly-established Diem government included mention of the large military expenditures of the regime and the continued dependence on the USA and France for over half the government's resources. The mission concluded that expenditures should have gone more in the direction of economic development and that increased self-sufficiency would have been preferred.

United Nations recommendations regarding industry were carried out by Diem only to the extent that there were a few government enterprises set up. These small enterprises did not make profits and they did not accumulate capital. According to an interview with the Deputy Minister of Economy in this period, Nguyen Hoang Cuong, the industries were mostly successful in enriching the style of life of their administrators.[6]

Regarding agriculture, Diem followed a policy of increased rice exports through re-establishing landlord control and marketing systems. Like the survey team he saw no problem with population growth and no compensating productivity increase. He assumed that the much larger population of South Vietnam in the mid-1950s could produce and export the large quantities of rice that were exported in the 1930s. As a result of the ending of hostilities, production grew during the first five years of the Republic of Vietnam. Because of Saigon government policies, however, Gross National Product did not increase in real per capita terms, even in this period of recovery from the First Indochina War (see Table 9.3). With people returning to the countryside, rice production increased by 50 per cent but rice exports did not go above 350 000 tonnes a year and averaged only 200 000 tonnes. Textile production increased slightly as did sugar, glass, pharmaceuticals, wood products, soft drinks and fishing. Rice production increases and small increases in other production in these areas were not sufficient, however, for a rising GNP per capita because rates of domestic investment were very low (1958 – 3.4 per cent of the GNP; 1959 – 1.8 per cent; 1960 – 4.8 per cent). According to Frank C. Child, an American advisor from the Michigan State University Vietnam Advisory Group, investments would have to double for economic growth to be a reality in South Vietnam. Money was available from the USA, but 'the real economic effort and hard economic decisions have not yet been made, economic progress waits upon the exercise of aggressive leadership by those persons responsible for economic policy'.[7]

Because of Diem's land policies (covered in the next section) and the disposition of foreign funds to the rich and middle classes, their incomes increased while incomes of the majority were stagnant or decreasing. There was a housing and real-estate boom confined mainly to the 'European' sections of Saigon and Western durables such as cars and refrigerators were traded in a rising market while the general economy stagnated.[8]

Table 9.3 Real per capita income

Year	1955		1956		1960		1961	1962
Source	UN[a]	Child[b]	UN	Ch	UN	Ch	UN	UN
Cost of living (base 1960)	94.10		104.90		100.00		105.90	108.90
GNP (billions of piastres)		64.20		69.40	83.00	86.00	85.80	95.50
Real GNP(base 1960)		69.10		65.30			80.80	88.20
Population (millions)	12.00	11.50	12.30	12.40	14.10	14.20	14.50	14.90
Income per capita (thousands of piastres)		5.58		5.61	5.90	6.05	5.92	6.40
Real per capita income (thousands of piastres)		6.01		5.28	5.90	—	5.57	5.90

Sources: [a]UN Statistical Office, *Yearbook of National Accounts Statistics.*
[b]Frank C. Child, Michigan State University Advisory Group,*Toward a Policy for Economic Growth in Vietnam.*

The US economic support in Vietnam was stongly military and police-oriented, even in the first years. There was strong *Viet Minh* influence in the countryside since at least 60 per cent of the countryside had been held by the *Viet Minh* before the signing of the Geneva Accords.[9] The Saigon government fought against this *Viet Minh* influence by force supported by US funding. During the period 1955–9, 80 per cent of US budgetary subsidies went to pay military expenses. The USA provided $3.162 billion in military and economic aid to the Saigon government and only $187 million of this went for development projects.[10]

US aid to Vietnam was directed through the Commercial Import Programme and this programme played an important role in US policy in Vietnam and in the Vietnamese economy. Inflation had been a problem in other Asian countries which had received large amounts of US aid. In order to subsidise the military budget of the Saigon government heavily without causing inflation, dollar credits were provided to the government of South Vietnam for the puchase of commodities from American suppliers which were jointly agreed on by both governments. The Saigon government then sold the credits to local importers in return for Vietnamese piastres at the official rate of exchange. The piastres were then put in the governmental central bank in a counterpart fund and these were used as needed by the Vietnamese in ways previously agreed upon by the two governments.[11] The increasing expenditures on military personnel did not push up prices on the Saigon market to a significant extent because these personnel and others purchased American goods which were imported. Because of a disparity between the official rate of exchange and the real market value of the piastre, importers were able to acquire goods at prices way below their value on the Saigon market. Large profits were made by thousands of Vietnamese who were able to obtain licenses to import. Many of these Vietnamese resold the licenses to Chinese traders who were more familiar with markets and business. Thus the living standards of the urban middle-class Vietnamese and Chinese were raised substantially through the process of the Commercial Import Programme.[12]

Another effect of the Commercial Import Programme was to raise the level of consumption goods imported and to discourage imports of capital goods. Imported capital goods would not offset inflationary pressures as consumer goods would. Because inflation fighting was the primary aim, goods agreed on for import were almost totally consumer and not investment goods.[13] Economic development objectives were ignored because the policy was to favor price stability.

DIEM'S LAND REFORMS

Ordinance 2, issued by the Diem government in January 1955, was its first attempt to deal with land tenure. It provided for a maximum rent of 25 per cent of the crop, security of tenure, and release from rental obligations in case of crop failuer. To enjoy these provisions, the tenant had to sign a contract acknowledging the land as belonging to the owner of record according to the Saigon regime and not to the operator, as in the *Viet Minh* reform.[14]

Ordinance 2 was viewed in many rural areas as simply a means of confirming the land titles of absentee landlords. Since no rents had been paid to absentee landlords in large areas of the countryside under the *Viet Minh*, the rent of 25 per cent was not a reduction from the traditional amount of 50 per cent but an increase from nothing![15] Price Gittinger, US Land Reform advisor to the Diem government, assessed the situation as follows:

> As implementation began, an interesting paradox in landlord and tenant attitudes emerged. Much of Free Viet Nam either recently had been recovered from Communist control or *Viet Minh* Communist forces still retained paramount influence. In these areas, particularly those in South Viet Nam, landlords had sometimes not collected rent for as long as eight years. Now, landlords looked upon the contract program as a means to assure them a rental of at least 25 per cent of the crop. On the other hand, tenants in these areas resisted the program since they had been paying no rent at all.[16]

This tenancy law, or reverse land reform, was thought necessary because tenancy was 'essential to achieving a highly productive and modernized agricultural sector'.[17] Land-to-the-tiller policies which would abolish most tenancies would not provide large amounts of rice for export because much of the rice would be consumed rather than sold for rent payments.

The true purpose of the ordinance dealing with rents was made obvious by its enforcement procedures. The government made sure to register more than 700 000 rent contracts initially affecting one-half of South Vietnam's tenant farmers, but after the initial three-year period when landlord rights were returned, there was essentially no further enforcement. Most of the three-year contracts, which were later changed to five-year contracts, were allowed to lapse.[18] Enforcement procedures imposed criminal penalties equally on tenant and landlord. Tenants who were pressed to pay more than the legal minimum would therefore not find it in their interest to take the landlord to court, even if they could afford to do so and most often they could not. The result of this policy was that the average rate for rentals was 34 per cent, well above the legal maximum of 25 per cent.[19]

In the countryside, Ordinance 2 created considerable resistance. In part to quell some of this and also to satisfy his US land-reform advisors, Diem embarked on a very limited land-redistribution programme, Ordinance 57. The measure restricted landlords to 100 hectares of land plus 15 hectares of family worship property (284 acres in all). This was about thirty times the retention limits of other American-advised land-reforms in Asia. The landlords were allowed to select the particular area which they wished to maintain. Regulations also ultimately gave landlords eight years in which to prove that they had made transfers to others prior to, not after, the new law. One land-reform adviser reported that transfers to relatives and strawmen were common and that years after the land redistribution, he had met men who openly admitted that they still owned 2000 acres.[20]

If all the land that was expropriated had been redistributed, the land reform might have affected 10 per cent of the South Vietnamese peasantry. These peasants would have had to pay for the land, however. Tenants who happened to be farming the expropriated land were eligible to receive land, and they were to pay for it in six instalments. The government was to repay the landlord with a 10 per cent cash down-payment and twelve-year government bonds carrying a 3 per cent interest rate. Cultivators who had taken land assigned to them by the Viet Minh, and had not paid back-rent and land taxes for those years, were ineligible for this reform.

Land expropriation began in 1958 and by 1961, 422 000 hectares had been taken by the government but only 244 000 hectares had been distributed to former tenants.[21] The former French-owned lands, which were mostly a gift to the Diem government from the government of France amounted to 230 000 hectares but very little (only about 10 per cent) of that was distributed. Renewed fighting against the Diem regime became widespread in 1961 and at this time continued implementation of the programme was halted. Henceforth, local and provincial officials retained rent from the undistributed land.[22]

If the purpose of Ordinance 57 was to win friends for the Diem goverment in the countryside, the limited conception of the law and its lack of enforcement prevented it from having its desired effect. Only 115000 tenant households or about 7 per cent of tenants in the country, actually benefited from the reform. The reform was arbitrary in that only tenants who happened to rent certain lands were affected at all and the poorest of the rural population – the agricultural labourers – could not receive any land.

Diem was in favour of preserving and extending communal land in the villages, but only as a source of revenue for local government, not for redistribution. He decided that rentals of communal land should be auctioned off to the highest bidder and that revenues should be retained for local expenses.[23] Locally-appointed officials never got the increases in communal land that Diem had wanted but, as we have seen, they did gain control of undistributed land that had been expropriated under Ordinance 57 and they also controlled former French land.

The Diem land-reform programmes ran into two major difficulties, according to Bernard Fall. The people most likely to be hurt by the reforms were in charge of applying them, and the reforms themselves had a limited and conservative outlook.[24] Diem himself was from the Central Lowlands and he was not a big landowner, but much of his support came from professional people and officials from landowning families as well as from landlords themselves. Vice President Nguyen Ngoc Tho tried to protect the interest of the landowners as did the Minister of Land Reform. Diem's party, the National Revolutionary Movement, was led by people from landowning families. The predominance of landowners in important positions was not solely in national offices; this tendency also extended done to the provincial and village level. High-ranking village officials were almost always landowners who were nominated by the Ministry of Interior in accordance with a proposal of the province chief.[25]

Through Ordinance 57, Diem seemed to think that he could increase the power of his appointed officials, including some medium and small landlords from the Central Lowlands, and his friends who were Roman Catholic refugees from the North, without antagonising the largest landowners too much. Although this power shift was one of the purposes of Ordinance 57, the law was subverted by the largest landowner supporters of the Saigon government, particularly Diem's Vice President. Vice President Tho had his friends appointed to the land-reform directorate but he was not completely successful in stopping distribution under the land reform until 1961. It was then that he reorganised government departments thus depriving a pro-Diem, pro-land reform official, Nguyen Xuan Kuong, of all authority.[26]

THE LANDLORDS AND THE WAR

The large amount of military and police aid which the USA put in the hands of Diem's government was used for political repression of *Viet Minh* sympathisers in the countryside and it was also used for the repression of the religious sects, the *Hoa Hao* Buddhists and the *Coa Dai*. As the Buddhists turned to demonstrations in the streets of Saigon, and self-immolations by fire were televised around the world, the US government realised that there was a significant lack of support for the Diem government and therefore President Kennedy withdrew political support from Diem. Because of this withdrawal, there was a coup and a group of military officers took over the Saigon government. The succession of governments which followed represented large landlord interests even more directly than Diem had, but these new governments were also receptive to Buddhist, and particularly *Hoa Hao* interests.

As the military situation deteriorated in the countryside, the USA entered the war with massive military support of the Saigon goverment. The Vietnamese landlords were able to use the military support of the USA continuously to reassert their position in the countryside. Landlords would ride in on government jeeps as the army reoccupied an area which had been held by the National Liberation Front.[27] Where this was not possible, they sometimes made agreements with local military commanders to collect their rents on a commission basis. A third method was to have the rents collected by local officials:

> In Dinh Toung, Bac Lieu, Gia Dinh, and An Giang provinces, for example, local officials have been observed performing the role of rent collector, following the troops as they advance into contested areas. In some cases they keep as much as 30 per cent of the proceeds in exchange for this service. One veteran regional observer estimates that 50 per cent of the popular forces in the countryside, working out of fortified positions, are among other things 'tax' and 'rent' collectors. In at least one case, it was

reported that the Army itself engaged in the operation, with officers sharing the collections with enlisted men.[28]

These practices evidently started during the Diem period when there was a circular near the end of the regime which asked each Chief of Province to help the landlords to collect rent.[29] The political reason for this policy was not only to maintain the support of the landlords for the government, but also this policy was geared to prevent the rice harvest from getting into the hands of the National Liberation Front. The mechanism used was described in the following interview:

> There was a particular convention [agreement] between the proprietor and the Chief of Province, district or village, to gather crops and get the rent. From 30 to 50 per cent of it went to the official. The village chiefs had guards which were well armed, even in 1960. Between villages there were agreements to let the village guard go in. Sometimes you had to make a raid, surround the village with troops, and tell the farmer to bring his crops and escort them to the district or province. The operation lasted all day ... The province administration had to do this many times after the harvest. If you didn't do that you would lack big quantities of rice. The Chief of Province would order these operations on the demand of the proprietor or the order of the government.[30]

For several reasons this process was incomplete, from the landlords' point of view. First of all, many landlords had land which was in the hands of the National Liberation Front and operations such as those described above could not take place. Second, even where rents were collected in this manner, the military and government officials took large percentages and left less for the landlords than they were formerly getting. The military and civilian officials gained from this mechanism, and there was a rise in the power of the military group in South Vietnam, *vis-à-vis* the landlords. The landlords depended on the civilian official or military commander in their area to tell them how much had been collected and the landlords had to accept what was told to them. Although there was thus some reduction of the influence of the landowners as the military gained in power, the governing class stayed the same to the extent that there were family ties between the two groups. Chiefs of provinces, for example, frequently conducted military operations for their uncles and fathers to get their rents.[31]

The amount of rent that landlords could charge in 'insecure' areas depended on the political and military strength of the National Liberation Front in that area. Insecurity usually meant that Saigon government forces, local officials and the military could only appear in the village during the daytime. In insecure areas, the Front cadres put pressure on the landlords on rent reduction and rent payments were lowest in these areas. An AID official describes the situation:

> In Dinh Truong province, for example, landlords are not even able to collect the 25 per cent rents permitted by law ... because peasants were able to use VC [*Viet Cong*] activity to keep rent collectors out; they pay only a fixed annual fee. In An Giang, Ba Xuyen, and Long Binh provinces on the other hand, rents are reportedly 40–50 per cent in the stable areas; in parts of Bien Hoa province they are even higher.[32]

As the revolution in the countryside proceeded, the former landowners moved to the provincial capitals or to Saigon or France. Since many were no longer able to collect rents, they found other means of supporting themselves and many, if not most, maintained powerful positions. Despite continuous protestations that southerners did not do well in business, many opened shops in the provincial capitals or in Saigon or became involved in importing operations. It is true, however, that the northern refugees did even better in these operations, considering that many of them started with little capital.

Besides business, there were other pursuits for former landlords such as professions, civil services and the military. Many of the landowners who did not consider themselves good at business and who did not have the required education for professions or civil service, became urban landlords. The most lucrative position to be in as an urban landlords was to rent to the Americans who were using office space and housing in large quantities in Saigon and in the provincial capitals.

It would seem that with massive US military intervention and expensive losses, the policy of protecting Vietnamese landlords would eventually have to be questioned despite the US and Saigon government interest in making South Vietnam a rice-exporting country. This questioning finally began in 1965 and the US Agency for International Development (AID) conducted a survey on the urgency of land reform which disclosed little interest in land titles on the part of the peasantry.[33] This result is not surprising, given what we have learned in previous chapters about the Vietnamese peasantry. They did not care about Western-style land titles; they were interested in the use and control of land and an acceptable standard of living for their families as defined in the Vietnamese context. The design of the AID survey, which asked about titles instead of rights, ensured the wrong result.

Another US government financed study on the question of supporting Vietnamese landlords was completed by Rand Corporation. This study by Edward J. Mitchell contended that the appeal of the Front had nothing to do with the Front's land policy.[34] He 'proved' his conclusions by showing that the Front's centres of power were not where land was most unequally distributed, as would be the case, he argued, if land-to-the-tiller were really important. Even if the data used in this study are correct (and there are reasons for suspicions about data measuring National Liberation Front influence and control), there could be many reasons for the results Mitchell arrived at. First, it would make sense that since the absentee landlords were strong in the Saigon government, they would try to keep their own lands within the control of the government, as we have seen, by directing the army into these areas. Second, the peasants in areas which had preserved communal rights, such as the Central Lowlands, would be particularly open to the socialist programmes of the Front government and would welcome the Front in these areas. 'Scientific studies' by AID and Rand continued to justify US support for the landlords of South Vietnam and the conservative land policy from 1965 to 1968.

The escalation of the war which culminated in the Tet offensive finally caused the US advisors to switch to a liberal land policy. The strength of the Front was suddenly realised by Americans and this finally made US advisors more willing to drop their strong alliance with Vietnamese absentee landlords. The USA had at long last determined that the primary goal of winning the war against the communists was more important than preserving the large-landownership pattern and exports of rice. Rice exports had averaged only 200 000 tonnes from 1958 to 1964 and had never reached over 350 000 tonnes a year. With US saturation bombing of the countryside starting in 1964, population in urban areas had increased from about 25 per cent of the population to over 36 per cent of the population of South Vietnam. Rice imports were needed to feed this growing urban population and imports increased from zero in 1964 to over 700 000 tonnes in 1967 and nearly that level in 1968. The power of the large landholders was broken in the countryside as NLF power grew and only then did the USA realise that their former policies were untenable.

US policy-makers then decided to combine a liberal land reform with technical aid in agricultural production and other aid services in projects called 'pacification programs'. Along with land reform, the distribution of new high-yielding rice varieties and mechanical water pumps for irrigation were supposed to win the 'hearts and minds' of the Vietnamese peasants.

The change in policy with regard to land is immediately obvious when looking at statistics on land distribution. Although virtually no Ordinance 57 or former French land had been distributed since 1961, distribution was resumed and 20 400 hectares were distributed in 1968 and 75 000 hectares changed hands in 1969.[35] 100 000 permanent titles were also issued in this period for lands that had previously been distributed.

In addition to these programmes, ordinances were passed to try to stop the landlords from resuming control in the countryside when the armed forces reoccupied an area. In November 1968 a decree prohibited officials and soldiers in newly secured villages from reinstalling landlords or helping to collect rents.[36] In February 1969 there was a decree creating a rent freeze in newly 'pacified' areas. This freeze on occupancy and rent was for one year from the date when the area was secured by Saigon forces. There was to be no change in occupancy or rent for the farmers actually cultivating the land if they had been cultivating that land for at least one year. After the freeze and after signing a legal contract, the landlord could continue to charge rent. This measure was one way for the Saigon government to buy time for the settlement of confused tenure in anticipation of the Land-to-the-Tiller law which was being drafted. In April, the rent freeze was made nationwide in anticipation that landlords would try to change the status of land in order to not have it expropriated by the Land-to the-Tiller law.

Along with this decision to create a liberal land policy expropriating large landlords, US advisors decided to diverge from the real-estate-transaction type of land reform which had been carried out in other countries where the USA had power (Korea, Taiwan, and Japan). The war had become so costly to the Americans that advisors calculated that if the new land policy would change the direction of peasant sentiments and help the USA win the war, this would be well worth the Americans donating the money to the Saigon government to pay the landlords. According to a decree issued in July 1969 all instalment payments on land already distributed were discontinued.[37] The USA, in addition, financed the whole Land-to the-Tiller programme which included an automated titling process using aerial photography and computers to print out the titles.

The economic reasoning behind the change in US policy was explained by Roy Prosterman, an originator of the new policy, at a US Agency for International Development Land Reform Conference in 1970. He stated that the cost of supporting massive land reform in all underdeveloped countries aided by the USA would be $1 for every $7 then being spent in foreign aid. Compensation being paid to the landlords by the USA was critical because if landlords were afraid they would not be paid for their land, they would attack land reform. He explained that support of land reform would cost the Americans only 5 per cent of what was then being spent in Vietnam and that the existing situation of the USA in Vietnam was caused by the Americans not being able to deal with land reform.[38]

THE LAND-TO-THE-TILLER LAW

The Saigon government's Land-to-the-Tiller law was signed by President Thieu in March 1970 and implementation was begun late in that year. The stated purpose of the law was to enable the tillers of the soil to receive all the benefits of their labour. The law specified that this purpose would be accomplished by providing the cultivators with ownership rights and putting a low rentention limit on landlords (20 hectares).

This law was the result of continued US concern with winning the war and questioning of the validity of continued support of the landlords. US Agency for International Development contracted with Stanford Research Institute to do a comprehensive study of land reform in Vietnam. In addition to reviewing the history of Saigon government land reform efforts and the National Liberation Front's land reforms, the Institute conducted two surveys of attitudes about land reform. They found, interestingly enough, that in the Southern region the peasants had an overwhelming desire to own land.[39] The landlords, however, were overwhelmingly against selling land. The report, based on their surveys, recommended legal and administrative reforms and organisational changes which would further land-reform efforts. Their main recommendations were as follows:

(a) 80 per cent of tenants interviewed wanted to own their own land.
(b) Farmers interviewed considered large landholding a violation of social justice.
(c) There are 500 000 families in the southern region who would need land in a thorough land reform.
(d) With only the land immediately available to the government for redistribution, only 76 000 families could receive land if they were given as much as they could adequately manage.
(e) The optimum retention limit for a new government land reform should be 30 hectares because this would keep landlords happy while satisfying peasants.[40]

Prosterman, the land reform advisor associated with this study, then wrote a land reform law which was handed to President Thieu for implementation.[41]

President Thieu who had initially been against a comprehensive land reform came to support this issue very strongly and, reportedly, even made payments to Assembly representatives in order to get the bill quickly through the National Assembly.[42] The attitude of most government officials to this law, however, was very negative because it was so heavily sponsored by the Americans.[43] These officials still held some hope of recovering some of their own or their family's land from the NLF or they, or their families, currently held lands which would be confiscated in the reform. Since these officials ultimately had to enforce the law, their continued disagreement proved to be a serious problem in some areas.

The law outlined a programme with much wider distribution plans than had previously been legislated by the government. The retention limit for landlords cultivating their own land was 15 hectares plus 5 hectares of land cultivated for religious purposes. All land above the retention limits was to be distributed to tenant-farmers. All non-agricultural land was excluded from coverage of the law because it was designed to cover rice land and some other crop land. Industrial crops which were generally cultivated in plantation type farms were excluded (coffee, tea, cotton, jute, indigo, rush, coconut, and mulberry). Vegetable garden land, orchard land and pasture land was also excluded, as was land owned by religious organisations and land cleared after the law was promulgated. Rice land and secondary cropland growing sweet potatoes, corn, sorghum, manioc, peanuts, soybeans, beans and sesame were included.

The Landlords were to receive compensation for the land which was expropriated. The compensation was to equal 2.5 times the annual crop yield which was defined as the average yield for the past five years. 20 per cent of the compensation was paid immediately when the land was taken and the rest was to be paid in eight-year bonds bearing 10 per cent interest. This 20 per cent immediate payment was an attempt to solicit landlord support because it was an improvement for the landlords over the Diem land reform which had only 10 per cent in immediate payment.

The distribution of the land was free to each farm family. The maximum area for distribution was 3 hectares in the Southern Region where plots were fairly large and 1 hectare in the Central Lowlands where double-cropping was frequent. The existing tenant-tillers had the first priority on plots to be distributed. Second in line were parents and spouses or children of war dead; next were soldiers and civil servants who had abandoned cultivation because of war. Last in order of priority were farm labourers and it is clear that these poorest of the rural population had little chance of receiving land. The terms of ownership specified that for a period of fifteen years persons receiving land under the law could not transfer ownership except with official authorisation and that the new owner must cultivate the land directly.

Approximately 1 million hectares of land were supposed to be distributed under this law. It was expected that the distribution would take at least three years and would affect over 600 000 of the 1.2 million families who rented land. By October 1970 713 641 hectares had been registered for exemption from expropriation – a rather high figure considering the low retention limit.

The Land-to-the-Tiller law itself provided for the distribution of communal as well as private land, but this was handled by a separate implementation decree. The 'sensitive nature' of communal land led to this special treatment.[44] The equally shared land (*cong dien*) was exempted from distribution in January 1972 when the implementation decree for rented communal land was issued. It was made clear, however, that this was a temporary situation and the *cong dien* would be distributed eventually.

The Land-to-the-Tiller programme was very similar to land distribution programs carried out in Taiwan and South Korea with US assistance and somewhat similar also to the Japanese reform. The retention limits were certainly much closer to those liberal reforms which the USA had previously supported than to the early Diem reforms. The major difference, which favoured the Vietnamese tenants, was the lack of tenant payments for the land since the USA was willing to pay the landlords as a mechanism for bailing out of an expensive war.

The effectiveness of the Land-to-the-Tiller programme varied throughout the country. In An Giang and Chau Duc provinces, where the Saigon government held strong control because of an alliance with the *Hoa Hao* Buddhist sect, the land reform ran into great difficulties. In most of the rest of Vietnam landlord collections had become sporadic, at best, because of Front influence or control, and the reform was much more successful.[45] This reverse correlation between government control and effectiveness of the reform was caused by the fact that the Land-to-the-Tiller essentially legitimised what the National Liberation Front had already accomplished in the country-side – a rural revolution which displaced the absentee landlords.

In areas where the landlords were still strong, they often found ways of getting around the reform. As previously stated, absentee landlord power in rural areas was greatly reduced before the LTT law was passed. Resident landlord power was still strong, however, in many areas. Most of the village and provincial administrators as well as the judges in areas with Saigon government influence were from the landlord or landlord-allied classes. A government study done prior to implementation of the law found that only a small proportion of village and hamlet officials were at that time landlords, but the study neglected to find out how many were related to landlords. Landlords in this period seldom held village positions but they were sure to have relatives or friends who did.[46]

Judges from the landlord class decided cases in the interest of their friends and relatives. They tended to use technicalities favouring the landlords rather than following the intent of the law.[47] Judges honoured backdated papers establishing worship land and also papers ceding back cultivation rights to the landlords which the tenants had been deceived into signing (documentation follows, pp. 193–5). Special land courts to decide land cases were never set up and the judges of superior courts tried land cases in addition to their regular duties. This, according to one advisor, was unfortunate for the administration of the law:

These individuals have no special qualifications in land affairs or training in the Land-to-the-Tiller law and it appears, at least in My Tho, that they are not above letting their personal feelings about the law influence their decisions.[48]

The backdating of papers establishing worship land and other 'irregularities' were common and greatly reduced the amount of land which could have been distributed. An observer mentions the extent of the reduction for one village:

> Shortly after the LTT law was passed by the National Assembly each village was asked to report how much of its paddy land would be subject to expropriation. Khanh-Hau reported 500 hectares and this figure was then listed as the village 'goal' for the Land to the Tiller program. Village officials now claim that 316 hectares is the maximum they will be able to expropriate.[49]

This observer also explained that some of the problems of enforcement of the LTT law came from a change in wording between the law and the implementation decree. The law stated that the worship property held by the *Gia Toc*, or head of the five-family group, was exempt from distribution. The implementation decree referred to the worship property of any property-owner who established it as being exempt. This subtle but important change was a clever trick of the landlords against the US-sponsored reform.[50]

In addition to these problems, there was dissension in the ranks of the Americans about the advisability of carrying out the land reform in areas where the Americans and the Saigon government were in control. Because of the landlord's power and their favourable attitude toward the USA, some advisors still questioned the LTT.[51]

There were hundreds of examples of lack of enforcement and landlord fraud which were collected and documented by the US advisors who favoured land reform. There was an investigating committee which was appointed to look into the false worship land problem in An Giang province. Out of 375 cases which were investigated, 374 seemed falsified. False worship land was not the only documented fraud, however. The following are examples which show the diversity in types of fraud:

> My Duc village, Chau Phu district, Chau Doc, VALRC (Village Agriculture and Land Reform Cadre) Tran van Hai is extorting money from title applicants. These same respondents together till 50 hectares belonging to La Than Sen, and reported that the same VALRC had told them all of this was worship land. They claim Sen made a backdated registration of worship land. Same agricultural VALRC of My Duc village, Chau Doc, also reportedly allying with landlords to cheat tenants. No action had been taken by high officials to correct this misbehaviour at the time of the survey although it had been going on for some time.

Wife of Nguyen van Phuoc of Vinh Qui hamlet, Vinh Kien village, Sam Chang district, Dinh Tuong: 'Landlord Mrs Le Thi Truoc (alias Mu Ba) had her people take my [4/10ths of a hectare] to lay up her garden in August 1970. The case was brought to the village. I was ordered by the village committee (including the village chief and his registrar) to give back the land and receive VN$2000 from Le Thi Truoc for my labor. I was also told that I was no longer to be authorized to farm the land. To date (17 November 1970) I have not gotten my harvest nor made any declaration.' (Other people in the hamlet confirmed that Mrs Phuoc should have been able to claim the land under LTT.)

Hoa Hiep village chief, Cai Be District, Dinh Tuong, after promulgation of LTT, hurried to sell 1 hectare to his tenant for VN$100 000. After the tenant heard about the law he came to claim back the money. At the time of the survey he had received no satisfaction.

The Village Land Distribution Committee (VLDC) of Hoa Hiep village avoided distributing lands of Tran van Binh and Tran Van Chu. When tenants came to apply for it they were told it was worship land or that there were no more application forms or that they were to wait until another time, etc.[52]

(Trung An Village, An Giang)
At Thanh Phuoc 2 hamlet, the tenant already seeded the field, but the landlord Le Thi Kim Chi, got her tractor to plough off all the seeds. Village police and PF came to guard her work because she had a court's judgement obliging the present tiller to return land to her.[53]

Avoidance of the law often involved not only mistreatment of the tenants, but also threats and sometimes violence:

Tenants so affected were: Mrs Luong thi Chan, Mr Luong van Te, Mr Nguyen van The, landlord Nguyen van Le, Vinh Trach village rented out to Ly Sen 2 hectares, Le van Hoa 2 hectares and Quach Mang 3 hectares. Recently his nephew Lt Chau, relying on his military power forced tenants to return the land not to cultivate, but to rent out for VN$15 000. He threatened to shoot down all who cultivated and would not pay him. The Village Administrative Committee (VAC) was unable to handle the case. They did report it to superiors, but no action was taken.[54]

Attached find a report by Mr Quang, Land Reform Area Specialist, which deals with the shooting of Nguyen van Quan of Thot Not

District, An Giang. As district leader of the Vietnamese peoples party (VNQDD), Quan championed many causes, among them land reform. He frequently took the side of tenants in landlord/tenant disputes. His death is widely interpreted by Thot Not peasants, all of whom seem to know of the killing, to have resulted from his outspoken advocacy of tillers' interests. The peasants hint darkly at the involvement of prominent district officials and seem to think that District Police are covering up for the killer.[55]

There were also conceptual problems with the land reform which were at least as important as its lack of enforcement in many areas. First, the reform was geared more toward the necessities of future tax collection than toward the well-being of the peasant population. Land reform was used as a method of registering the cultivator for future taxation because (i) many land records had been destroyed in the Tet Offensive, and (ii) landlords in the cities could not easily be taxed by the village.[56] If equal redistribution were the emphasis rather than registration of the current holder as a taxpayer, landless labourers might have been considered in the distribution and plots might have been more evenly distributed.

Second, people who could not cultivate their own plots suffered inequities as a result of the land reform. Soldiers, old and disabled people who lived off the returns from their land because they were not able to perform the cultivation themselves often lost their land under the new law. In fact, they were more likely to lose their land than were the larger landlords with influence in the village, because of the differential enforcement already discussed.

Last, there was an emphasis on Western-style ownership and titles in the programme which the tenants did not always understand. One US advisor met a large number of former tenants who had titles but did not realise that they were owners of the land and that they did not have to pay rent.[57] These peasants were used to having their rights determined in the context of the political economy of the village through oral agreement. The pieces of paper issued from computers, based on aerial photography, and brought into the village by foreigners were often unintelligible to the peasant. They would only have meaning if they were explained and promoted by local officials and advisors and this often did not happen because many of the officials and advisors identified themselves with the interests of the landlords.

Whether liberal or conservative, US land-reform policy never had the results expected by US advisors. In this respect the American experience followed closely the experience of the French in their rural policies. No matter what the specifics of the law or regulation, American and French 'reforms' would always be influenced by the pro-Western Vietnamese who were enforcing them. Reforms could always be turned, one way or another, to the advantage of this minority. Americans never seemed to learn the lesson that they could not impose democratic or progressive reforms on Vietnam. There were essentially two reasons for this result:

1. the private property and market institutions sponsored by the US in Vietnam were, by nature inegalitarian.
2. no really progressive reform could be effectively imposed by outsiders.

Vietnamese egalitarian and cooperative institutions stood in opposition to private property and market institutions imposed by the French and later by the Americans. Vietnamese control of public works and planning had from ancient times been important to the maintenance of production and the raising of production to match population growth. This was very different from the Western bias toward the use of anarchic forces of the market in directing economic life. When market institutions led to tremendous inequality and landlordism, piecemeal policies of reform always seemed too little and too late and never really appealed to the average Vietnamese peasant. These reforms were not understandable from the traditional egalitarian or cooperative frameworks.

The Vietnamese who had some understanding of Western land titles and Western *fee simple* property rights were sure to benefit. Even when some Western advisors could get beyond their alliance with this élite and understand some of the grievances of the average peasant, the advisors were not able to change policy to the advantage of this average peasant. Their policies were either naive or ineffective and they were often contradictory. Ultimately, with the American retreat, no answer to these problems was arrived at and Americans referred to the 'quagmire' that they were never able to really understand.

ECONOMIC RESULTS OF THE US INTERVENTION

In areas outside the Delta, and particularly in central Vietnam, cropped area and production decreased in Vietnam during the period of the air war (Table 9.4). The value of agricultural production for the whole of Vietnam increased from 1964 to 1970 because of large increases in high-value foods such as livestock, fish, poultry, and eggs. These products largely fed the increasing market for luxury foods in the cities. Per capita value of agricultural production decreased in this period, despite the rising production of these high-value protein foods. The greater part of the increased urban population as well as the rural population could not afford these luxury foods and had to depend on the staple, rice.

Despite the efforts of thousands of AID people in Vietnam which were directed to trying to make South Vietnam self-sufficient in agriculture and particularly in rice, Southern Vietnam increased its dependence on US-financed imported food. In 1964, food imports into South Vietnam were about 3 per cent of total food use for the country; by 1970, however, imported food made up nearly 15 per cent of total domestic food consumption.[58] In 1970, the South Vietnamese people consumed 3.15 million tonnes of grain for food, of which 826 000 tonnes, or 26 per cent were imported. In addition to 560 000 tonnes of rice imports, 250 000 tonnes of wheat and 17 000 tonnes of other food grains were imported. Feed grain for animals in 1970 consisted of 1.9 million tonnes of grain and bran, of which 140 000 tonnes or 7 per cent were imported.

In addition to grain imports there were large amounts of other agricultural and manufactured goods imports coming into Vietnam by 1970. Other agricultural products imported were vegetable oil, dairy products, fruit and vegetables, sugar, textiles and tobacco. In 1970, 40 per cent of the vegetable oil used in the country was imported. All the dairy products, or about 200 000 tonnes of whole milk equivalent were imported. Practically all the 107 000 tonnes of sugar consumed in the country was imported. In 1970, also 26 000 tonnes of US cotton went to Vietnam and 10 400 tonnes of synthetics and generated fibres and 4200 tonnes of cotton yarn and fabric were imported. About 3000 tonnes of the 11 000 tonnes of tobacco used in the country were imported also in 1970. In addition to these huge agricultural imports, there were large imports of industrial consumer goods. Meanwhile, the only remaining substantial export was rubber, of which 23 000 tonnes were exported in 1970.

The air war had substantial effects in the countryside in at least postponing for a number of years the NLF victory. The bombing also had the effect of producing a large urban population which could not be fed by the agricultural production of the country. The bombing created a very great food-deficit problem in Vietnam which was only alleviated through large imports.

Table 9.4 Regional value of production: rice, secondary crops, livestock, fish, and non-food, 1964 and 1970, 1964 prices

Item	Unit	South Vietnam Total	South West	South East	Central Lowlands	Central Highlands
1964						
Total value	Mil. VN$	50 411	27 989	6 441	13 635	2 346
Rice	Mil. VN$	20 169	13 872	1 566	4 454	277
Secondary food crops	Mil. VN$	7 673	3 131	1 458	1 808	1 276
Livestock, fish, poultry and eggs	Mil. VN$	20 770	10 859	1 957	7 187	767
Non-food crops	Mil. VN$	1 799	127	1 460	186	26
Rural population	1 000	11 543	5 916	1 480	3 643	504
Total population	1 000	15 711	6 316	3 979	4 722	694
Per capita, total	VN$	3 209	4 431	1 619	2 888	3 380
Per capita, rural						
Total	VN$	4 367	4 731	4 352	3 743	4 655
Food	VN$	4 211	4 710	3 365	3 692	4 603
Non-food crops	VN$	21	21	987	51	52

1970

Total value	Mil. VN$	59 914	34 050	8 176	12 278	2 410
Rice	Mil. VN$	22 026	15 925	1 732	4 132	237
Secondary food crops	Mil. VN$	7 138	1 264	1 264	1 463	1 550
Livestock, fish, poultry and eggs	Mil. VN$	26 611	15 112	4 436	6 483	580
Non-food crops	Mil. VN$	1 139	152	744	200	43
Rural population	1000	11 659	5 619	1 657	3 741	643
Total population	1000	18 332	6 830	5 080	5 482	940
	VN$	3 105	4 985	1 609	2 240	2 564
Per capita, total						
Per capita, rural						
Total	VN$	4 882	6 060	4 934	3 282	3 748
Food	VN$	4 784	6 032	4 485	3 229	3 681
Non-food crops	VN$	98	28	449	53	67

Source: Nancy Wiegersma, 'Agricultural Economy, an Economic Profile', p. 155. in Daly *et al. Agriculture in Vietnam's Economy.*

The greatest problem of underproduction was in the Central Lowlands. By 1970, agricultural production in this region was only two-thirds of production per capita in rural areas in the rest of South Vietnam, down from 87 per cent in 1964 (see Table 9.4). Consumption per capita was even lower because with the exception of some rice shipments, food imports went through the port of Saigon and did not reach the Central Lowlands areas. This was a heavily NLF area and the NLF may have received some shipments from North Vietnam or China but the Saigon government clearly did not serve the needs of this food-deficit area.

Industry in Vietnam did not fare better than agriculture in the 1960s. Although the consumer-goods importing business was booming, this was all based on US funding. Even the processing industries which grew during this period – sugar refining, cigarette production, soft drinks and alcoholic beverage production – depended for the most part on imports and not on domestic resources. These imports would not have existed without almost total US support, since this was a period of low exports from South Vietnam.

National Income figures grew from 99 billion piastres (1960 prices) in 1964 to 106 billion in 1968 but foreign donations grew by nearly seven billion piastres – the entire NI increase. Meanwhile, per capita income declined. The distribution of income in the country changed substantially during this period. As previously mentioned, the absentee landlords were not collecting ent in large areas of the countryside by 1964. There were gains to the peasants' incomes which had adverse effects on the landlords in the early 1960s. Many of the landlords, however, as we have seen, entered various commercial activities in the 1950s which prospered with the expanding US engagement in the war in the 1960s. The countryside was hit hard by the war but the cities prospered, albeit through a totally foreign-financed prosperity. With the new land reform policy in 1969, there was more landlord money to be spent on imported goods, since the USA was paying landlords for land that, in many cases, they were not able to take rent collections from. The prosperity in the cities however, was very unequal. Peasant refugees from the countryside came in search of work and they often did not find it, while those with money for investment in commerce expanded their holdings.

The increased inequality in income distribution is evident from structural changes in agricultural production which took place through market demands. We have seen that luxury foods such as meat and poultry increased in supply (Table 9.4). The subsistence food, rice also increased slightly in supply while production of secondary food crops decreased. The poorer sector of the population demanded more rice for subsistence reasons and less vegetables, oils and fruits. Meanwhile, a newly-enriched, mainly urban sector, demanded large quantities of protein foods.

The US failure in Vietnam was primarily a failure in the countryside where peasants, through their support of the NLF, finally broke the power of the landlords who were supported by the USA for so long. The Land-to-the-Tiller Programme and technical innovations supported by the USA did not change the basic direction of the war. The land reform, as we have seen, was often not enforced in some regions and it did not benefit landless labourers. The technical changes introduced through the market led to progress in some areas of the countryside but increased inequalities in incomes as well. The US failure was ultimately a failure in the cities also. Former landlords and officials turned to commerce and grew rich on commercial import activities which were made possible by large amounts of US aid. The character of the Commercial Import Programme ensured that almost all imports were consumer goods. Investment goods were seldom imported and a balanced manufacturing sector was not established in the cities of South Vietnam.

10 The National Liberation Front

The Second Indochina War was a very different conflict from the First Indochina War. The war against the Americans was fought on a much broader scale than the war against the French and there was much greater involvement of masses of poor and middle-peasant men and women in the struggle. There was a broad-based resistance to the Americans which pre-dated the formation of the National Liberation Front and therefore the composition of the Front was more diverse than that of *Viet Minh*, and the Front enjoyed more active mass support.

Despite the American government's contentions to the contrary, the North did not direct the struggle in South Vietnam. The North was busy in reconstructing their part of the country after the Geneva Accords were signed in 1953. Nguyen Thi Dinh complained in her memoirs that even in 1959, when armed struggle was being planned in many parts of the South, the North would not provide weapons. As a *Viet Minh* cadre, and member of the Workers' Party, she voiced her strong opposition to this policy before proceeding to lead an unaided and poorly armed insurrection in Ben Tre province.[1]

In the 1950s the US-sponsored leader, Ngo Dinh Diem, attempted to repress former *Viet Minh* sympathisers by killing 90 000 of them and imprisoning another 800 000, many of whom were tortured. Diem also antagonised practically the whole country by establishing Roman Catholicism as the state religion despite the fact that only 10 per cent of South Vietnamese were Roman Catholic. The many Vietnamese who were hoping that the Geneva Accords would be respected and the promised elections would be held, were also greatly disappointed in 1956 by Diem's refusal to hold the elections. In the countryside, as we have seen, landlords who had been dispossessed under the *Viet Minh* during the First Indochina War, were brought back under Diem. As a resistance movement developed among the peasants, many peasants were herded into protected villages called '*agrovilles*' and 'strategic hamlets' in order to separate them from the dissidents.

In reaction to Diem's outrageous policies, massive resistance developed among many sections of the population. Trade unions were active in the cities in this period and there were many strikes and

202

demonstrations protesting the lack of elections. In the countryside, villagers protested at being moved from their homes into *agrovilles*. By 1958 they were defending themselves with homemade shotguns and crossbows. To put down resistance in the countryside, government troops were sent in and they engaged in indiscriminate killing and stealing. As a reaction to these acts, tens of thousands of peasant women descended on towns which were district or provincial administrative headquarters and protested about the conduct of the government troops. The action led by Nguyen Thi Dinh in Ben Tre Province in January 1960 was large-scale and served as a model for later actions all over Vietnam. The population stormed rural militia posts and took control of them. When the Saigon government sent in troops to control the area, women demonstrators occupied the town for a week and forced the government to withdraw the troops.[2]

After the 1960 uprisings, local and regional groups which had been fighting against Diem saw the advantages of unification. The formation of the National Liberation Front was the crystallisation of the struggle which had been waged in all parts of South Vietnam for years. The groups forming the Front included *Cao Dai* and *Hoa Hao* religious sects, Cambodian and Mantanyard minority group members, representatives of farmers' organisations from the Mekong Delta, students and intellectuals. There were three political parties in the Front – the Radical Socialist Party, the Democratic Party and the Revolutionary Peoples Party (affiliated with the Workers' Party of the North). The Front group chose as its president Nguyen Huu Tho, an intellectual without party affiliation, who was a leader of the Saigon–Cholon Peace Group.[3]

The National Liberation Front was thus formed from diverse groups and individuals who had been driven underground or into armed resistance to the Diem government. With the help of his American advisors, Diem had pushed the most varied social, political and religious forces in Vietnamese society into each other's arms in a desperate search for a means of survival. Because of their broad-based support, local organisations of the NLF were able to develop as an integral part of the Social order of the countryside. Two additional policies aided in developing mass support in the countryside. One was the policy of developing cadres that belonged to the villages in which they worked, and the other was the land redistribution policy.

The NLF cadres lived with the peasants and they were usually local people known to the peasants. The cadres depended on the people for their own subsistence and this made them treat the people with respect instead of aloofness. The cadres were usually self-sacrificing people who were developing their own skills and working for goals which were laudable and sometimes seemed impossible to the local people. The peasants generally identified with the personal conduct of the cadres and their goals of overthrowing the US-supported Saigon regime.[4]

Recruiting mass participation from a frightened and discouraged peasantry was a very dificult and time-consuming job for NLF cadres. In working with Rand Corporation interview material, David Hunt found examples of cadres working one whole week with each family in a village just to get them to attend initial meetings.[5] Decisions on local policy were made through a process of the cadres coming to agreement resulting from their own political discussions and then taking the policy to the rest of the villagers for discussion. If large numbers of villagers could not be persuaded, the cadres had to rethink the soundness of the policy.[6]

Under the NLF, People's Revolutionary Committees, sometimes called 'Self-management Committees', were set up to be in charge of local government. These committees were made up of representatives of village associations of peasants, women, youth, Buddhists, small traders, etc. These groups have had many functions ranging from administration to revolutionary work. During the war they were in charge of resistance work, security and order, self-defence, economy and finance, education and health and land reform.

NATIONAL LIBERATION FRONT LAND REFORMS AND PROGRAMMES (1960–72)

Continuing in the *Viet Minh* tradition with regard to land, the NLF classified the rural population and used these classifications to determine policy. The classifications were a lot clearer than those of the *Viet Minh*, however, and they led to fewer difficulties with respect to interpretation. The categories are listed below, along with the percentage of the population in each.

The landless labourer in the southern region was a worker on other people's land. This labourer neither owned or rented land for cultivation. This classification included those peasants in the Central Lowlands who share-cropped their land under a system where the landlord provided all the inputs except for labour. The next category included poor peasants who rented or owned small amounts of land that provided little more than subsistence for their families. The

Class	Approximate proportion of rural farm population (%)
Landless peasant (sharecropper, farm labourer)	17
Poor peasant (tenant farmer)	45
Middle peasant (small landholder)	27
Rich peasant (large landholder)	11
Landlord	1

middle peasants owned land which they cultivated by themselves and through exchange of labour and they therefore had some income above their (culturally defined) subsistence needs. The rich peasants owned and rented up to 50 hectares and personally operated some of that area (in this book they have been referred to as local landlords). The landlord category was defined by the NLF as 'owning in excess of 50 hectares of land and operating none'.[7] (In this book these landlords have been referred to as absentee landlords).

In the early years of the liberation movement, the NLF followed a policy of unity of the landless labourers with the poor and middle-peasants and alliance with the rich peasants. In a united front policy against the USA and their supporters, the NLF recognised the rights of landlords to collect some rents if they were patriotic landlords, that is, if they did not support the USA. Only the land belonging to the supporters of the Saigon government was expropriated and redistributed. Land not cultivated because it had been abandoned because of the war was temporarily distributed. Rent reduction was the policy which was followed toward both patriotic landlords and rich peasants. There was no set rate for rent reduction, which varied locally with the extent of NLF control and its longevity. 15 per cent was the rate allowed in large areas which were securely under NLF control.

The communal lands which had been used to support the village budget, were redistributed by the NLF along with some other types of village communal lands. *Cong dien* was usually continued in the traditional distribution pattern but there was a lot of flexibility to allow for local conditions. Rich peasant's rights to *cong dien* were respected but they were encouraged not to accept their shares. Even enemy soldiers' rights were considered. The following is an NLF policy statement on community land:

Seize all community land and fishponds distributed by the resistance [*Viet Minh*] to the peasants which have been stolen by the US

Diemist authorities and village bullies. Divide them equally, logically and democratically among all citizens, with priority for poor peasants, families of liberation troops, self-defense members, and guerrillas. Rich peasants can receive community lands but they must be persuaded to refuse and give the land to people who have no land to cultivate. Enemy soldiers from the peasant class also have their plots of land. But this land will be given to another person to exploit and return when such leave enemy ranks. Their families will also receive their plots of land. When dividing public lands, one must carefully examine the ownership giving by US–Diem to peasants to preserve unity among peasants.[8]

The end of the period of emphasis on the united front with patriotic landlords came in 1963 after there were significant gains by the NLF in the delta of South Vietnam.[9] Thereafter, the unity of landless, poor, and middle peasants was stressed in coalition with rich peasants. Unity with landlords was no longer emphasised. Land reform was carried out in areas which were secure and where there were conditions of solidarity and cooperation in the village. All the landlords' land and much of the land belonging to rich peasants was redistributed in these areas. On the other hand, there were areas where conditions were not yet suitable for land reform because of the history of the area as non-*Viet Minh* or there was as yet insufficient leadership among the landless and poor peasant familes. Rent reduction was carried out in those areas.

Flexibility was the most characteristic aspect of the NLF land reforms in this period. Local conditions dictated which reforms were feasible and it is difficult to generalise and find overall rules:

Land taxes and land rents must depend upon the situation of rice fields in each region. In general, they must be based on the right principles acquired by peasants under the resistance. They can change a little to coincide with present conditions. When the harvest is bad, land rents must be re-examined to avoid hurting the peasants. If the harvest gets worse, peasants are exempt from taxation.[10]

There was also sufficient flexibility to make allowances for special circumstances and situations:

In principle, those who rent rice fields must reduce rents; but there are people who are unable to cultivate their own land because they are old, are widows, or their family members have joined the liberation troops. Their rice fields are for rent, so this problem must be solved through mutual help and free negotiation.[11]

The National Liberation Front's land policy cannot be seen in isolation from other policies in liberated areas. The Front emphasised solidarity of the peasantry and the justice of an equal distribution of land – or one which was at least aiming toward equality. These principles of equality and solidarity underlay the entire programme of the NLF. Every phase of the programme had to be supportive of the total effort for a people's war for national independence to be successful against such a strong enemy as the USA. Military policies, taxation, education and health care were fitted together with an equitable distribution of land. The battles which were fought and the collective activities completed made the organisation tighter and future collective activity easier.

The taxation depended on the classification of the rural population already described. Basically, the families paid from zero to 20 per cent of crop yield, depending on their social class and other conditions. As with rents, tax rates varied because of a number of circumstances but in large sections of the Mekong delta in the period 1961–4, the following schedule was followed: the very poor farmer who harvested less than fifteen bushels of rice a year was exempt from tax; the poor farmer paid from 5 to 10 per cent; the middle farmer paid 10 to 15 per cent and the rich peasant and absentee landlord paid from 15 to 21 per cent.[12] In the event of failure of crops there was no tax.

Closely associated with the land reform, were the programmes for acceleration of production in liberated areas. Mutual assistance groups were encouraged to develop and were affiliated to the Farmers' Associations. Everyone in the village, including officials, soldiers and students, worked on the mutual assistance teams. For large areas, the aim of production during the war was self-sufficiency because of the difficulties of transportation and communication. Irrigation and drainage canals were organised and built by the villages. This could be easily accomplished with the tight organisation of the village and the lack of emphasis on individual ownership rights in land.

Even under wartime conditions, there was an expansion of educational and other social services. Community projects to build and administer social services were developed by the NLF in areas under their control and they were also initiated in 'insecure areas'.[13] Where the population was in need of a service, like a school, the NLF often took the initiative in organising the project.

By comparison, the American and Saigon governments during the 1950s and 1960s supported the property relations developed by the French in Vietnam. Areas which had been freed by the *Viet Minh* from landlord control were brought back under their control in a rent contract system which reduced rates from the traditional 50 per cent to 25 per cent (as we saw in the last chapter, actual payments were closer to 33 per cent). The very limited land redistribution programme was not even completed. When it became clear that the reactionary policy of bringing back and supporting the landlords was not working and the NLF showed great strength in the Tet offensive, the American and Saigon policy changed to a liberal land reform programme, which redistributed private-ownership rights to tenant farmers. The importance of preserving individual private ownership was underscored in both the liberal and conservative land programmes, however. In one case the ownership was held by the landlord, in the other by the former tenant.

The National Liberation Front, on the other hand, distributed usufruct rights of confiscated lands to landless labourers and poor peasants. The NLF land reform basically moved from support of *Viet Minh*-type distributions (rent reduction and confiscation of land which belonged to those landlords supporting the Saigon government), to a programme of additional confiscation of all large landlords in many areas. The NLF stressed collective organisation of social services and canal-building. Increased production in liberated areas was mostly the result of these efforts which were organised by the NLF. During the last part of the war, new seed varieties passed into NLF areas through the market and some were brought by the North Vietnamese, and these also increased production.

Whereas the Vietnamese peasants understood and supported the cooperative projects of the NLF and their land distribution to all poor villagers, Western-style ownership contracts were as foreign to them as the Western originators of the Saigon government's policies. The NLF land-reform policies won them considerable support, especially among the poorer segments of the population.

WOMEN IN THE NATIONAL LIBERATION FRONT

The NLF also depended on the support of women, as a group. In addition to their role in demonstrations in the towns and administrative centres, women played a very active role in all phases of the NLF armed forces. Women were active in guerilla units, in self-defence and in the regular armed forces. Women concentrated on self-defence and non-military work until 1965 when a shortage of soldiers resulted in a drive to mobilise the female population into the regular army.[14] By the time of the NLF victory, ten years later, women had taken on very important roles in the armed forces and Nguyen Thi Dinh had become Deputy Commander in Chief of the Liberation Armed Forces.

Women also played important political roles in the National Liberation Front organisation and the Provisional Revolutionary Government (PRG) which the Front established. About 25 per cent of the top-level leadership positions in the PRG were held by women. Nguyen Thi Binh was Foreign Minister, Nguyen Dinh Chi was a member of the PRG advisory council and both the Minister and Vice Minister of Public Health, Duong Quynh Hoa and Bui Thi Me, were women. More than 30 per cent of the NLF cadres were women and they encouraged women's participation in local politics. Women's contribution to village-level political committees was most often equal to or more than men's participation and women held more than 30 per cent of the positions on district and provincial level committees.[15]

The Front was actively engaged in women's issues, and the village Women's Associations were encouraged to be at the forefront of village politics. The Associations were particularly strong in fighting against the daughter-in-law system. Although most extended families in the South no longer lived together, there were still cultural expectations of obedience to the mother-in-law which came into conflict with Vietnamese women's new political and military roles. The Women's Association also pushed forward the Front slogan 'equality between men and women' and at least some women from the villages took this quite literally by refusing to eat separately from the men and wash dishes after celebrations.[16]

Among the peasants, there was a considerable lag in cultural values about women and a negative reaction to women taking on new roles and acting in an untraditional manner. Women cadres had to pay an emotional price for their activity in the Front because in order to be effective they had to develop styles of which men (including men in the

Front) and many women in the village disapproved. One older woman describes her impressions of female cadres as the complete opposite of the traditional female:

> female cadres [have]... ridiculous ways of living, which are completely out of step with the traditional manner. They are educated by the Front and so they have that manly way of talking and behaving. They liked to use terms that I had no idea what they meant, lived with male cadres and don't care about cooking and housekeeping. As soon as they open their mouths, words like construction, criteria, struggle, etc., come out.[17]

In the traditional Vietnamese Confucian perspective, political talk would be considered manly talk. The women cadres therefore had an extremely complex and difficult task in reaching the typical peasant woman.

Despite these problems, most women cadres won the respect of the villagers through their dedication and hard work. David Hunt, in his comments on women in the NLF, gives the impression that many of the women cadres came from poor peasant families and that some had decided against marriage in order to fulfil their political duties. The villagers respected these female cadres at the same time that they ridiculed them for their 'manly way of living' or their talking to everyone without 'caution or care'.[18]

ECONOMIC CHANGE WITH RURAL REVOLUTION

The appeal of the NLF programme in the countryside was not confined to poor-peasant men and women and it was not limited to areas that the NLF controlled. The NLF anti-landlord policies influenced the whole countryside and the technological advances which were accomplished in the 1950s and 1960s were mostly as a consequence of NLF policies.

The exit of absentee landlords from essentially all areas except for broadcast rice areas (An Giang and Chau Doc Provinces where the *Hao Hoa* were predominant) caused many economic changes in the villages in the 1960s.[19] With rents greatly reduced or non-existent because of NLF activity, peasants were able to afford expenditures on new technology such as motor pumps, fertilisers and new varieties of rice. Increased cooperation in canal-building was also a result of decreased landlord-power in many areas. These were general changes in the countryside and they were not confined to areas where the NLF had direct influence. By the middle 1960s there was an alteration in power relationships in the entire countryside resulting from NLF activities.

Despite these changes which increased land productivity, war-related population shifts decreased agricultural output per capita, especially in food crops. The country became more dependent on agricultural imports in the late 1960s. This, added to an already existing dependency on the USA to furnish industrial consumer goods, resulted in complete reliance on the USA to bolster the economy.

Modern inputs were purchased with the increased funds which ended up in the hands of the rural population because of rent decreases. The US Agency for International Development (AID) made available new varieties of rice and these were distributed throughout South Vietnam via the private market. Fertiliser had become popular in the 1950s in Vietnam and use of this input was greatly expanded in the 1960s. Motor pumps also became available and were marketed throughout South Vietnam in the 1960s.

Despite these technological changes, military operations, and particularly saturation bombing, resulted in population shifts which were the largest determinant of changes in cultivated area and production in the 1960s. Part, though not all, of this change can be seen through looking at statistics on rural and urban Vietnam before the air war in 1964 and after the bombing policy was well under way in 1970. For the whole country, urban population increased from 26 per cent in 1964 to 36 per cent in 1970 (see Table 10.1). For the Delta (Western part) urban population tripled, increasing from 6 per cent to 18 per cent of total population. There were also movements of people from rural areas which were being bombed to other rural areas, but these movements were not measured.

The effects on production of the bombing and the new organisational and technological changes in agriculture largely offset one another in the Delta so that the total cropped area did not decrease, as it did in other areas of South Vietnam. Table 10.2 shows regional cultivated areas for two 'normal' years for South Vietnam. 'Normal' years are here defined as years where there was not an unusual amount of bad weather or war activity. While the total area cultivated decreased in the delta, the area cultivated per capita increased. In the eastern part of the southern reigon and in the Central Lowlands, both cultivated area as a whole and cultivated area per capita decreased as a result of the war.

212

Table 10.1   Rural and urban population by region, 1964 and 1970[a]

	South Vietnam Total		Southwest		Southeast		Central Lowlands		Central Highlands	
	pop.	%	*pop.*	%	*pop.*	%	*pop.*	%	*pop.*	%
1964										
Total	15 711		6 316		3 979		4 722		694	
Urban	4 168	26	400	6	2 499	63	1 079	23	190	27
Rural	11 543	74	5 916	94	1 480	37	3 643	77	504	73
1970										
Total	18 332		6 830		5 080		5 482		940	
Urban	6 673	36	1 211	18	3 423	67	1 741	32	297	32
Rural	11 659	64	5 619	88	1 657	33	3 741	68	643	68

[a]There were two series on population published in Republic of Vietnam sources. One series was based on reports from provinces and municipalities and was published by the Agricultural Economics and Statistics Service (AESS), *Agricultural Statistics Yearbook, 1959–1970* (Saigon: 1959–1970). Another series, computed by the National Institute of Statistics (NIS) was based on an assumed 2.6 per cent increase (3.0 per cent for later years) [NIS, *Vietnam Statistical Yearbook 1967, 1969, 1970* (Saigon: 1967, 1969, 1970)]. The estimated rate of increase was based on surveys conducted by NIS. The AESS series tend to run lower than the NIS series although at varying rates. For some years, the two series are nearly equal, for others they are quite far apart. For some years, the AESS population series grows at unreasonable rates. Vietnamese officials may have been reporting sections of the population that were not reported in previous years.

There was no urban–rural population breakdown by regions published in Vietnamese sources. There was, however, an urban–rural break in the Hamlet Evaluation Survey data for the late 1960s and early 1970s (US Government Military Assistance Command, Vietnam, 'Hamlet Evaluation Survey', computer copy of survey sheets). The definition used for urban 'hamlet' was based roughly on the following guidelines: the urban hamlet contains part of a population mass of 20 000 or more; the population density is high; there are many shops and restaurants present; the primary occupation is business or commercial activity. This definition would not include many small commercial hamlets scattered throughout the countryside of Vietnam. The rural population is, therefore, not the same as the agricultural population but rural population is the closest approximation available. To arrive at rural population for 1964, the percentage change in the population of province capitals and autonomous cities was computed between 1964 and 1970 for each region. This rate of change was applied to the HES urban population of 1970 to work back to the urban population of 1964. The bias in this exercise is to make the 1964 urban population too high. The rate of growth of smaller cities was larger than bigger cities. The rate of change between the two years is, therefore, biased on the low side.

Table 10.2 1964 and 1970 regional cultivated area: rice, secondary food crops, non-food crops

1964	Unit	South Vietnam Total	Southwest (Delta)	Southeast	Central Lowlands	Central Highlands
Total	1000 ha.	3 067	1 907	369	665	126
Rice	1000 ha.	2 562	1 779	180	34	70
Secondary crops	1000 ha.	352	124	68	124	39
Non-food crops	1000 ha.	151	5	121	7	17
Rural population	1000	11 543	5 916	1 480	3 643	504
Per capita						
Total	ha.	0.266	0.322	0.249	0.182	0.249
Rice	ha.	0.222	0.301	0.120	0.147	0.143
Secondary crops	ha.	0.031	0.021	0.046	0.034	0.077
Non-food crops	ha.	0.013	0.001	0.082	0.002	0.034
1970						
Total	1000 ha.	2 844	1 963	292	506	81
Rice	1000 ha.	2 511	1 854	191	418	48
Secondary crops	1000 ha.	283	105	60	84	33
Non-food crops	1000 ha.	50	4	41	4	—
Rural population	1000	11 659	5 619	1 657	3 741	643
Per capita						
Total	ha.	0.244	0.349	0.176	0.135	0.127
Rice	ha.	0.215	0.330	0.115	0.111	0.075
Secondary crops	ha.	0.024	0.019	0.036	0.022	0.051
Non-food crops	ha.	0.004	0.001	0.025	0.001	—

Source: Nancy (Wiegersma) Hancock, 'The Agricultural Economy: An Economic Profile', *Agriculture in the Vietnam Economy*, US Department of Agriculture, Economic Research Service, FDD Field Report 32 (Washington, DC: US Government Printing Office, 1973) p. 153.

Technological and organisational changes affected production through area under cultivation, such as a move from single- to double-cropping, and not through increases in yields. This seems surprising since the new high-yielding varieties of rice were widely used, reaching 25 per cent of the total use by 1970. Table 10.3 shows yields of rice per hectare for South Vietnam for a twelve-year period and there is no perceptible increase in yields. In order to understand why this is true and to understand the effects of technology more precisely, we need to take a closer look at each of the technological innovations and organisational changes in the context of Vietnam.

Canal-building was one of the services organised by the NLF at the village level in many areas and US advisors also sponsored some projects. In the South, between 1960 and 1964, double-cropping increased from 30 000 to 77 000 hectares, largely because of canal-building.[20] The NLF irrigation projects were small, encompassing at the most one or two villages, while the few US projects attempted were on a larger scale.[21] As we have seen, canal-building was a task usually handled at the village level in traditional Vietnam and still accomplished in a cooperative manner in the Central Lowlands. It is not surprising, therefore, that once the power and control of absentee landlords disappeared, and the remaining landlords were constrained by the NLF movement, canal-building was renewed in the Delta, even where the NLF was not directly in control.[22] This organisational change increased production through increasing cultivated area, not yields per hectare, for each crop.

Water pumps were another change which increased cultivated area. More people acquiring water pumps farmed larger areas. Adopters averaged 2.5 hectares as opposed to 1.2 hectares for those who did not acquire pumps in areas studied by Robert Sansom.[23] Sansom exaggerated the effect of the water pump in Vietnam by taking the experience of two villages in Dinh Tuong province, within twenty-five miles of Saigon, to be that of the whole of the Upper Delta. Although cultivated area, and therefore production, increased in Dinh Tuong, these increases were not typical of all of the provinces in the Upper Delta (See Table 10.4). In summing up his argument about the advantages of investments like the motor pump for the Vietnamese peasants, Sansom brought in as comparison a province in the Lower Delta to show the contrast of an area which did not have the motor pump.[24] Table 10.4 shows that for the late 1960s increases in production in that very province, Bac Lieu, were in line with the Dinh Tuong increases. This was a heavily NLF area which utilised

Table 10.3 Area, production, and yield of rice

Unit	1959	1960	1961	1962	1963	1964	1965	1966	1967	1968	1969	1970
1000 M.T.	5041	4955	4607	5205	5321	5185	4822	4336	4688	4336	5115	5716
1000 Ha.	2269	2318	2353	2479	2538	2562	2429	2295	2296	2394	2430	2511
Kilos/Ha.	2220	2138	1958	2100	2099	2024	1985	1889	2042	1811	2105	2276

Source: US Department of Agriculture, Economics Research Service, Foreign Regional Analysis Division, Far East Branch.

Table 10.4   Changes in cultivated area in rice for selected provinces, Upper and Lower Delta, 1964 and 1968

Area	1964–5	1968–9
Upper Delta	*ha*	
Dinh Tuong	84 000	120 000
Long An	83 600	90 000
Kien Haa	101 100	105 000
Vinh Binh	178 700	130 000
Lower Delta	*ha*	
Bac Lieu	92 400	120 000
Ba Xuyen	175 200	197 000
Phong Dinh	116 200	90 000
An Xuyen	103 200	110 000
An Giang	179 000	165 000

Source: Republic of Vietnam, *Agricultural Statistics Yearbook, 1968* (Saigon, Vietnam: Agricultural Economics and Statistics Services, 1969) p. 31.

canal-building. Traditional mechanisms for increasing cultivated area were much more effective than Sansom realised – production increased considerably in Bac Lieu in the years immediately following Sansom's study.

The use of new 'miracle' varieties of rice was introduced in Vietnam in 1967 and their use grew to 30–40 per cent of the crop in 1972. Although the high-yielding varieties performed outstandingly under experimental conditions in the Philippines, yielding from six to eight tonnes per hectare, Vietnamese conditions are very different. Very good water control and very large quantities of fertiliser are needed for the new varieties to perform as they are supposed to do. Most Vietnamese farmers did not have the appropriate conditions for the new varieties and could not afford the appropriate inputs. Richer farmers in the villages who could afford the appropriate inputs benefited from investments in the new varieties much more than poorer farmers. The introduction of new varieties thus tended to exaggerate the inequalities in rural Vietnam in areas of Saigon government control.

A ten-year update on the *My Thuan* village study (discussed in

Chapter 6 of this book) analysed introduction of the new varieties in this village. Larger farmers used fertiliser with their new variety seeds. A small farmer who had started to use the new varieties on his plot of 0.5 hectare could not afford fertiliser but forecast that with larger output that year, the next year he might afford fertiliser in addition. My Thuan was an area where the growing season was long enough for two crops of the the new faster-growing varieties to be grown, doubling output in some parts.[25] The advantage in using the new varieties was in multiple-cropping and even the small producer might benefit if he could acquire the new seeds but he would not benefit as much as the richer farmer.

In a village in Chau Doc Province, when the new varieties became available, only those with financial resources for irrigation during the dry season could use them. (Chau Doc is mostly a broadcast rice area.) These rich farmers found it advisable to plant two crops of new varieties, hire labour for the extra tending of crops and skip cultivating the traditional floating rice which was broadcast. When the floods came and there was no floating rice on their areas, the currents ruined the crops of poorer farmers who were still planting rice. The smaller farmers then had either to switch to the new varieties or hire themselves out as labourers for the larger farmers.[26]

New varieties and water pumps were certainly not restricted to Saigon-controlled areas. The new seed varieties crossed easily into NLF territory and were accepted there. Because of the organisation of the village in NLF areas and their progressive tax policies, the innovations did not lead to excessive inequalities in income. The NLF issued propaganda against buying water pumps, however, because they were imported under the US Commodity Important Programme and came complete with AID emblems. NLF reasoning was that the peasants paying for the pumps directed funds toward the USA which helped them to continue the war. Where peasants bought pumps anyway, they were encouraged to share the resource with other farmers.

In the Delta of South Vietnam, technical innovations and canal-building were responsible for increased output through expansion of multiple-cropping. These two types of changes affected income distribution in opposite ways. The traditional canal-building tended to equalise incomes while the water pump and new varieties increased inequality. The larger farmers who received increased income from using water pumps and new varieties were then able to invest in further labour-saving technical innovations such as roto-tillers and tractors.

Some also invested in motor boats for transportation and sewing machines for home production. Consumer goods such as radios and small generators for lights and even televisions were purchased by some villagers.[27]

Since not only these innovations but also the war affected the supply of rice in Vietnam, there was no increased supply and no price decreases accompanying technological advances. In fact, because of shortages, rice prices were rising in the late 1960s. With this price situation and the decreased population in the rural areas, demand for labour did not decrease in most parts of the Delta despite the labour-saving technology being introduced. Wage labourers were able to increase their real wages in some areas, although not nearly as much as the richer farmers increased their incomes.[28]

The net effect of rural change in the 1960s, when both technology and the elimination of rents are considered, was income-equalising. It is ironic that technological advances sponsored by the USA were a lot more effective, on a broad basis, because of the policies and influence of the NLF. US development strategies are not nearly so effective in countries where the USA is more successful in its support of existing hierarchies.

COMPARISONS BETWEEN THE VIET MINH AND THE NATIONAL LIBERATION FRONT

The level of economic development and the changed social structure in the South in the 1960s ensured a much different interaction between the NLF and the peasants than was possible for the *Viet Minh* in an earlier period. The traditional village hierarchy no longer existed in the South. NLF cadres could organise in their own villages without concern that they might be associated with the traditional hierarchy. This difference was very important in determining the amount and type of local support that each of these organisations was able to generate.

A large segment of the traditional village hierarchies supported the *Viet Minh* because they were anti-French. These village notables wanted political power in their own hands as opposed to French hands. The *Viet Minh* instituted change which was much more profound than these village notables anticipated. Change was forced by the Workers' Party by sending cadres whose own roots were elsewhere, into the village. But, as we have seen, village hierarchies were reconstituted in the North and caused 'family economy' and 'middle peasant' problems later.

Conditions in the South in the 1960s were very different. The village governments working with the Saigon regime and the Americans did not have the same status in the countryside as the village notables. The peasants' traditional values were not in harmony with support of these officials, who upheld the rights of absentee landlordism as well as foreign intervention. The NLF cadres found fertile ground for organising against the Saigon government because their form of modernisation was more consistent with Vietnamese social values than American–Saigon style capitalism.

The local NLF cadres had the knowledge of the local situation needed to administer land reform in a flexible manner. This was an improvement over earlier *Viet Minh* reforms. NLF cadres were trusted and supported by the local population partially because their income came from local revenues. Benefits of the Front government were obvious to the poor peasants and they, in turn, offered their support to the NLF in very large numbers.

Another part of the tendency to recruit more broad-based support on the part of the NLF as opposed to the *Viet Minh*, was the greater participation of women at all levels of the NLF in both civilian and military roles. Women were active in the mass movement against Diem, from its inception, and, later they took their places in NLF structures. Their greater independence from the traditional extended family made women more available to the struggle. The struggle having a mass base, on the other hand, made women's recruitment easier.

Many characteristics of Southern organisation: the political diversity, flexibility and independence, were not necessarily looked upon favourably by the South's northern allies. The northerners were stronger politically and economically and they had experienced two decades of socialism by the end of the war with the USA. Northerners tended to think that southern diversity came from the decadence of the French and American influences in the South. Since the South developed a dependent economy under the French and under the Americans, the region was not in a position to exert a lot of influence at the time of integration with the North at the end of the war.

11 Integration of the Country

The two parts of Vietnam, the North and the South, have had very different experiences in recent history. While the northern part of the country was undergoing socialist transformation for over two decades, the southern region operated under a dependent form of capitalism. Because of this great difference in experience, it was initially expected that there would be a long period of adjustment in the south before the country could be reunited and both regions could move toward socialism. After the war, however, thinking changed rapidly and in 1976 the Vietnamese embarked on a course of reuniting their country. In the next period, when southerners stubbornly resisted methods of transition which had been used in the North, southern individualism was pointed to as the cause of the problem. The southern experience of intense class struggle and the mass character of their revolution was overlooked in the northern assessment of the southerners as backward in terms of socialist consciousness.

In the process of the development of markets and modernisation in the south, many traditional social structures had broken down. Traditional collectivism and the power of the village patriarchs had disintegrated in this region and therefore some of the programmes that depended on patriarchal collectivism were unsuccessful. This chapter reviews problems of socialist development in the northern and southern parts of Vietnam in the present period in light of the historical development of capitalism and socialism in these regions.

The Provisional Revolutionary Government of the South was formally merged with the government of the Democratic Republic of Vietnam in 1976, and the Socialist Republic of Vietnam was formed. The established institutions of the North became dominant in reunified Vietnam because the North had undergone socialist revolution earlier, had far more experience in socialist policies and planning, and was in far less critical economic condition following the war. The attitude of northern communists toward the South was that the North had more experience on which to draw and therefore the integration of the country should mean that the South would 'catch up' with the North by moving in the directions in which the North had moved. This attitude made southern participation in a national direction problematical.

Another problem which prevented full participation for southerners in the new integrated structure was that the revolutionary organization, the National Liberation Front, was combined with the northern broad-based organisation, the Vietnam Fatherland Front. The Vietnam Fatherland Front was under the direction and dominance of the Vietnamese Communist Party which was itself a coalition of the Workers' Party of the North and the Peoples Revolutionary Party of the South. During the struggle in the South, the NLF, which was made up of numerous parties and organisations, had greater decision-making power on its own and it was not simply the tool of the People's Revolutionary Party. Officials in the NLF lost considerable power in the transition if they were not also members of the People's Revolutionary Party. People of diverse backgrounds, and particularly women, lost power in this transition, thereby narrowing the base of the new southern leadership.

The eleven years since the integration of the country can be divided into two periods. In the first four years, 1976–9, some grave policy errors were made in agriculture and trade and the communist leadership was forced to face the reality that their form of agricultural collectivism was no longer working. In the midst of Vietnam's economic problems, China withdrew its aid, Vietnam invaded Cambodia and China invaded the northern part of Vietnam, but was pushed back. The second period, 1980–7, had been a period of reassessment and the development of an alternative growth path. The Vietnamese have decided to use market incentives and encourage progress in the peasant family sector to help the nation to recover from a disastrous economic bind. The latest phase of these reforms consists of a recent major shift in the Party and Government in the direction of southern leadership and southern flexible alternatives to economic growth and development. The Vietnamese see themselves on a more gradual path to socialist transformation, since the reforms.

AGRICULTURE IN THE TRANSITION PERIOD

In the liberated zones, land redistribution had already taken place long before 1 May, 1975 when the Provisional Revolutionary Government became the government of the whole of South Vietnam. In the rest of the countryside, there were few large landlords left, but in some places where there were, land redistributions were carried out. The formation of mutual aid teams was also well under way in the liberated areas even before 1975. After 1975 there was a movement for the rest of the villages of the southern area to form mutual-aid teams.

The countryside in the South received many new inhabitants from the city. Over 700 000 people left the Saigon area alone in the two years following liberation. Some have returned but there has still been a large net exodus. About 4 million people moved from one place to another in South Vietnam in that first period; either from cities to countryside, or from one area in the countryside to another.[1] Recruits for resettlement were given provisions to compensate for difficulties which their inexperience in the countryside brought. These resettlements were not organised directly into cooperatives, but rather they organised much like the other villages in the South. They were then supposed to undergo cooperativisation later. The areas which were moved directly to socialised production were the State farms and the cooperatives which were constructed by the army in the Mekong Delta and also the State farms which were formerly tea and rubber plantations. The army, which was still mobilised after the war, aided in the clearing of land and the establishment of many state farms and cooperatives in the South.[2]

Cooperativisation proceeded slowly in the south, and was actually completed in only about 30 per cent of the villages by 1980. As we saw in the last chapter, changes in factor inputs in South Vietnam were the result of NLF anti-landlord policies combined with large imports of agricultural inputs sponsored by the USA. Modern inputs, like tractors, were particularly necessary because of all the draft animals which were killed during the war. Many peasants, particularly middle and rich peasants, gained financially from the use of the new inputs and they did not want to give up their private gains with cooperativisation. There were also negative financial incentives for collectivisation for this group. State prices for rice were running very low in relation to private market prices. In the past few years, as market prices were allowed to rise and cooperative roles have allowed for much more differentiation among family economies, the majority of villages have formed cooperatives.

The difference that the political–economic history of the different regions made in the rapidity of acceptance of the North's policies is evident when we observe that villages in the Central Lowlands region of the former South Vietnam collectivised quickly. 85 per cent of households in that region had joined collectives by 1979. The problem was in the Southern Region, the former Cochin China. Some sources say that in this area, less than 10 per cent of peasants had become collectivised by the early 1980s.[3]

Meanwhile in northern agriculture, the crisis caused by low productivity in collective agriculture, which had its roots in the 1960s, finally came to be recognised in the late 1970s. After an initial increase in grain production in 1976, production of grains for all of Vietnam decreased by 1 million tonnes and then stagnated (Table 11.1) in the late seventies. Meanwhile, population increased rapidly following the war, causing food supplies per capita to fall drastically. This production problem was a crisis in organisation and incentives rather than in lack of inputs. Hiebert mentions 80 000 hectares of arable cooperative land that was left fallow during this period.[4]

Table 11.1 Grain production in Vietnam

Year	Cereals Output (1000 metric tons)
Average	
1969–71	10 198
1974	11 350
1975	10 830
1976	12 470
1977	11 318
1978	10 560
1979	11 269
1980	12 134
1981	13 065
1982	14 977
1983	15 241
1984	16 104

Source: *FAO Production Yearbook*, Food and Agricultural Organisation of the United Nations , vols 30–9.

The conflicts between collective production and peasant family production are analysed in Chapters 7 and 8 of this book. In addition, problems in the northern collectives are enumerated in Vietnamese sources and by Adam Fforde in a study of five collectives in the Tonkin Delta. Managers wasted collective property, including tools, implements, and draft animals. Cooperators took over collective property without permission, as well as devoting more time and attention to family economies.[5]

The family economy was not stifled in Vietnam in these years. In fact, it seems that the peasant family economy was strengthened and made more prosperous in the North despite a high level of collectivisation. Not only did the peasant families have their small plots to use as the patriarchal family head chose, but also the cooperatives had been subcontracting to families for part of the labour process, such as drying rice and cart transportation. Considerable handicraft work also was done by a putting-out system in the family home. In 1979 a strengthening of the family economy in North Vietnam and considerable prosperity in the peasant family sector was observed:

> Before the revolution, only a handful of landlord and rich peasant families in each village had tile-roofed brick houses and brick courtyards to dry their rice. Now a very large percentage, and in many areas the overwhelming majority of Vietnamese peasant familes enjoy such living quarters.[6]

Vietnamese peasants owned their houses outright.

NEW MANAGEMENT

In the mid-1970s North Vietnamese officials embarked on yet another programme to solve collective problems through management changes. The direction of the New Management System was to reorganise collectives by centralising power over decision-making in the Management Committee, thereby taking such power away from production brigades which were usually organised by hamlet or neighbourhood. The Management Committee would then control planning, production and distribution through a system of contracts with production brigades or teams.[7]

The campaign for new management took place at a time when there were shortages of goods within the state-controlled distribution sector, low prices for state-collected goods and a thriving free market. The New Management System, however, was a complete failure. Not only did agricultural production decrease, but labour productivity also decreased.[8] The programme was the last hurrah in attempts to socially control the peasant patriarchs through socialist collectivisation and collective management schemes.

The reforms which began in 1979 took a dramatic new direction in legitimising the place of the peasant patriarch in the family economy in agriculture, handicrafts and small-scale industries and services. The socialist sector maintained control of large scale industry, state farms and government administration but control of all small-scale undertakings thereafter was ceded to the family patriarchs through the 'family economy'.

INTEGRATION IN THE INDUSTRIAL SECTOR

In Ho Chi Minh City, formerly Saigon, conditions were very antagonistic to transition following liberation. Saigon was a consumer society living off US-financed imports. Only 20 per cent of the work-force were involved in manufacturing production activies, the rest were in services and trading.[9] The manufacturing production which did exist was mostly made up of enterprises which processed imported goods. A million people were unemployed in the capital at the time of the liberation and one estimate shows that with the disintegration of the former government and army, 3.5 milllion were unemployed in the whole country.[10]

Two programmes were constructed to solve the unemployment problem. The programme for resettlement of people in the countryside has already been mentioned. The government also established manufacturing industries, especially many handicraft cooperatives, producing goods for export.

Socialist transformation of private industry proceeded a lot faster in the South than was expected, partly because so many of the capitalists fled Saigon just before liberation. The State asssumed control of their enterprises. By October 1975, 8000 large and small industrial enterprises had resumed production in Ho Chi Minh City (about 95 per cent of the enterprises) and 5000 of these had been made the responsibility of the Industry Department.[11] The power of the remaining private enterprise owners changed significantly despite the fact that they had not been expropriated. Trade-union power was one of the reasons. The trade unions, which took an active part in the liberation of the cities, also took a strong position in initiating the resumption of production. The changed power relationships between workers and private producers caused by this initiative is evident in the following quotation from a newspaper article:

At 7:00 in the morning of 19 July 1975, a cordial meeting was held at the headquarters of the Liberation Trade Union Federation of Thanh My Tay District between comrades heading the Trade Union

Federation and the owners of the eight principal enterprises in the district ... The Chairman of the Thanh My Trade Union Federation clearly explained to the enterprise owners the revolution's policy of encouraging and assisting the enterprises to resume production of products serving the national economy.[12]

The workers in southern industry met many challenges and used their self-reliance and creativity in order to replace raw materials and machines formerly imported. For example a sewing-machine factory which previously imported all its machine parts started producing 80 per cent of them. Paper mills successfully experimented with domestic bamboo and wood to replace imported paper pulp. Workers at a salad-oil enterprise successfully produced two kinds of artificial butter from vegetable oil in a quantity sufficient to supply enterprises specialising in the production of condensed milk and instant noodles.[13]

As a mechanism for transferring capital from the private to the goverment sector, the government entered into many joint state–private contracts. The joint enterprises were used as a stepping-stone to state control of industry. In one example of such a mechanism, the people's self-management committee in an area of Ho Chi Minh City persuaded the owners of two presses to become a mixed enterprise. The committee appointed a management team consisting of three members of their committee and the two former owners.[14] The former owners continued to be paid for their labour but the state essentially established socialist control through this mechanism.

Whereas the national bourgeoisie in manufacturing were dealt with in this careful manner, the capitalists in wholesale and retail trade (mostly Chinese) were considered 'comprador' bourgeoisie and were expropriated by the state. The wholesalers were given some payment for their stocks, with large payments at first, tapering off to smaller payments.mMany wholesalers collected the first couple of payments and then left Vietnam (the 'Boat People'). On the other hand, the small retailers who were also expropriated had few stocks and received little payment. Some were able to shift to handicraft manufacture but many ended up in street-trading or begging.[15]

The economic impact of expropriation in the trading sector was considerable since the state trading network was not usually established prior to the expropriation. The shut-down of trading networks therefore led to cut-backs in production.

ECONOMIC PLANNING

Material incentives in worker motivation were a major focus in the North after the war years. The introduction of a second five-year plan in 1976 initiated a trend which had a strong focus on 'economic management' including cost accounting and material incentives. Nguyen Nieu wrote in 1975:

> it is necessary to correctly apply the principles of socialist economic management, especially the principle of democratic centralism, the principle of cost accounting and the principle of material incentives.[16]

The party plenums of the early 1970s emphasised the necessity of overcoming the decentralised and 'handicraft' method of management of small-scale industry in order to set up a centralised system capable of managing large-scale socialist production. What was proposed looked very much like a Soviet-style planning system complete with profitability criteria and an extensive reliance on material incentives such as bonuses.

The basic plan for socialist transition in Vietnam has called for three simultaneous revolutions, the revolution in production relations, the technical and scientific revolution and the ideological and cultural revolution. The technical and scientific revolution has been seen as the keystone in industry throughout the present period. The problem with this formulation is that modern management techniques are often seen as 'scientific' rather than methods which are reflections of the social system, the relations of production and the ideologies which spawned them (capitalism). In the period 1975–6, such factors as cost accounting and operating enterprises at a profit were heavily stressed.[17] Economic methods in planning semed to be synonymous with material incentives, beginning in this period.

At this time, also, the strengthening of labour discipline was stressed and management control was strengthened. Complaints about labour and suggestions for changes read like endorsements of the principles of scientific management. According to a resolution of the 22nd plenum of the Party:

> We must heighten labour discipline, closely manage labour in accordance with work norms, manage work by grasping norms, have timely and accurate rewards for people with a large number of work days and work hours.[18]

This statement looks like material from a bourgeois management textbook on strict management control of the work process rather than a socialist government statement about worker discipline! Principles of scientific management became 'science' in Vietnam rather than being seen as a change in relations of production.

In retrospect, the second five-year plan (1976–80)was wildly optimistic. The first five-year plan (1961–5), carried out before the Second Indochina War affected the North, had been largely sucessful and this gave the northern planners false promise. The North had attained self-sufficiency in agriculture in the late 1950s and, with the help of both the Soviet Union and China, industrial development proceeded rapidly. A decade later, after the war with the USA, conditions were different. The economy could not sustain the developmental focus on large-scale industry. Integration with the South did not go smoothly in either the manufacturing, trade or agricultural sectors. The world-wide energy crisis made oil imports extremely expensive, therefore hampering both industrial and agricultural growth. The final blow to the plan was the cessation of Chinese aid and the war with China.

VIETNAMESE ALLIES AND ENEMIES

Chinese Communism has profoundly influenced the Vietnamese both historically and in the contemporary period. While Vietnam's top leaders, Ho Chi Minh and Le Duan, have been pro-Soviet and somewhat critical of the Chinese even before the present period, other important leaders, like Truong Chinh, have been profoundly influenced by Chinese Communist ideology. The Vietnamese land reforms and their collectivisation process were a lot more like the Chinese than the Soviet model. Reliance on the peasantry for the main support of revolutionary movements and the use of guerilla tactics can also be traced to Maoist Chinese influence.

On the other hand, the Vietnamese have always been wary of the Chinese because of a history of political and economic dominance and threat of dominance by the Chinese. Although the Vietnamese nation was never subsumed by China, the threat of the Vietnamese losing their national identity was real enough to have a permanent impact on relations between Vietnam and China.

The Vietnamese see themselves as more pragmatic than the Chinese. They view the periods of the 'great leap forward' and the 'cultural revolution' in China as idealistic forays away from a practical development path. The Soviet Union, on the other hand, is a developed country which has achieved that status by taking a more stable path. These ideological and pragmatic concerns combined with the fact that the Soviet Union is at some geographical distance, made the Soviet Union a more appealing ally when a choice had to be made.

During the war with the USA, Vietnam did not have to make a choice of alliances and she received considerable help from both the Chinese and the Soviets. The Chinese contributed half a million tonnes of rice a year and in addition there were many developmental and military contributions. The Chinese claim to have given the Vietnamese 20 billion dollars worth of aid.[19]

The Vietnamese antagonism toward their former allies, which eventually led to complete breakdown, stems mostly from some foreign policy moves on the part of the Chinese. There were old wounds such as the fact that, at the Geneva talks in 1954, China had pressured Vietnam to accept a boundary which was 350 miles further north than the one that the Vietnamese wanted. The really crucial event for the Vietnamese, however, was that China had asked President Nixon to visit China in 1972, when Vietnam was still fighting the USA in the South. The *rapprochement* between China and the USA was seen as a betrayal of the Vietnamese revolution and Vietnamese–Chinese relations started down a dangerous descending path in the aftermath of that event. The Vietnamese even started to question the loyalty of the ethnic Chinese in their own party. During the Christmas bombing by the USA in 1972, at least one ethnic Chinese –Tai Niu Sieu – and possibly more, were purged from the Vietnamese Workers' Party.[20]

The actual break in the deteriorating relations with China did not come until six years later and it was over an alliance between China and the Stalinist Pol Pot in Cambodia. This alliance was seen as an encirclement of Vietnam and an act which meant grave danger to Vietnamese national security. There were a number of border incidents which concerned the Vietnamese and in December 1978 there was a larger-scale attack by Pol Pot's forces. There were also substantiated reports of wanton killing of between one and two million Cambodians by Pol Pot. A number of Khmer Rouge wanted to break with Pol Pot and ally with the Vietnamese because of the slaughter. The Vietnamese saw the opportunity to depose a hated regime and help to set up a government more friendly to their own interests when they carried out their invasion of Cambodia in January 1979 (see **Table** 11.2).

Table 11.2 Chronology of events leading to the Vietnam–China War

Event	Date
Nixon's China visit	1972
Vietnam abolishes capitalist (Chinese) trading in the South	March 1978
Rich Chinese leave South	March–April 1978
China encourages northern ethnic Chinese to cross border	May 1978
China cancels aid contracts in Vietnam	July 1978
Pol Pot launches an attack on parts of southern Vietnam	December 1978
Vietnam attacks Cambodia	January 1979
China attacks Vietnam	March 1979

Conflicts within Vietnam, between the Vietnamese and Chinese ethnic groups also heightened the Vietnam–China Conflict. In March 1968, the Vietnamese abolished capitalist trading in the South. Many Chinese ethnic Vietnamese, called *Hoa*, were involved in this trading. For a cash payment, many southern *Hoa* boarded boats going to Taiwan, Hong Kong, and Singapore in the next couple of months. China then became active in organising among the *Hoa* in northern Vietnam, encouraging them to move across the border to China. The Chinese were accusing the Vietnamese of discrimination against their Chinese minority. At that time, May 1978, the Vietnamese tried to dissuade the northern *Hoa* from leaving. Later, however, after the Chinese invasion of Vietnam in March 1969, the Vietnamese actually encouraged a renewed *Hoa* exodus from northern Vietnam.

Vietnamese leaders must have know what some of the results of their decision to invade Cambodia would be, but it is hard to imagine that they accurately assessed the total cost.[21] They had already lost Chinese aid and the Western response to the Cambodian invasion cost them Western aid as well. Perhaps as much as a decade of development was lost to a poor country which had just experienced over three decades of almost uninterrupted war. The loss of more than $300 million a year from China and $200 million from the West does not nearly assess the real damage. Western explorations for oil in the South China Sea were discontinued and Vietnam's Soviet allies did not have the technology for deep enough drilling. (Oil production was only recently begun in late 1986, after a costly decade of delay.) Vietnam lost precious foreign reserves in order to import costly fuel, when oil lay beneath her territorial waters, if only she could reach it!

The human cost of the war with China in Cambodia has been staggering for the Vietnamese. In 1979, during a period of decreasing food allotments per capita and poor crop yields, the European Economic Community suspended shipments of powdered milk to Vietnam. The USA then rejected licensing requests from American relief agencies which wanted to send food aid to Vietnam. In 1981, when typhoons destroyed 2.5 million tonnes of rice and the FAO requested international donations, the European Economic Community, Japan and the USA all refused. In that year, malnutrition among urban children was measured at 38 per cent and the situation was probably worse in parts of the countryside.[22]

Another developmental setback occurred as a result of the Chinese invasion of Vietnam in March 1979. A phosphate fertiliser plant was destroyed. Six years later, the plant had still not recovered its full capacity.

Vietnam's disastrous economic situation and her isolated trade and aid situation caused her to default on foreign debt of approximately $4.6 billion in 1982. That situation was renegotiated, but Vietnam was without international financing for even urgent projects and countries have shied away from contracts with Vietnam, given her default status.[23]

This picture puts into some perspective Vietnam's close alliance with and dependence on the Soviet Union in the contemporary period. The Vietnamese have had considerable admiration for Soviet ideology, and the Soviet development model, as compared with the Chinese model. In the 1950s, 1960s, and 1970s, however, Vietnam supported non-alignment and independent socialism. In the 1980s, however, she is very economically dependent on the Soviet Union and the Soviets have been providing Vietnam with approximately $1 billion of aid a year. In return, Vietnam has been exporting fruits, rubber and light manufactured goods to the Soviet Union at very low negotiated prices. The most important *quid pro quo*, however, for the Soviet Union, is the use of Vietnamese bases at Da Nang and Cam Ran Bay for their Pacific fleet. Vietnam's dependent position will only change when there is movement in the Cambodian situation and more normal ties with other countries are possible.

REFORMS

By the time of the meeting of the Sixth Plenum of the Vietnamese Communist Party in 1979, both the industrial and agricultural sectors of the Vietnamese economy were in poor condition. The Party decided on changes in the direction of encouraging groups (cooperatives) and individuals to set up small factories and handicraft workshops to produce goods for consumption in Vietnam and for export. By resolutions of the Sixth Plenum, both the collective and private family economic sectors were encouraged to grow. The idea was that the production of more consumer goods in handicraft industries could be offered to the peasants and would, in turn, spur agricultural development and help to solve the food shortage.

The Sixth Plenum criticised the too-zealous officials who had moved too quickly in the South to set up institutions resembling those already established in the North, without considering developmental effects. They decided that it was a shortcoming to carry on transformation to socialist forms without linking these transformations to construction:

> The desire to eliminate right away the non-socialist economic components and to carry on transformation without linking it with construction has to some extent affected the development of production and consolidation of the new production relationships.[24]

In the future the desirability of socialist transformation would be measured by its developmental effects on labour productivity, standard of living and total production.

The Sixth Plenum found it an 'objective necessity' to allow the individual economic sector (family economy) and some national bourgeois elements to do business or productive work in a number of sectors. The state-operated economic sector would continue to play the leading role, but some national bourgeois elements would continue to be accepted in manufacturing in the South. The family economy and cooperative elements would be especially important for the coming period.

There was also a redirection of power relations between cooperative and neighbourhood and family economy elements. The New Management System in agriculture was negated and power was put back in the hands of production brigades (by hamlet or neighbourhood). Consolidation of control of production in the hands of cooperatives would not be a goal for the next period. Subcontracting to individual family patriarchs, which had been practised in the village anyway, was legitimised.

Since the new economic guideline of the Sixth Plenum was instituted, families have been encouraged to raise their own buffalo and cattle (renting them out to the cooperative) and even to farm any land that the cooperative leaves fallow. This ruling and others since the Sixth Plenum allow the cooperatives of the South to remain below the 'high' level of collectivisation established in the north where the animals were the property of the collective and most work was collectivised.

The price structure was also adjusted over the next few years. State prices were allowed to rise as they were reconciled to private market prices. The *dong* was devalued, in international markets, in order to improve Vietnam's export situation. Meanwhile, internal prices rose quickly in the cities as state prices were adapted to economic realities. Civil service and other urban workers paid a heavy price for these readjustments. Their cost of living rose quickly in relation to their incomes and many civil servants and cadres fell into abject poverty. The policy favoured the agricultural sector, however, and these price changes produced renewed efforts to increase production and productivity in the peasant family economy and in the collectives.

In 1980 and 1981 reforms went even further when a contract system was initiated. Agricultural contracts were tried, on an experimental basis, in 1976 and 1977 in Vinh Phu Province. In the urban context, Vo Van Kiet, party leader in Ho Chi Minh City (1977–81) initiated and experimented with contracts. Kiet wanted a specific southern direction to economic development. He argued for public/private ventures, greater reliance on the market, and contracts.

In 1980 and 1981, the Final Product Contract Quota System replaced the work or labour contract in Vietnamese agriculture. Formerly, as we have seen, cooperative members were paid according to work points accumulated during the planting and harvesting seasons. Under the new system, the cooperative makes a contract for the delivery of final products with groups of farmers or individual farmers. The cooperatives see to the supply of water, seed and fertiliser and the producers agree to fulfil or overfulfil their production quota, in terms of rice paddy, and they keep the rest for their own consumption or private market trading.[25]

As part of the attempt to attain self-sufficiency in agricultural production and improve food rations per capita, the government also embarked on a population programme which includes target rates of population increase and renewed population redistribution programmes. Vietnam has a population of 60 million people, which is currently growing at a rate of 2.2 per cent per year. The target rate of growth for 1985 was 1.7 per cent and Vientam would like to approach the developed countries' low rate of less than 1 per cent.[26] The population-control method that Vietnam is using is to set a target of only two children per family – less restrictive than the Chinese one-child family – and to encourage birth-control programmes. Emphasis on public employees setting an example on population control is particularly strong. In 1984, 75 per cent of public employees had signed up for family-planning programmes. By 1984, about 33 per cent of all women of child-bearing age were regular users of contraceptives.[27]

Population migrations in Vietnam have occurred from cities to rural areas in the South and from the overpopulated North to southern New Economic Zones. Over 500 000 northerners have gone south to the New Economic Zones, while others in the crowded northern provinces have built New Economic Zones in the hills. These new settlements concentrate on the production of secondary agricultural products and agricultural products for industrial use. The New Economic Zones became so popular in the early 1980s that chief planner Kiet announced that the five-year plan of 'redistributing' 300 000 of the population, had been met in four years.[28]

In line with the new direction in economic reform, the third five-year plan (1981–5) emphasised Soviet-style pragmatic planning, promoting consumer goods and agriculture as opposed to heavy industry. The fervour over the war with China coupled with the failure of northern-style collectivisation methods in the South, meant that Maoist-type thinking within the Vietnamese Communist Party was criticised and the failure of the unrealistic second plan was blamed on these elements. With the promotion of Vo Van Kiet, from his position in Ho Chi Minh City, to chief planner, a pro-market, anti-centralisation direction was taken in the plan. A considerable amount of liberalism, as regards private entrepreneurship, was allowed for in the Southern Region. Mixed state/private enterprises and private small-scale enterprises were continued in this region. Increased production of consumer goods was promoted in order to act as incentives for increased agricultural production in general, and southern agricultural production in particular.

Except for some large-scale dam projects which will increase electrical output and increase possibilities for irrigation, by the third plan investments in heavy industry had ceased to be emphasised. Small-scale industry and handicrafts increased production during the third plan but, interestingly, not as quickly as state-produced consumer goods. In the first three years of the plan, production of paper increased by 27 per cent, of silk cloth by 33 per cent and of bicycles by 66 per cent.[29]

Without Chinese aid, and with the cessation of economic aid from the Western powers after the Cambodian invasion, Vietnam has relied heavily on the Soviet bloc for industrial and technological advancement during the third five-year plan. In addition to the hydroelectric projects already mentioned, the Soviet Union has been constructing machine-tool and phosphate-fertiliser plants. Important imports from the Soviet Union in the early-to mid 1980s have included metals and oil as well as food and fertiliser.[30]

Even pre-dating the recent dynamic changes coming with the Sixth Party Congress in December 1986, there were further significant economic changes in the winds. Resolutions over the past several years have called for decentralisation in economic planning and the elimination of state subsidies. In an attempt to eliminate bureaucracy and encourage efficiency in all the enterprises and cooperatives in Vietnam, the government attempted to push decision-making down to the basic level. They wanted all the units to be cost-efficient and work toward producing a surplus without relying on subsidies from above. Although these new policies influenced some of the planning apparatus and some production units became more efficient, most of the economy remained strongly centralised and bureaucratic.[31]

The currency reform of 1985 was an attempt to devalue the *dong* in order to solve the problem of rapidly rising inflation. The leadership's attempt to devalue, however, made matters even worse for the urban sector. There were rumours preceding the change which caused a run on the market for goods. This was followed by hoarding and speculation when the change occurred. There was an attempt, in this same period, to eliminate the rationing of basic goods to state employes at low prices. The employees were given a wage increase to compensate for their loss in rations, but price increases on the private market soon outran their wage increases. The wage increases and price increases on the private market encouraged a renewed round of inflation. Early in 1986, limited rationing in major cities was re-established in order to discourage inflation, but price increases remained out of hand. Some officials estimated price increases in 1986 at 700 per cent.[32]

In the economic atmosphere of rising costs of living, it is not surprising that many government workers and cadres have developed side-line occupations in order to make ends meet. It is also not too surprising that corruption and lack of attention to duty have characterised many officials. The events of 1986 are partly the result of the contradictions that have developed as a result of economic policies and other problems with the economy. In 1985, a year of criticism and self-criticism was declared in preparation for the Sixth Party Congress. The Sixth Party Congress decided to change the top-level leadership of the country and many who had been responsible for, and supportive of, the types of dynamic programmes developed in the South were promoted to the highest levels of office.

The year of self-criticism forced changes to bureaucratic attitudes on the part of cadres and government officials and corruption was also tackled. There were meetings in cooperatives and state enterprises throughout the country and the feedback of workers and cooperative members was written down. Many changes and replacements were brought on by the process. The newspapers, especially *Saigon Giai Phong*, were very active in the campaign. The *Saigon Giai Phong* received 2540 letters and printed 235 of them.[33] The officials in cities were often criticised for their overbearing attitudes and for stealing state goods. As an example of criticism in the countryside, in one village reporters interviewed the secretary of the cooperative, who was an old war veteran, and the chairman. The secretary was criticised for his lack of leadership ability, his neglect of the village and for not observing the planned parenthood plan. He was 56 years old and he had six children, the youngest of whom was 2 years old! But this was the 'good official' example since he had agreed to retire and let younger people have their chance. The chairman, on the other hand, had no intention of resigning. He was accused of not working and being drunk and of being arrogant toward the people. He was also criticised because his family had not entered the cooperative and because he favoured his own family in opportunities for selling local specialty crops.[34]

The criticism and self-criticism campaign was also geared toward taking stock of the social and economic spheres and making changes. The criticisms coming from the villages mentioned shortages of insecticides and fertilisers and the problem of these supplies often arriving late. In the cities, there were problems with lack of autonomy. For example, in Ho Chi Minh City, one observer pointed out that in one joint enterprise, raw materials are supplied to each of the individual enterprises and they merely deliver the finished products. The director of these enterprises actually acts merely as a shop foreman.[35]

In preparing for the Sixth Party Congress, the Party reassessed the economic situation and decided to initiate reforms in the direction of decentralisation and autonomy for the enterprises which would be more effective than previous attempts. They decided to 'dismantle the management mechanism based on bureaucratic centralism and state subsidies and institute economic accounting and socialist business practices'. They have been quite frank in criticising their recent reforms for not going far enough and not being comprehensive enough. This time, they intend to work toward 'thoroughly revamping the whole of the country's economic management'.[36]

The new plan calls for each enterprise to be responsible only to the agency directly above it and to formulate their plan independently. Enterprises will have the authority to open additional sources of supplies and markets for their products through export–import contracts that comply with state law. Although the state will continue to set prices for primary materials, the enterprise may formulate their own price plan within the scope of prices established by the state. The enterprise may also, on its own initiative, decide the technical plans pertaining to production and products and they can perform their own research. They are allowed to retain the additional profits accruing from the application of scientific and technical advances for a period of several years.[37]

It is not too surprising, given this plan for sweeping change, that the 'old guard' leadership decided to retire and that new people took their place at the Sixth Party Congress in December 1986. Truong Chinh, Secretary General since Le Duan died six months before, retired, as did Pham Van Dong and Le Duc Tho. The new leaders, Nguyen Van Linh, Pham Hung, and Vo Chi Cong, all favour economic reform and they will now have a chance to carry out thoroughgoing reform. General Secretary Nguyen Van Linh formerly presided over many of the economic reforms in the South, and Vo Van Kiet, already the chief planner, has also moved up in the party ranks.

SUCCESSES AND PROBLEMS

In a broad sense, the Vietnamese reforms have been successful in doing what the policy-makers were hoping. Production of staples increased steadily from 15.1 million tonnes in 1981 to 18.2 million tonnes in 1985. Food rations per capita are more reasonable now, at last reaching the wartime levels achieved when foreign donations made up a substantial part of rations, but a large percentage of children – estimates vary from 25 to 70 per cent – are still malnourished because of growing up in a period of extreme food shortage.[38]

With the new system of contracts and local control, there has also been much more progress in collectivisation in the southern region. Over 80 per cent of peasants are in mutual aid teams and well over half have now joined production cooperatives. In 1983 and 1984, land was redistributed to families with little or no land in regions where rich and middle-peasant interests formerly stood in the way of redistribution.

The third five-year plan was very successful, when compared with the disastrous second five-year plan. As Table 11.3 shows, industrial output grew very rapidly, averaging an increase of 13.6 per cent per year. This increase was clearly the result of reform policies, since there were slightly less average capital investments in the third plan than the second plan. National income grew at almost three (2.72) times the rate of the second plan![39]

Table 11.3   Main indices of SRV economic development

	Average Annual Increase (%)	
	Second Five-Year Plan (1976–80)	Third Five-Year Plan (1981–5)
Index		
Produced national income	2.5	6.8
Gross industrial production	2.5	13.6
Gross agricultural production	3.6	4.9
Volume of capital investments	9.7	8.4

Source: *Ekonomicheskaya Gazeta*, no. 28, July 1986, p. 20. JPRS, SEA-86-155, p. 91.

Private trading has expanded rapidly since the 1979 reforms, but marketing cooperatives have also increased. There are now more than 2 000 such cooperatives in the Southern Region, and the state continues to push for further increases. Most of these cooperatives, however, sell state products and do not purchase local products, which are sold through the private market.[40]

In Ho Chi Minh City small industry and handicrafts have increased at a very rapid rate in the years since the 1979 reforms. In 1985 this sector contributed 47 per cent of the value of the city's industrial output.[41] Since export producers in this region have been allowed to use foreign-exchange earnings to purchase their own imports, exports have increased dramatically and they have exceeded planned targets.

The new smaller industries often have close ties to the areas of dynamic change in the countryside. In the Mekong Delta, subsidiary food crops and short-term industrial crops like pineapple, sugar cane, soya beans and shrimp have been developed for export. In the eastern part of the southern region, coffee, rubber, groundnuts, soya beans and cashews have been developed. Small industries, like machine shops, rice mills and building materials have also increased throughout the countryside. In short, the south has been an area of considerable dynamic economic change and economic development.[42]

Meanwhile, the reforms have also lead to a breakdown of cooperation at the village and production brigade level. Family labour has increased and cooperative labour has decreased. Many seed-breeding, seed-selection, tilling and manuring teams have been dissolved. Public works have not been kept up, as before because private family labour is better renumerated than is collective labour.[43] Patriarchs have overworked both their families and their draught animals in efforts to increase production and their own private well-being. In one hamlet over a third of the draught animals died as a result of the production push.[44]

Particularly depressing, considering the incredible price which Vietnam paid to choose socialism over capitalism, market reforms have led to some of the same injustices and flagrant abnegations of collective welfare experienced under the previous system. There have evidently been renewed quarrels between families over water rights, as families impatiently drain water into their own fields when it is needed in the fields of others. Some families, meanwhile, are trapped in indebtedness when they lack able-bodied-labour power. Family patriarchs with a surplus make interest-bearing loans, and cooperatives sometimes also charge interest on unfulfilled contract quotas. The process of debt entrapment in the present era is illustrated by a recent story in the *Nhan Dan* newspaper letters column:

> The Tich Giang Cooperative in Phuc Tho District is also collecting interest on the balance of the paddy that cooperative members must deliver to meet their product contract quotas. One family has been

in debt from one season to the next for several years now because it is short of help and has been unable to deliver all the paddy required under its contract. The paddy harvested is only enough to pay the annual interest charge to the cooperative. After harvesting their crops, they have no paddy left for themselves.[45]

Some of these problems became clearer during the recent discussions in villages around the nation in preparation for the national Sixth Party Congress. In Nam Ha village, for example, one of the issues raised was the lack of appropriate and timely investments, like fertiliser and insecticides. Another problem was the increase in inequalities in the countryside. Some families had a surplus of paddy while others were short of food. Those who were well off became so through 'labour, intensive cultivation and capital from a variety of sources'. Those who did poorly, did so because of 'shortages of labour, substandard farm work techniques, lack of knowledge of methods, and a lack of abilities appropriate to the new system'.[46]

CONCLUSIONS

Southern Differences

With a very different historical experience from the North in the past century and a half of capitalist penetration and social revolution, the southern part of Vietnam developed a stronger worker-oriented politics and a more mass-based mode of struggle. In the North, the influence of middle and rich peasants on the overall political direction has been stronger and the political struggle has been more closely directed by a vanguard party. Because of the patriarchal family-based production system, this party has had little permanent success in controlling the more well-to-do peasant classes.

The Northern section of the country had more experience in socialist transformation than the South and it was in a stronger position, politically and economically, at the end of the war with the USA. For these reasons, northern institutions were initially extended to the South. Southern deviations from these institutions were seen as the result of the impact of imperialist culture in the South. Little attention was paid to the greater participation of peasant and worker masses and women in the southern struggle and southern cadres were initially not able to attain positions of power and influence in the party or the government. Partly as a result, mistakes were made in the southern transition, particularly in trying to collectivise peasants too quickly without showing them concrete advantages, and in moving too quickly with the expropriation in the trading sector. More importantly, in terms of long-run issues of social change, the bias of the Party in reinforcing the patriarchal peasant family has been a regressive policy especially for the South, where economic forces had partially disintegrated the partriarchal peasant family economy.

While people in the Central Lowlands responded well to northern programmes and policies, the southern region has been an anathema to policy-makers in Hanoi. The 1979 reforms helped to encourage southern peasants to participate in the market, but the party realised that it must go further. The current attack on bureaucracy and decision-making from the top down in management comes closer to what the southerners want. This direction has encouraged them to participate more fully in a national direction. It seems that very recently the party leaders may really have begun to tap into the democratic, mass activism from the bottom up, that the National Liberation Front cadres generated during the war.

The Vietnamese have linked bureaucratism in their administration and their party structures with mandarin influences from an earlier time. In fact, the Vietnamese word for bureaucracy is derived from the word for mandarin. The arrogance of some party officials has been under attack since the Communist Party's Fifty Party Congress. Le Duc Tho criticised the tendency in certain localities to grant party membership only to 'yes-men' as a way of preserving their power.[47] As we have seen, the Vietnamese are currently (1987) struggling against their management structures being heavily bureaucratic and interventionist. This is now considered the major factor holding back the use of science and technology in promoting economic development in Vietnam.

It is difficult to determine how far the new participatory direction of openness in the press will go in Vietnam. A recent editorial in southern Vietnam's *Saigon Giai Phong* explains how the Municipal Party Committee in Ho Chi Minh City adopted the policy of carrying out open self-criticism and criticism in the press throughout the Party Congress period. The editors criticised the administrative–bureaucratic journalism of the past and opted for open criticism. Although there was some evidence of retaliation for criticisms in all sections of Vietnam, as a result of the criticism and self-criticism campaign, this phenomenon does not seem to have been greater in the Ho Chi Minh City area, where criticisms have been very candid.[48]

There seem to be two continuing obstacles to the Communist Party's success in fighting arrogance in bureaucracy and lack of democracy: vanguardism and patriarchy. The first, vanguardism, is the hierarchical structure which depends on initiatives from the Party apparatus in promoting change. The Party is seen as the dynamic element and the mass organisations in the Front are seen only as the coordinators in development policies. Not until the masses and their organisations have a stronger role in actual conception of policies, are the policies likely to be stronger in implementation. Recent changes may reflect this realisation.

Accommodating the Patriarchs

The other limiting problem for Vietnamese policy-makers is the lack of Vietnamese analysis of the patriarchy and the role of the patriarchy in limiting socialist development. Like the 'middle peasant' problem of an earlier period, the problems of management and bureaucracy now may actually be a foil which prevents socialists from seeing the *real* problem as one in which patriarchial interests predominate.

The interests of the family patriarchs have subverted the collective process not only in agriculture, but also in industrial collectives and to some extent in the democratic centralist process in the Party policies and state administration. Patriarchal interests are so established that they interact with, interconnect with, and support socialism as well as subverting ultimate socialist goals. The patriarchal system is so entrenched as to be invisible to many practitioners of Vietnamese socialism. A recent article in *Doc Lap* points out that most of the 1100 production teams in industrial and handicraft collectives in Hanoi are not run by collective, but instead by family, i.e. patriarchal, processes. These teams average approximately fourteen members each and they are supposed to be operating according to collective regulations but only about 10 per cent are actually operating correctly. Most team chiefs have a boss–worker relationship with a number of temporary or casual workers and family members. 'One learns only on inspection that the team chief is the father and the team members are the son, son-in-law, daughter-in-law and wife.[49]

The writer is very clear that the family nature of the relationship is antithetical to socialist principles and that family is synonymous with dominance by the father (which we have termed patriarchy):

> Due to the family nature, power is concentrated in the hands of the team chief and there is no discussion. So, the team chief can do as he

pleases and, because of profits, can spend money to sway cadres, bend economic contracts, even financial principles.[50]

Most of the production from these teams goes to private markets and much goes to the black market. Still, the author does not suggest disbanding the teams. He points out the need for consumer goods and employment in Hanoi and hopes, rather furtively, that the majority of teams that are socially incorrect (60 per cent), and those that are partially incorrect (another 30 per cent) can be brought up to standard.

Another area where the patriarchy affects the socialist sector is in the area of family influence in the state and party administrations. The extent of family influence on promotions is hard to measure, particularly from outside Vietnam, but its existence is so prevalent that Vietnamese fiction has tackled the issue by portraying an enterprise administrator who promotes members of this own family above others.[51]

Despite these ways in which the patriarchy has subverted socialist goals, it is clear that an accommodation has been struck between patriarchy and socialism with Vietnam's reform policy of the past eight years (1979–87). The interconnected forces of patriarchy and socialism are working together. In the agricultural collectives, family economies are producing vegetables, fruits, meat, fish and clothing and simple handicrafts and the collective is providing most subsistence goods. In the collective sector, either family patriarchs or production brigades are responsible for certain amounts of collective land where subsistence crops are grown. The patriarchal system of production now predominates even on collective land in most areas. The accommodation between socialism and patriarchy, interestingly enough, is very similar to the accommodation which the emperors made with peasant patriarchs in the pre-French era. This seems like a more stable condition than the one which was attempted in the 1960s revolutionary village (Chapter 8). Of course, both situations were vastly more stable than the past colonial Southern village (Chapter 6) where friction, inequality and stagnation were predominant.

It seems that women are the major losers from the socialist leaders' accommodation with a patriarchal system of production in agriculture and small-scale industry. In the North the revolutionary system described in Chapter 8, was patriarchal also and it was much too contradictory to operate smoothly. Accommodating to patriarchy in the South is a different matter. Women have lost influence with the imposition of northern political institutions and production systems. As we have seen, women held important positions in the National

Liberation Front and the People's Liberation Army. The fact that Nguyen Thi Binh, who was Foreign Minister for the NLF, is now Minister in charge of Elementary and Secondary Education, and Nguyen Thi Dinh, Assistant Commander of the People's Liberation Armed Forces, is now head of the Women's Union, is symptomatic. The Vietnamese Communist Party is the dominant political organisation in reunified Vietnam. There are no women members of the *Politburo* and there are only four women on the 116-member Central Committee.[52] Women have lost a considerable amount of political power in the South and millions of ordinary peasant women are caught in a reinstituted system of patriarchal peasant production at the village level.

Women started having more children throughout Vietnam when the men came home after the war. Because of the Vietnamese attitude, which is reflected in the Party, that women should carry out most household responsibilities, women's public positions have decreased in the northern and central regions, as well as in the South. Nguyen Thi Dinh has complained that slogans like 'The New Woman Builds and Defends the Fatherland' discourages women from joining the Women's Union. Women's incredible responsibilities and trying schedules make more admonitions and request for greater efforts fruitless and counterproductive.[53]

The people who actually do most of the work under the family contract system are women. They do the planting out, weeding, and most of the harvesting and threshing. Men contribute only 40 per cent to agricultural production because many are away in military service fighting the war on two fronts (Cambodia and the border with China), or they have jobs in the cities. Since they are responsible for the last stages of the production cycle, women are often considered at fault when contracts are not filled. Meanwhile, state and village officials, who are usually men, have often not kept their end of the bargain by providing adequately for the five tasks: soil preparation, stocking seed, fertilising, watering and applying insecticides. Thien Thanh asks who is going to be responsible for changing this situation:

> If the women who do contracted work are a catty of rice short they are punished, but the production unit heads, the management boards, and the cooperative directors allow water buffaloes to die and seedstock to be in short supply, and do not ensure that the five tasks are carried out, but are still as insensitive as earthenware jars.[54]

Given that women are doing most of the work, we might think that women would be taking on more leadership posts in agricultural cooperatives, but the reverse seems to be true. Some officials from Women's Union have given an interesting justification for this. In the countryside:

> especially village chairmen and heads of cooperatives, must be able to do very hard physical work, to confront problems such as severe storms and mobilize the people in these emergencies. It is better for men to do jobs like that.[55]

This is an interesting argument, given that Vietnamese studies have shown that production has generally exceeded the norm in cooperatives with women leaders.[56]

Women have been pushed in every way, including being pushed by the Women's Union, to work harder on the family economy and improve their production. There is a 'women's animal husbandry movement' and the Thien Giang Provincial Women's Association reports the launching of a movement to develop the family economy by switching to higher-value crops and export crops and increasing kitchen gardens.[57]

Women's workload cannot continue to increase indefinitely without there being other resulting social strains. Nguyen This Dinh, head of the Women's Union, reports an increase in the number of violations of law stemming from family friction.[58] Children's nutrition is also a problem, despite the increases in agricultural production in recent years. 80 per cent of the children suffering from malnutrition in Vietnam are in the 1–3-year-old group. One important reason for this seems to be the early-weaning practices of contemporary Vietnamese women resulting from their huge workloads, and the lack of sufficient nutritional value in the traditional weaning food, thin rice gruel.[59]

On the other hand, Nguyen Thi Dinh has made a very strong statement in the official journal of the party in preparation for the Sixth Party Congress. She mentioned that the directives and resolutions of the party and policies of the state concerning women's issues have not been well implemented during the past ten years and more. She believes that there must be organisations directly responsible for researching the status and position of women in society, for proposing policies for each period and supervising and inspecting the implementation of these policies. She believes that the party's leadership of the women's movement is a matter of strategic importance to the country's revolution.[60] It remains to be seen whether her male comrades will listen to her.

What about the socialist goals of equality between the classes and between men and women? The Vietnamese have been saying that their transition to socialism is going to be slower than originally expected. When the technological and scientific revolution is completed, when mechanisation has replaced intensive labour in agriculture, the wage labour form will presumably return to southern agriculture and 'pre-capitalist' and 'pre-socialist' peasant economies will be defeated all over the country.

The contrast in the experience of the two parts of Vietnam bring into focus several important issues concerned with socialist transformation. In the case of Vietnam, the region of greater capitalist penetration developed socialist politics with a stronger working-class and less peasant-oriented bias and a greater mass character to the revolutionary struggle. The part of Vietnam which retained more aspects of the traditional, non-capitalist, mode of production, based on the peasant patriarchy, developed politics which were more centralist. The politics of this region moved in the direction of supporting a modernised (non-feudal) version of the patriarchal peasant family as a very strong, and perhaps very limiting, institution in contemporary Vietnam. The Vietnamese case leads us to question the progressiveness of peasant-based revolution in areas where the peasantry has not undergone massive transformation through the impact of capitalist markets.

Afterword

In late 1987, and after I had completed the manuscript for this book, the United Nations asked me to travel to Vietnam for an evaluation and appraisal mission for the World Food Programme (WFP) there. My specific responsibilities involved interviews of village women about their work on irrigation projects sponsored by the WFP and how this work influenced their family responsibilities. This assignment was part of an emphasis that the United Nations agencies have been putting on women in development issues. The concern is that development projects often affect women differently from men and that United Nations funded projects should be careful about possible negative impacts on women.

After interviewing forty-three women peasants and talking to twenty women from the Women's Union in six districts and four provinces in the Central Lowlands and the Red River Delta, I became convinced that the irrigation projects which paid workers in kind were very progressive. The mostly women workers worked harder in these projects, but they were compensated significantly better than they were for their family or collective work. The projects also changed the long-run prospects for villagers in the areas affected by the dams, canals and dikes that were built.

After the Soviet Union the United Nations is the most significant donor for development projects in Vietnam. If the three irrigation projects which I saw in Vietnam are typical of United Nations efforts, and I have no reason to question this assumption, then multilateral aid is having a positive impact on the poorest of people in this poor country. The contrast between these projects and US Agency for International Development projects which I observed in Vietnam fifteen years before was startling. The poorest of the peasants in the most vulnerable areas for typhoons and flooding were affected by these World Food Programme projects. On the other hand, in that earlier period the richest of villagers owned the new breeds of hogs and chickens brought to Vietnam by the Americans.

The better design of the modern international projects, which are linked to permanent improvements in the country's own food supply, is part of the difference between the two types of projects. The nature of international, as opposed to bilateral, aid is another factor. For every somewhat imperious international adviser, there are other more down-to-earth advisers who communicate with locals in the process of carrying out the development projects.

A comparison of internationally financed projects with development projects sponsored by the Soviets was not possible on this trip. The impression was that Soviet aid more often goes to larger projects, like hydroelectric projects, which are less visible to ordinary people. I also have the impression that this is a conscious policy choice of the Soviets. Given the nationalism of the Vietnamese, they do not want to make the mistakes that some powerful nations have made in the past by intervening in Vietnamese politics on the local level.

Of course, it is significant that Vietnam is a socialist country receiving the aid. The careful administration of the project relies on the administrative ability of local government officials. The international organisations require record-keeping that is so comprehensive and detailed that the process might be overwhelming for a country not geared to administrative controls and central planning. The one really significant problem that our mission ran into was one of local officials proceeding with a project which the central government was seeking outside aid to start. Such embarrassing problems might be even more frequent in a less centrally administered economy. The history and tradition of government involvement in irrigation projects in the Vietnamese case also certainly helps.

Impressions I had gained from reading the literature, that women's position in the northern village is still very much a product of patriarchal control, was, unfortunately, verified by my interviews with women in the villages. Patrilocal residence and the mother-in-law system are still very much intact in the villages. There are sometimes women leaders who are politically very active in the countryside, but usually they are single women or widows. Married women I talked with in the 25–40 group had an average of four children and women in the over-40 group had an average of five children. They were very much tied down by family responsibilities and very much tied to their husbands' families. When I asked where they lived after marriage, they thought that was a very strange question. The response was: 'With our in-laws, of course, where else would we live?'

Women in the cities, on the other hand, seem to have fewer children, and patrilocal residence does not seem to be the rule. The situation of families in the cities has been financially very difficult in the current period because of rising costs for basic foodstuffs but it is in the urban areas where women are moving past patriarchal family constraints.

The other area of hope for women in the countryside is that party officials seemed to be very aware of some of the contradictions of the present policy with regard to the 'family economy'. One male commune official called the situation a 'vicious cycle' of poverty because families with more children are given larger plots to farm, and this encourages more population growth. Although people from outside Vietnam may see the present rural policies as a permanent shift in the direction of private property values, the Vietnamese officials may see it as an expedient necessity, until more development is possible.

Economic reforms were very obviously having an impact on the northern part of the country in the Fall of 1987. Traders from Australia, Japan and the United States (operating out of Hong Kong) were making the rounds of Vietnamese enterprises. According to one American import-exporter we met, each enterprise has their own translator and the Ministry of Commerce (he said Chamber of Commerce) had organised his business trip very efficiently. The Vietnamese were selling rugs and handicrafts and buying high-technology equipment.

Private internal trading has also reached a new level of activity in Hanoi. I found unexpected items, like calculators made in Texas, that were selling at prices very close to the price I would have paid for them in the United States. These items evidently come into Vietnam through Thailand and Laos. The goods that are very much less available in Hanoi are the large consumer items and machinery that cannot easily get through the US trade blockade of Vietnam. There are very few household consumer goods available and few cars or buses on the streets of Hanoi. Bicycles are the typical mode of travel for people in Hanoi.

In the cultural area, also, there were noticeable changes. We listened to a Vietnamese-Latin rock band that was very modern and the dance atmosphere and stylish dress of the dancers could have placed the scene anywhere in the world. According to people in the international community, that scene would have been unheard of in the puritanical Hanoi of just a year before.

We were told that the campaign against corruption was proceeding apace and that the jail that formerly housed US prisoners of war now held corrupt former bureaucrats as inmates. According to our guide, the US prisoners were treated much more favourably than these internal enemies will be.

From several sources I got the impression that the structural changes being initiated by Nguyen Van Linh in Vietnam are on the order of the changes being made by Gorbachev in the Soviet Union. However, some Vietnamese and international friends of Vietnam are concerned that Linh may get himself too far out on a limb and that more traditional forces may take back control. The discussion about this issue seems very similar to talk about Gorbachev's vulnerability in the Soviet Union. In both cases, those who are used to the old system are not quite sure that change of a significant magnitude is possible within a short period of time.

The face of socialism is changing very rapidly throughout the world and Vietnam is a part of that change. The success or failure of reform in the Soviet Union and Eastern Europe will certainly have an impact on Vietnam. The success of the current dynamic southern leadership depends, at least in part, on forces in the wider socialist world's political economy.

Notes

To avoid duplication only the names of authors, the title of the book or article and the relevant page numbers are given here. Readers who wish to follow up the reference will find full publication details in the Bibliography, which follows this section.

1 Peasants and Socialism

1. Nguyen Khac Vien (ed.) 'South Vietnam: *From the NLF to the Provisional Revolutionary Government*', p. 113.
2. Le Thanh Khoi, *Histoire du Viet-nam*, p. 353 (The translation of the quotation is mine.)
3. John McAlister and Paul Mus, *The Vietnamese and Their Revolution*, p. 112.
4. Frances Fitzgerald, *Fire in the Lake*.
5. Ibid, pp. 291–2.
6. McAlister and Mus, *The Vietnamese and their Revolution*, pp. 61–3.
7. Ibid, pp. 116–19.
8. Fitzgerald, *Fire in the Lake*, p. 226.
9. Ibid, p. 206.
10. Ibid, p. 216, brackets mine.
11. Ibid, pp. 204–9.
12. William J. Duiker, *The Rise of Nationalism in Vietnam, 1900–1941*, pp. 287–91 and Alexander B. Woodside, *Community and Revolution in Modern Vietnam*, pp. 163–4.
13. James C. Scott, *The Moral Economy of the Peasant*; and Samuel L. Popkin, *The Rational Peasant*.
14. Duiker, *Rise of Nationalism*; and Woodside, *Community and Revolution*.
15. Woodside, *Community and Revolution*, p. 167.
16. Scott, *Moral Economy*, p. 92.
17. Ibid, pp. 56–90.
18. Ibid, pp. 2–9.
19. Popkin, *The Rational Peasant*, pp. 1–28.
20. Nguyen Khac Vien, *Tradition and Revolution in Vietnam*, pp. 36–7 and 210.
21. Ibid, pp. 41–3.
22. Ibid, pp. 45–6.
23. Ibid, p. 47.
24. Hla Myint, *The Economics of Developing Countries*, pp. 46–8.

2 Collective Property and the Rise of the Confucian Patriarchy

1. Mai Thi Tu and Le Thi Nham Tuyet, *Women in Vietnam*, pp. 11–13.
2. Vu Van Hien, *Communal Property in Tonkin*, p. 10.

3. Nguyen Khac Vien, *Tradition and Revolution in Vietnam*, p. 37.
4. Arlene Eisen-Bergman,*Women of Vietnam*, pp. 30–2.
5. See Esther Boserup, *Women in Economic Development*.
6. Mai Thi Tu and Le Thi Nham Tuyet, *Women in Vietnam*, pp. 13–14.
7. Ibid, p. 16.
8. Ibid, p. 23.
9. Jean Chesneau, *The Vietnamese Nation*, p. 18.
10. Vu Van Hien, *Communal Property*, pp. 6–7.
11. Ibid, p. 7.
12. Nguyen Khac Vien (ed.)*Traditional Vietnam: Some Historical Stages*.
13. Mai Thi Tu and Le Thi Nham Tuyet, *Women in Vietnam*, p. 37.
14. Ibid, pp. 35–6.
15. Vu Van Hien, *Communal Property*, p. 25. A *mau* is 0.36 hectare (0.9 acres).
16. Helen B. Lamb, *Vietnam's Will to Live*, p. 22.
17. Vu Van Hien, *Communal Property*, pp. 26–7.
18. Ibid, p. 27.
19. Ibid, p. 29.
20. Ibid, p. 30.
21. Mai Thi Tu and Le Thi Nham Tuyet, *Women in Vietnam*, p. 46.
22. David Marr, *Vietnamese Anticolonialism*, p. 15.
23. Vu Van Hien, *Communal Property*, p. 35.
24. Ibid.
25. Joseph Buttinger, *The Smaller Dragon*, pp. 223–40.
26. Nguyen Khac Vien, *Traditional Vietnam: Some Historical Stages*, pp. 103–20.
27. Mai Thi Tu and Le Thi Nham Tuyet, *Women in Vietnam*, pp. 80 and 86.
28. Vu Van Hien, *Communal Property*, p.37.
29. Ibid.
30. René Gueffier, *Essay on the Land System in Indochina*, p. 67.
31. Ngo Vinh Long, *Vietnamese Women in Society and Revolution*, pp. 8–9.
32. David Marr, *Vietnamese Anticolonialism*, p. 24.
33. Charles Robequain, *The Economic Development of French Indochina*, p. 353.
34. Vu Van Hien, *Communal Property*, pp. 11 and 14.
35. Ibid, p. 16.
36. Ibid, pp. 13–14.

3 Land and Economy in the Traditional Village

1. René Gueffier, *Essay on the Land System in Indochina* (Annamese Countries) pp. 16–56.
2. J. Lan, *Rice: Legislation, Cult, Beliefs*, p. 6.
3. Joseph Buttinger, *The Smaller Dragon*, pp. 42–3.
4. The material in this section is based on my Ph.D. dissertation, 'Land Tenure and Land Reform: A History of Property and Power in Vietnam'. Some major original sources were:

René Gueffier's *Essay on the Land System in Indochina*, first published in 1928. Gueffier elaborated on the history and development of family land (which he called private land) in Vietnam. He pointed out numerous mistakes in the official French interpretation of the traditional Vietnamese land law and went on to elaborate on errors in French policy, especially with respect to family land.

Pierre Gourou contributed two standard works, *Peasants of the Tonkin Delta*, translated by Richard R. Miller, and *Land Utilization in French Indochina*. Gourou, a professor of human geography at the University of Bordeaux did field work in 1927 through 1935 and in 1939. Gourou catalogued almost every aspect of Vietnamese society and land formations in order to establish geographical determinism.

Jean Baptiste Eliacin Luro wrote *The Country of Annam*, first published in Paris in 1878. Luro was one of the early French administrators in Saigon, holding the office of Inspector of Native Affairs. The field dates for his study are 1864–76. The work is an early treatment of Vietnamese social and political organisation.

P. Ory's work, *The Annamite Commune at Tonkin*, was originally published in Paris in 1894. This is a clear study of the political and social organisation at the village level, complete with details of social relations.

Vu Van Hien's study, *Communal Property in Tonkin*, was originally published in Paris in 1939. This work is a history of communal land tenure, and an elaboration of Vietnamese land laws in the traditional period.

5. Charles Robequain, *The Economic Development of French Indochina*, p. 396.
6. Literally, the phrase means 'incense and fire'.
7. Gueffier, *Essay on the Land System*, p. 43.
8. Vu Van Hien, *Communal Property*, p. 84.
9. A *mau* is 0.36 hectare, or 0.9 acre; a *sao* is one-tenth of a *mau*, a *thoc* is one-fifteenth of a *sao*.
10. Later the village collected a large rental share from those who cultivated the *tu dan dien* property.
11. Pierre Gourou, *Peasants of the Tonkin Delta*, p. 392.
12. After the 1711 regulation residents who possessed rice fields by themselves or through their wives no longer had a right to *khau phan*. When their personal property was small, they were allowed a portion of *khau phan* to increase their rice fields to a sufficient amount (Vu Van Hien, *Communal Property*, p. 35). Adherence to this law was not observed by our sources in the Tonkin Delta but this regulation could be the origin of the tradition later observed in the south among villages with little communal land, that only those without family patrimony should use the *cong dien*.
13. Vu Van Hien, *Communal Property*, p. 104.
14. Two other methods of distribution of the *khau phan* were noted by the French, but these were exceptional in spite of a regulation passed in the nineteenth century outlawing the traditional distribution of equal-sized lots in order of hierarchy. In some places the plots of *khau phan* were

distributed by drawing lots, but this was rare. More usual was the method of beginning with a new inhabitant at each distribution, following a regular rotation with all the recipients occupying all the shares one after the other.

15. Vu Van Hien, *Communal Property*, p. 114.
16. Gourou, *Peasants of the Tonkin Delta*, p. 393. Most other cults, such as the cult of Budda and the cult of the village spirit were administered by the village and fell under the category of *tu dan dien*.
17. Gourou, *Utilization of the Soil*, pp. 284–5.
18. Gourou, *Peasants of the Tonkin Delta*, p. 109. A 'Ligature' is ten strings of sixty zinc coins.
19. Ibid, pp. 582–4.
20. Ibid, pp. 610–11.
21. Ibid, pp. 611–12.
22. Gerald Hickey, *Village in Vietnam*, p. 299.
23. Gueffier, *Essay on the Land System*, p. 57.
24. Ibid, p. 65.
25. Ibid, p. 65.

4 The Colonial Impact

1. Virginia Thompson, *French Indochina*, pp. 221, 225.
2. René Gueffier, *Essay on the Land System in Indochina*, p. 94.
3. Bernard B. Fall, *The Two Viet-Nams*, p. 294.
4. Joseph Buttinger, *Vietnam: A Dragon Embattled*, vol. I: *From Colonialism to the Vietminh*, p. 124.
5. Ibid, p. 24.
6. Paul Kresser, *The Annamese Commune in Cochinchina*, pp. 24–5.
7. Thompson, *French Indochina*, p. 238.
8. Kresser, *The Annamese Commune*, pp. 1–2.
9. René Gueffier, *Essay on the Land System*, p. 97.
10. Ibid, p. 97.
11. Ibid, pp. 97–102.
12. Ibid, p. 101.
13. Ibid, pp. 102–4.
14. Ngo Vinh Long estimated the impact of concessions as being somewhat greater (Ngo Vinh Long, *Before the Revolution: The Vietnamese Peasants Under the French*). He assumed that all concessioned land was cultivated. Even with his estimates of 40 per cent of the cultivated lands being given in concessions, however, a large percentage of the land would still have changed hands through market forces.
15. René Gueffier, *Essay on the Land System*, p. 77.
16. Pierre Gourou, *Land Utilization in French Indochina*, p. 375.
17. The details of this transition are reported by Gueffier, *Essay on the Land System*, pp. 77–87.
18. Le Than Khoi, *Histoire du Viet-nam*, p. 422.
19. Vu Van Hien, *Communal Property in Tonkin*, p. 121.
20. Gueffier, *Essay on the Land System*, p. 75.
21. Ibid, p. 66.

22. Ibid, p. 67.
23. Gourou, *Land Utilization*, p. 380.
24. Vu Van Hien, *Communal Property*, pp. 57–8.
25. Ibid, p. 58.
26. Ibid, pp. 57–62.
27. Ibid, p. 67.
28. Joseph Buttinger, *Vietnam: A Dragon Embattled*, vol I., pp. 105 and 523. A similar estimate is given by Gueffier who states that French period interest rates were 60, 90, and 100–240 per cent. Gueffier, *Essay on the Land System*, p. 59.
29. Gueffier, *Essay on the Land System*, p. 104.
30. Thompson, *French Indochina*, pp. 221 and 225.
31. Ibid, p. 225.
32. Ibid.
33. Ibid, p. 226.
34. Gourou, *Land Utilization*, p. 281.
35. Ibid.
36. Ngo Vinh Long, *Vietnamese Women in Society and Revolution, vol I: The French Colonial Period*, p. 45.
37. Ibid, p. 42.
38. Buttinger, *Vietnam: A Dragon Embattled*, p. 171.
39. Ibid, pp. 165–6.
40. Thompson, *French Indochina*, p. 125.
41. Buttinger, *Vietnam, A Dragon Embattled*, p. 526.
42. Ibid.
43. Ibid, p. 171.

5 The Nationalist–Communist Resistance

1. Christine Pelzer White, 'Vietnamese Revolutionary Alliances' (unpublished paper), p. 46.
2. Ibid, p.15.
3. Marr, *Vietnamese Anticolonialism*, pp. 84–155.
4. Ibid, pp. 120–60.
5. White, *Politics*, p. 15.
6. Ibid, p. 16.
7. Ibid, p. 17.
8. Jean Lacouture, *Ho Chi Minh: A Political Biography*, p. 19.
9. Ibid, p. 24.
10. Lacouture, *Ho Chi Minh*, p. 31.
11. Ibid.
12. Ibid, p. 47.
13. Nguyen Khac Vien, *The Long Resistance*, p. 61.
14. White, *Politics*, p. 23.
15. Nguyen Khac Vien, *The Long Resistance*, p. 61.
16. Ibid, pp. 62–4.
17. Ibid, p. 64.
18. Marr, *Vietnamese Anticolonialism*, p. 263.
19. White, 'Vietnamese Revolutionary Alliances' *(unpublished paper)*, pp. 25–26.

20. Lacouture, *Ho Chi Minh*, pp. 55–6. Summarised from a history published by Hanoi University and edited by Tran Van Giau.
21. Ibid, pp. 58–9.
22. James C. Scott, *The Moral Economy of the Peasant*, p. 134.
23. Christine Pelzer White, 'The Peasants and the Party in the Vietnamese Revolution', p. 8. White's study follows Vietnamese historian Tran Huy Lieu's account.
24. Democratic Republic of Vietnam, *An Outline History of the Vietnam Workers' Party* (Hanoi: Foreign Languages Pub. House, 1970), p. 25.
25. Ibid, pp. 25–6.
26. Truong Chinh and Vo Nguyen Giap, *The Peasant Question*, pp. vii–x (the introduction by White).
27. Ibid, p. 14.
28. Ibid, pp.14–16.
29. *Selected Readings from the Works of Mao Tse Tung* (Peking: Foreign Languages Press, 1971) pp. 12–20.
30. Ibid, p. 74.
31. Milton Sacks' 'Marxism in Vietnam', p. 129.
32. Ibid, pp. 127–9.
33. Ibid, p. 133.
34. Ibid, pp. 30–6.
35 Ibid, p. 142.
36 Ibid, p. 143.
37. Christine Pelzer White, 'The Vietnamese Revolutionary Alliance', p. 88.
38. Ibid, pp. 90–1.
39. White, 'Vietnamese Revolutionary Alliances' (unpublished paper) p. 65.
40. Lacouture, *Ho Chi Minh*, p. 66.
41. Nguyen Khac Vien (ed.) *A Century of Struggle*, p. 20.
42. Ibid, p. 116.
43. Buttinger, *A Dragon Embattled*, vol. I, pp. 233–6.
44. Democratic Republic of Vietnam, *History of the August Revolution*, (Hanoi: Foreign Languages Publishing House, 1972) pp. 20–3.
45. Ibid, pp. 29–30 and p. 44.
46. Chesneaux, *The Vietnamese Nation*, p. 164.
47. Christine Pelzer White, *Agrarian Reform and National Liberation in the Vietnamese Revolution : 1920–1957*, p. 122.
48. Ibid, pp. 118–21.
49. Chesneaux, *The Vietnamese Nation*, p. 175.
50. White, *Agarian Reform*, p. 153.
51. Ibid, pp. 167–70.

6 The Post-Colonial Village

1. Two short studies were done of the village of My Thuan: John D. Donoghue, *My Thuan, A Mekong Delta Village in South Vietnam*, and Truong Ngoc Giau and Lloyd W. Woodruff, *The Delta Village of My Thuan*. There were also two studies of the village of Khanh Hau: James B. Hendrey, *The Small World of Khanh Hau* and Gerald Cannon

Hickey, *Village in Vietnam*. Both villages were controlled by the Saigon government, but were under some NLF influence during the time of the studies. In Khanh Hau, which was the more 'secure' of the two villages, the researchers did not feel safe enough to spend nights in the village.

A study of Ma Xa Hamlet in Central Vietnam was done by Nicholaas Luykx in 1959: 'Some Comparative Aspects of Rural Public Institutions in Thailand, the Philippines and Vietnam'. This village was under the control of the Saigon government, but the *Viet Minh* had had influence on the development of the village. In addition, Wolf I. Ladejinsky gives impressions of four villages in the central lowlands in 'Field Trip Observations in Central Vietnam'. Two of the villages had been under *Viet Minh* control and two had not.

2. Donoghue, *My Thuan*, p. 11.
3. Hickey, *Village in Vietnam*, p. 9 and Luykx, 'Comparitive Aspects', p. 811.
4. Hickey, *Village in Vietnam*, p. 191.
5. Hendrey, *Small World of Khanh Hau*, p. 264.
6. Hickey, *Village in Vietnam*, p. 235.
7. Ibid, p. 34.
8. Giau and Woodruff, *The Delta Village of My Thuan*, p. 50.
9. Hickey, *Village in Vietnam*, p. 253.
10. Ibid, p. 258.
11. Ibid, p. 42.
12. Republic of Vietnam, Department of Rural Affairs, *Report on the Agriculture Census of Vietnam*, p. 27.
13. Ladejinsky, 'Field Trip Observations', p. 5.
14. Edward Fitzgerald and Henry Bush, *Village Use of Communal Rice Land*, p. 10.
15. Ibid, pp. 4–5.
16. Luykx, 'Comparative Aspects', p. 709.
17. Ibid, p. 713.
18. Hendrey, *Small World of Khanh Hau*, p. 164.
19. Hickey, *Village in Vietnam*, p. 233.
20. Ibid, pp. 133–5.
21. Luykx, 'Comparative Aspects', p. 820.
22. Ibid, p. 72.
23. Hickey, *Village in Vietnam*, p. 143.
24. Donoghue, *My Thuan*, p. 47.
25. Luykx, 'Comparative Aspects', p. 22.
26. Hendrey, *Small World of Khanh Hau*, p. 238.
27. Hickey, *Village in Vietnam*, p. 229.
28. Lloyd Woodruff, 'Local Administration in Vietnam, Village Finance', p. 46.
29. Luykx, 'Comparative Aspects', p. 613.
30. Hickey, *Village in Vietnam*, p. 91.
31. Ibid, p. 29.
32. Ibid, p. 112.
33. Ibid, p. 113.
34. Ibid, p. 117.

35. Ibid, p. 136.
36. Hendrey, *Small World of Khanh Hau*, pp. 120–1.
37. Ibid, p. 256.
38. Ladejinsky, 'Field Trip Observations', p. 7.
39. Luykx, 'Comparative Aspects', p. 703.
40. Hendrey, *Small World of Khanh Hau*, p. 205.
41. Ibid, p. 221.
42. Ibid, p. 208.
43. Ibid, p. 216.
44. Ibid, p. 213.
45. Luykx, 'Comparative Aspects', p. 703
46. Ibid, p. 705.
47. Hendrey, *Small World of Khanh Hau*, p. 162 and Donoghue, *My Thuan*, p. 47.
48. Hendrey, *Small World of Khanh Hau*, p. 128.
49. Luykx, 'Comparative Aspects', p. 705.

7 Socialism in the North

1.   Christine Pelzer White, *Agrarian Reform and National Liberation in the Vietnamese Revolution: 1920–1957*, p. 265.
2.   Ibid, pp. 318 and 326.
3.   Edwin E. Moise, 'Land Reform and Land Reform Errors in North Viet Nam', pp. 79–82, quoting from *Nhan Dan*, 11 May 1956.
4.   Ibid, p. 72.
5.   White, *Agrarian Reform and National Liberation*, p. 364.
6.   Moise, 'Land Reform', p. 81.
7.   Ibid, pp. 73–5.
8.   Ibid, p. 84 and White, *Agrarian Reform and National Liberation*, pp. 423–34.
9.   Christine Pelzer White, 'Family and Class in the Theory and Practice of Marxism: The Case of Vietnam', pp. 17–20.
10. White, *Agrarian Reform and National Liberation*, pp. 332–4.
11. Le Duan, 'Hold High the Revolutionary Banner of Creative Marxism, Lead Our Revolutionary Cause to Complete Victory', pp. 63–4.
12. Irene Norlund, 'The Role of Industry in Vietnam's Development Strategy', pp. 95–7.
13. Ibid, p. 65.
14. Norlund, 'The Role of Industry', p. 98.
15. Bernard Fall, *The Two Vietnams*, p. 176.
16. Alec Gordon, 'North Vietnam's Collectivization Campaigns: Class Struggle, Production and the "Middle Peasant" Problem', p. 21.
17. Ibid, pp. 30–2.
18. Lam Quang Huyen, 'Economic Activities of a Cooperative Household', p. 9.
19. Robert Hewlett and John Markie, *Cooperative Farming as an Instrument of Rural Development: Examples from China, Vietnam, Tanzania and India*, pp. 43-5.
20. Duang Quoc Cam, 'Correct Solution of the Relationship Between the

Collective Economy and the Supplementary Economy of the Families of Individual Members', pp. 71–9.

21.   Ibid, p. 76.
22.   Adam J. Fforde, *Problems of Agricultural Development in North Vietnam*, pp. 379–83; 'Collectivization in the Democratic Republic of Vietnam, 1960–66: A Comment', *Journal of Contemporary Asia*, Vol. 12, No. 4, 1982, p. 486.
23.   Fall, *The Two Vietnams*, pp. 163 and 294.
24.   'Irrigation Projects', *Nhan Dan* (newspaper) 28 July 1963, JPRS #, 21, 217, 26 September, 1963.
25.   Canh Sinh, 'Correctly Understanding the Problem of Improving the Standard of Living', p. 53.
26.   'Our Acute Lesson in Building the Party in Bac Ninh Province', *Hoc Tap*, December 1962, JPRS #17666, 15 February, 1963, p. 10.
27.   Nguyen Dang Kieu, 'A Uniform Financial and Production Plan for Agricultural Cooperatives'.
28.   Pham Van Tiep, 'Waste of Agricultural Technicians in Kieu An Province'; Nguyen Thi Kim Oanh, 'Agricultural Technician in Wrong Job'; and Nguyen Van Thoai, 'Agricultural Technician Rears Children'.
29.   Dao Thi Dinh, 'Training and Promoting Female Cadres'.

8   The Revolutionary Village

1.   Gérard Chaliand, *The Peasants of North Vietnam*. Chaliand interviewed people in villages and hamlets in four provinces. A picture of ordinary life in the villages emerges from his many interviews.
2.   Pham Coung, *Revolution in the Village of Nam Hong (1945–75)*. This is the most detailed and complete study of a revolutionary village. Most of the field work appears to have been done in the early 1960s. Nguyen Yem, 'The Thanh Oai District' and Pham Toan 'The Ngo Xuyen Cooperative'. These two studies of the rural areas in revolutionary times are more widely read but they are less detailed than the Nam Hong study.
3.   Pham Cuong, *Revolution in the Village of Nam Hong*, p. 57–8, Chaliand. *Peasants of North Vietnam*, p. 126.
4.   Chaliand, *Peasants of North Vietnam*, p. 62.
5.   Ibid, pp. 74 and 185.
6.   Pham Cuong, *Revolution in the Village of Nam Hong*, p. 33.
7.   Chaliand, *Peasants of North Vietnam*, p. 77.
8.   Pham Cuong, *Revolution in the Village of Nam Hong*, pp. 32–3.
9.   Chaliand, *Peasants of North Vietnam*, p. 223.
10.   Pham Cuong judged this a negative solution. *Revolution in the Village of Nam Hong*, p. 35.
11.   Chaliand, *Peasants of North Vietnam*, p. 79.
12.   Pham Toan, 'The Ngo Xuyen Cooperative', p. 212.
13.   Pham Cuong, *Revolution in the Village of Nam Hong*, p. 36.
14.   Chaliand, *Peasants of North Vietnam*, pp. 122–5.
15.   Ibid, pp. 124–5.

16.   Ibid, p. 177.
17.   Pham Cuong, *Revolution in the Village of Nam Hong*, p. 90.
18.   Ibid, p. 100.
19.   Pham Toan, 'The Ngo Xuyen Cooperative', pp. 224–7.
20.   Pham Cuong, *Revolution in the Village of Nam Hong*, pp. 70–4.
21.   Ibid, p. 66.
22.   Pham Toan, 'The Ngo Xuyen Cooperative', p. 221.
23.   Ibid, p. 119 and Pham Cuong, *Revolution in the Village of Nam Hong*, p. 45.
24.   Pham Cuong, *Revolution in the Village of Nam Hong*, pp. 55–6.
25.   Pham Toan, 'The Ngo Xuyen Cooperative', p. 220.
26.   Pham Cuong, *Revolution in the Village of Nam Hong*, p. 61.
27.   Ibid, p. 107.
28.   Nguyen Yem, 'The Thanh Oai District', p. 197.
29.   Pham Toan, 'The Ngo Xuyen Cooperative', p. 231.
30.   Pham Cuong, *Revolution in the Village of Nam Hong*, p. 79; and Nguyen Yem, 'The Thanh Oai District', p. 200.
31.   Nguyen Yem, 'The Thanh Oai District', pp. 182–90.
32.   Ibid, pp. 132–83.
33.   Pham Cuong, *Revolution in the Village of Nam Hong*, pp. 47–8. This assumption about a shift in the division of labour is made partly because the positions of officials and clerks were typically given to men in North Vietnam in this period but the assumption is made also because of certain statements in the Nam Hong village study. Statements were made about leaving ploughing (a man's job) to take on accounting and retailing work. When complaints were made about members of cooperatives spending time at markets, a footnote explains that women were freed from household tasks by cooperative nurseries. Presumably, the author thought that the women *should* have been grateful and worked on the cooperative and not in private trading.

9   US Intervention

1.   Gareth Porter, 'Commercial Import Programme', unpublished paper, p. 4.
2.   Frances Fitzgerald, *Fire in the Lake*, pp. 108–10.
3.   Ibid, pp. 109–11.
4.   Economic Survey Mission to the Republic of Vietnam, 'Toward the Economic Development of the Republic of Vietnam'.
5.   Ibid, pp. 1 and 2.
6.   Interview of Gareth Porter, Indochina Resources Center, with Nguyen Hoang Cuong, 16 October 1971. Mr Cuong was a large landowner in South Vietnam in addition to his post in the Ministry.
7.   Frank C. Child, 'Toward a Policy for Economic Growth in Vietnam', pp. 4–11.
8.   Ibid, p. 64.
9.   Roy L. Prosterman, 'Land Reform in Vietnam', p. 329.
10.   Porter, 'Commercial Import Programme', p. 5.
11.   Ibid, pp. 6–7.

12. Ibid, pp. 8–9.
13. Ibid, p. 13.
14. Jeffrey Race, 'South Vietnam'.
15. Robert Scigliano, *South Viet Nam: Nation Under Stress*, pp. 121–23.
16. Price Gittinger, 'Agrarian Reform in Free Vietnam', p. 4.
17. Donald MacPhail and Mary Vaughan, 'Comments on Stanford Research Institute Report on Land Reform in Vietnam', p. 3.
18. John D. Montgomery, 'Land Reform and Political Development: Prospects in Vietnam'.
19. MacPhail and Vaughan, 'Comments on Stanford Research', p. 4.
20. Prosterman, 'Land Reform', p. 330.
21. Republic of Vietnam, National Institute of Statistics, *Vietnam Statistical Yearbook, 1967–68*, Table 83.
22. Prosterman, 'Land Reform', p. 330.
23. William Bredo *et al.*, *Land Reform in Vietnam: Working Papers, Volumes I–IV*, vol 3, p. 43.
24. Bernard Fall, *The Two Vietnams*, p. 309.
25. Gareth Porter's interview with Le Van Toan, Chief of the Land Reform Court, 10 November 1971.
26. The author's interview with Nguyen Xuam Kuong.
27. Race, 'South Vietnam', p. 19.
28. Montgomery, 'Land Reform', p. 10.
29. Gareth Porter's interview with Le Van Toan, 10 November 1971.
30. Gareth Porter's interview with Vice President Nguyen Ngoe Tho.
31. Gareth Porter's interview with Nguyen Doy Xuan, 3 September 1971.
32. Montgomery, 'Land Reform', p. 10.
33. Ibid, p. 11.
34. Edward J. Mitchell, 'The Significance of Land Tenure in the Vietnamese Insurgency'.
35. Republic of Vietnam, Agricultural Economics and Statistics Service, *Agricultural Statistics Yearbook, 1968*, p. 140.
36. Prosterman, 'Land Reform', p. 332.
37. US Agency for International Development Vietnam, Office of Domestic Production, 'Review of Land Tenure Programs'.
38. Comments by Roy L. Prosterman Transcribed by the author from a speech given at the Spring Review of Land Reform, an AID Conference, Washington, DC, 2–4 May 1970.
39. MacPhail and Vaughan, 'Comments on Stanford Research' p. 2.
40. Bredo *et al.*, vol IV, pp. 87–137.
41. Department of State Telegram, Subject: Land Reform (No 6344), 28 April 1970.
42. Gareth Porter's interview with Au Ngoc Ho, Minister of Economy 1968–9, 29 September 1971.
43. Department of State Telegram, No 6344, p. 1.
44. USAID, Vietnam, Associate Director for Land Reform, Land Reform Memo Number 19, 10 February 1972.
45. Gareth Porter's interview with Bui Huu Tien, in land reform directorate 1958–71, 31 August 1971.

46.   C. Stuart Callison, 'Progress Report on Dissertation, the Economic, Social and Political Effects of the Land to the Tiller Program', and an interview with the author on his findings in the villages, Saigon, Vietnam, April 1972. Callison has more recently written a monograph which gives high marks to the implementation of the Land-to-the-Tiller law and which sees subsequent investments in the countryside to be a consequence of this law, rather than the Front's actions in ridding much of the countryside of landlord influence. He reports on three villages not in Chau Doc or An Giang where interviews show a favourable response to LTT and one village in An Giang Province where there was significant criticism. In general, he sees the 15–20 per cent rate of complaints about the land reform as favourable, Charles Stuart Callison, *Land to the Tiller in the Mekong Delta.*

47.   Callison, *Progress on Dissertation.*

48.   Letter from Paul Walter, An Giang Province, to Dick Eney, Director of Land Reform, CORDS/MR4, 29 October 1971.

49.   Callison, *Progress on Dissertation,*

50.   Ibid, pp. 20–2.

51.   US Government Memorandum from Donald Melville, Supervisor, Government Land Distribution Project to Richard Hough, Assistant Director for Land Reform, 10 November 1969. Mr Melville was reporting on the attitudes of some US officials in An Giang Province.

52.   US Government Memorandum entitled An Giang LTT SOS – no date.

53.   US Government Memorandum from R. A. Luedte, Land Reform Advisor to John A. Riggs, Subject: LTT Grievances and Disputes, 15 April 1971.

54   Ibid.

55.   Letter from Douglas B. Archard, Land Reform, to Richard Eney, Director, Land Reform Division, MR IV, 19 October 1971.

56.   Christine White, 'Report, Thesis Research in South Vietnam', November 1971–March 1972, unpublished manuscript.

57.   Report of John F. Keane, District Senior Advisor, Hoa Tan District, Go Cong Province, Subject: Land Reform and Politics in Go Cong 20 (March 1971).

58.   Rex Daly, Nancy (Wiegersma) Hancock *et al.*, *Agriculture in the Vietnam Economy*, p. 1.

10   The National Liberation Front

1.   Nguyen Thi Dinh, *No Other Road to Take*, pp. 62–3.

2.   Vu Can, 'The NLF and the Second Resistance in South Vietnam', p. 22.

3.   The sects later changed sides and supported the Saigon government. It is not only people writing from the US Government perspective who make claims of northern dominance over the southern struggle. Gabriel Kolko, while noting divergence on the part of the Party's southern branch (the People's Revolutionary Party) in the early years of the war, claims that the Party dominated the National Liberation Front throughout the years of its existence. He claims that the Party played

the dominant role in the NLF's Liberation Committees despite the fact that they had a non-party majority. Gabriel Kolko, *Anatomy of a War*, p. 127.

4. Vu Can, 'The NLF and the Second Resistance', pp. 25–6.
5. David Hunt, 'Organizing the Revolution in Vietnam', pp. 25–36.
6. Ibid, pp. 34–5.
7. William Bredo *et al.*, *Land Reform in Vietnam*, vol. III, p. 45.
8 'National Liberation Front Land Policies' (Long An Province, May 1963) reprinted and translated in Bredo *et al.*, vol. III, p. 120.
9. Christine Pelzer White, 'Land Reform and Revolution: Vietnam', unpublished manuscript (January 1967).
10. 'National Liberation Front Land Policies', Bredo *et al.*, p. 118.
11. Douglas Pike, *Vietcong*, p. 279.
12. Mark Selden, 'The National Liberation Front and the Transformation of Vietnamese Society', *Bulletin of Concerned Asian Scholars*, vol. II, no. I, p. 39.
13. David Hunt 'Organizing the Revolution in Vietnam', p. 138.
14. Arlene Eisen-Bergman, *Women of Vietnam*, pp. 187–8.
15. Hunt, 'Organising the Revolution', p. 147.
16. Ibid, p. 146.
17. Ibid, pp. 147–8.
18. Ibid, p. 147.
19. Rice is broadcast in these areas instead of being transplanted in rice paddies. When the rains and floods come, the top of the rice plant floats on top of the water. After the floods, the rice is harvested. The product is called 'red rice' and it is used for food in the local area and sold for animal feed to other parts of Vietnam.
20. Robert Sansom, *The Economics of Insurgency in the Mekong Delta of Vietnam*, p. 152.
21. The author's interview with Nguyen Xuam Kuong, former Director of the Cadaster (April 1972).
22. Sansom, *The Economics of Insurgency*, p. 15.
23. Ibid, p. 173.
24. Ibid, p. 179.
25. Department of State Airgram A-90, 'Ten Year Update of Village Studies', Attachment 4, p. 4.
26. This was observed by Randy Cummings (State University of New York-Binghamton, Anthropology Department), and reported to the author in 1975.
27. Department of State Airgram' 'Ten Year Update of Village Studies', Attachment 1, p. 5.
28. Gareth Porter's interview with Bui Huu Tien (Land Reform Directorate 1958–1971) 31 August 1971.

11 Integration of the Country

1. Stewart E. Fraser, 'Vietnam Struggles with Expanding Population', p. 6.
2. 'VNA Reports Army Production Activities in South, North Vietnam', JPRS microfiche no. 67427 (June 1976) p. 7.

3. Ngo Vinh Long, 'Agrarian Differentiation in the Southern Region of Vietnam', p. 297, and 'View from the Village', *Indochina Issues*, No. 12 (December 1980), p. 7.

4. Murray Hiebert, 'Contracts in Vietnam: More Rice, New Problems', p. 1.

5. Adam Fforde, *Problems of Agricultural Development in North Vietnam*, pp. 130–3.

6. Melanie Beresford, 'Household and Collective in Vietnamese Agriculture', p. 11.

7. Fforde, *Problems of Agriculture Development*, pp. 105–6.

8. Huu Tho, 'Contractual Quota System in Agriculture Reviewed'.

9. 'Saigon–Ho Chi Minh City', *Vietnam Courier*, no 59 (April 1977) pp. 1–4.

10. Wilfred Burchett, 'Reorganizing the Vietnamese Economy', p. 47.

11. 'Economic Restoration, Production Gains Reported', Hanoi Radio in Vietnamese (31 October 1975) JPRS Microfiche no. 66182, p. 12.

12. 'Trade Union Federation Explains to Owners Policy of Aiding Private Enterprises', *Saigon Giai Phong* (23 July 1975) pp. 1, 4, JPRS microfiche no. 65766 (September 1975) p. 5.

13. Ngo Vinh Long, 'The Tasks of Reconstruction', p. 5.

14. Lasclo Bogos, 'The Transformation of South Vietnam'.

15. Erich Wulff, 'Must We Make All the Old Mistakes Again'.

16. Nguyen Nieu, 'Correctly Coordinating and Using Administrative and Economic Methods to Adjust Economic Relationships in the Present: Improvement of Enterprise Management', p. 24.

17. Ibid, pp. 24–8.

18. 'The Direction, Missions and Major Measures for Strengthening Labour Organisation and Management of Labour During the Coming Period', *Xay Dung*, no. 9 (Hanoi: September 1974) JPRS microfiche, p. 41.

19. Paul Quinn-Judge, 'The Vietnam–China Split: Old Ties Remain', p. 3.

20. Ibid, p. 5.

21. This is not to say that the decisions of Vietnamese leaders would have been different if they were aware of the total cost. To them, their national integrity was at stake and Pol Pot was a madman who had to be dealt with.

22. Murray Hiebert, 'The Food Weapon: Can Vietnam be Broken?', pp. 1 and 5.

23. Alexander Casella, 'The Case of Catch 22'.

24. Christine Pelzer White, 'State, Cooperative and Family in the Political Economy of Vietnamese Agriculture', p. 9.

25. 'Improve the Quality of Socialist Transformation', *Nhan Dan* editorial, p. 33.

26. Fraser 'Vietnam Struggles', pp. 1–3 and Dang Thu, 'Some Urgent Population Questions', pp. 45–50.

27. Fraser, 'Vietnam Struggles', p. 3. Since most pressure to use contraceptives seems to be on civil servants and not on peasant women, at the present time, Vietnamese peasant women are not experiencing the intense contradiction of being pressured to produce labour power for

peasant agriculture and being limited to one child, as is true in China. The Vietnamese, at this point, see the Chinese as excessive in their methods of lowering population.

28. Fraser, 'Vietnam Struggles', p. 7.
29. Huong Giang, 'Positive Changes in the Economy of Our Country Under the Illumination of Resolution 6 of the Party Central Committee'.
30. John Spragens, Jr, 'Vietnam and the Soviets: A Tighter Alliance', p. 3.
31. *Tap Chi Cong San* (editorial) 'Revamping the Management of Basic Economic Units', p. 1.
32. Murray Hiebert, 'Vietnam Begins Leadership Transition', pp. 3–4, and Hiebert, 'Call for Radical Surgery'.
33. 'Four Months of Self-Criticism and Criticism in *Saigon Giai Phong*', editorial, 31 August 1986, pp. 1, 4. JPRS, SEA-86-194, p. 60.
34. Phong Ha, 'The Truth about a Village', pp. 82–7.
35. *Saigon Giai Phong* 'Enterprises Still "Subsidized"'.
36. *Tap Chi Cong San* (editorial) 'Revamping the Management of Basic Units', pp. 1–3.
37. Ibid, pp. 3–6.
38. M. Hiebert, 'Contracts in Vietnam', p.1, and 'Agricultural Production Progress', Socialist Republic of Vietnam Government Brief, 16 October 1986, JPRS, SEA-86-200, p. 104.
39. *Ekonomicheskaya Gazeta*, no. 28, July 1986, p. 20, JPRS SEA-86-155, pp. 90–3.
40. *Nhan Dan* (editorial) 'Land Reorganization in Nam Bo', pp. 85–6.
41. Tran Xuan, 'Ho Chi Minh City Steps Up Small Industry and Handicraft Production', *Tap Chi Cong San*, No. 7, July 1986, pp. 71–5, JPRS, SEA-86-171, p. 89.
42. 'Industrial Development in Southern District', JPRS, SEA-86-1512, pp. 85–6.
43. M. Hiebert, 'Contracts', p. 3.
44. John Spragens, Jr, 'Cautious Policy Reforms', p. 3.
45. Do Chu and Xuan Giang, 'Let's Help One Another, Not Lend Money for Interest'.
46. Vu Kiem,'Member Comments on Party Congress in Nam Ha Village'.
47. John Spragens, Jr, 'Vietnamese Fiction Tackles the Bureaucratic Plague', p. 4.
48. 'Four Months of Self-Criticism and Criticism … ', p. 59.
49. Nhat Linh,'Cooperation Teams – Good and Bad Aspects'.
50. Ibid, p. 60.
51. Spragens, 'Vietnamese Fiction', p. 3.
52. Sophie Quinn-Judge, 'Vietnamese Women: Neglected Promises', p. 3.
53. Ibid, p. 4.
54. Thien Thanh, 'To Avoid Giving "Blank Check" Contracts, Management Must be Based on a Strict System of Material Responsibility', *Pu Nu Vietnam*, 3–9 September, pp. 2, 3; JPRS, SEA-86-197, pp. 104–6.
55. Karen Gellen, 'Vietnam Women: A New Agenda'.
56. Arlene Eisen, *Women and Revolution in Vietnam*, p.297.
57. *Nhan Dan*, 'Tien Giang Encourages Women to Develop the Family Economy'.

58. Nguyen Thi Dinh, 'Toward the Sixth Party Congress', *Tap Chi Cong San*, pp. 50, 54, JPRS, SEA-86-193, p. 64.
59. Linda Gibson Hiebert, 'Malnutrition Among Children'.
60. Nguyen Thi Dinh, 'Toward the Sixth Party Congress', pp. 61–6.

Bibliography

BOOKS, JOURNAL ARTICLES AND DISSERTATIONS

Beresford, Melanie. 'Household and Collective in Vietnamese Agriculture', *Journal of Contemporary Asia*' vol.15, no. 1 (1985).

Boserup, Esther, *Women in Economical Development* (London: Allen & Unwin, 1970).

Bredo, William; Shreve, Robert O. and Tater, William J., *Land Reform in Vietnam, Working Papers*, vols I–V (Menlo Park, California: Stanford Research Institute, 1968).

Burchett, William, *Inside Story of the Guerilla War* (New York: International Publishers, 1965).

Burchett, William, 'Reorganizing the Vietnamese Economy', *Vietnam Quarterly*, no. 1, (Winter 1976).

Buttinger, Joseph, *The Smaller Dragon* (New York: Praeger, 1958).

Buttinger, Joseph, *Vietnam: A Dragon Embattled*, vols I–II (New York: Praeger, 1967).

Callison, Charles Stuart, *Land-To-The-Tiller in the Mekong Delta* (Lanham, New York: University Press of America, 1983).

Chaliand, Gerard, *The Peasants of North Vietnam*, (Baltimore: Penguin Books, 1969).

Chesneaux, Jean, *The Vietnamese Nation*, translated by Malcom Salmon (Sydney, Australia: Current Book Distributors, 1966).

Child, Frank C., *Toward A Policy of Economic Growth in Vietnam* (East Lansing, Michigan: Michigan State University Advisory Group, 1962).

Clauson, Rishard, *Communal Land Tenure*, Agricultural Studies no. 17 (Rome: Farm and Agriculture Organisation, 1953).

Daly, Rex; Hoffman, Robert; Nelson, Frederick; Weingarten, Hyman; Hancock, Nancy (Wiegersma); Chugg, Boyd and Rojko, Anthony, *Agriculture in Vietnam's Economy* (International Development Center, US Department of Agriculture, 1973).

Dang Thu, 'Some Urgent Population Questions', *Tap Chi Cong San* (August, 1984) JPRS no. SEA-84-145.

Dang The Binh, 'The Vietnamese', *Ethnic Groups of Northern South-east Asia*, South-east Asian Studies (New Haven: Yale University, 1950).

Democratic Republic of Vietnam, *An Outline History of the Vietnam Workers Party* (Hanoi: Foreign Languages Publishing House, 1970).

Democratic Republic of Vietnam, *History of the August Revolution* (Hanoi: Foreign Languages Publishing House, 1972).

Donoghue, John D., *My Thuan, A Mekong Delta Village in South Vietnam*, Michigan State University Advisory Group (Washington DC: Agency for International Development, 1963).

Duang Quoc Cam, 'Correct Solution of the Relationship Between the Collective Economy and the Supplementary Economy of the Families of Individual Members', *Hoc Tap* (October 1962) JPRS no.16815.

Duiker, William J., *The Rise of Nationalism in Vietnam, 1900-1941* (Ithica, New York: Cornell Unversity Press, 1976).

Economic Survey Mission to Vietnam, *Toward the Economic Development of the Republic of Vietnam* (Rome: United Nations, 1956).

Eisen, Arlene, *Women and Revolution in Vietnam* (London: Zed Press, 1984).

Eisen-Bergman, Arlene, *Women of Vietnam* (San Francisco: Peoples Press, 1975.

Fall, Bernard B., *The Two Viet-Nams*, revised ed (New York: Praeger, 1964).

Fitzgerald, Edward and Bush, Henry, *Village Use of Communal Rice Land*, Saigon: Control Data Corporation, United States Agency for International Development, 1970).

Fitzgerald, Francis, *Fire in the Lake* (New York: Random House, 1972).

Fitzgerald, Frances, 'The Struggle and the War', *The Atlantic Monthly*, LLXX (August 1967).

Fforde, Adam J., 'Problems of Agricultural Development in North Vietnam', Ph.D. dissertation, Clare College, Cambridge, 1982.

Furnival, J. S., *Colonial Practice and Policy* (New York: New York University Press, 1956).

Gordon, Alec, 'North Vietnam's Collectivization Campaigns: Class Struggle Production and the Middle Peasant Problem', *Journal of Contemporary Asia*, vol 11, no. 1 (1981).

Gough, Kathleen, *Ten Times More Beautiful: The Rebuilding of Vietnam* (New York: Monthly Review Press, 1978).

Gourou, Pierre, *Land Utilization in French Indochina*, translated by Guest, Clark and Pelzer, (Washington, DC: Institute of Pacific Affairs, 1945).

Gourou, Pierre, *Peasants of the Tonkin Delta*, translated by Richard R. Miller, (New Haven: Human Relations Area Files, 1953).

Gueffier, René, *Essay on the Land System in Indochina*, translated by Claude Reed, (New Haven: Human Relations Area Files, 1955).

Hendrey, James B., *The Small World of Khanh Hua* (Chicago: Aldine Publishing Company, 1964).

Hewlett, Robert and Markie, John, *Cooperative Farming as an Instrument of Rural Development: Examples from China, Vietnam, Tanzania and India* FAO Land Reform Paper, no 2, 1976.

Hickey, Gerald Cannon, *Village in Vietnam* (New Haven: Yale University Press, 1964).

Ho Chi Minh, *Selected Works* (Hanoi: Foreign Languages Publishing House, 1961).

Hoc Tap (editorial), 'Our Acute Lesson in Building the Party in Bac Ninh Province', *Hoc Tap* (December 1962) JPRS no. 17666.

Hunt, David, 'Organizing the Revolution in Vietnam', *Radical America*, vol. 8, nos 1 and 2 (January–April, 1974).

Huynh Kim Khanh, *Vietnamese Communism, 1925–1945* (Ithica, New York: Cornell University Press, 1982).

Kolko, Gabriel, *Anatomy of a War* (New York: Pantheon Books, Random House, 1985).

Kresser, Paul, *The Annamese Commune in Cochinchina*, translated by K. Botsford (New Haven: Human Relations Area Files, 1964).

Lacouture, Jean, *Ho Chi Minh: A Political Biography* (New York: Random House, 1968).

Lam Quang Huyen, 'Economic Activities of a Cooperative Household', *Nghien Cuu Kinh Te* (August 1961) JPRS no. 15066.

Lamb, Helen B., *Vietnam's Will to Live* (New York: Monthly Review Press, 1968).

Lan, J., *Rice: Legislation, Cult Beliefs'*,translated by Keith Botsford (New Haven: Human Relations Area Files, 1953).

Le Duan, 'Hold High the Revolutionary Banner of Creative Marxism, Lead our Revolutionary Cause to Complete Victory', in *On Some Present International Problems* (Hanoi: Foreign Languages Publishing House, 1964).

Le Than Khoi, *Histoire du Viet-nam* (Paris: Les Editions de Minuit, 1955).

Luro, Jean Baptist Eliacin, *The Country of Annam*, translated by Mrs Claude A. Lopez (New Haven: Human Relations Area Files, 1956).

Luykx, Nicholaas, 'Some Comparative Aspects of Rural Public Institutions in Thailand, the Philippines and Vietnam', Ph. D. dissertation, Cornell University, 1962.

Mai Thi and Le Thi Nham Tuyet, *Women in Vietnam* (Hanoi: Foreign Languages Publishing House, 1978).

Mandel, Ernest, *The Formation of the Economic Thought of Karl Marx* (New York: Monthly Review Press, 1971).

Marr, David, *Vietnamese Anticolonialism* (Berkeley: University of California Press, 1971).

Marr, David, *Vietnamese Tradition on Trial, 1920–45* (Berkeley: University of California Press, 1981).

Marx, Karl, *Precapitalist Economic Formations*, edited by Eric J. Hobsbawm, (New York: International Publishers, 1964).

McAlister, John T., and Mus, Paul, *The Vietnamese and Their Revolution* (New York: Harper & Row, 1970).

Mitchell, Edward J., 'The Significance of Land Tenure in the Vietnamese Insurgency', *Asian Survey*, vol. VII (August 1967).

Moise, Edwin E., 'Land Reform and Land Reform Errors in North Vietnam', *Pacific Affairs*, no. 49 (Spring 1976).

Myint, Hla, *The Economics of Developing Countries* (New York: Praeger, 1964).

Ngo Vinh Long, *Before the Revolution: The Vietnamese Peasants Under the French* (Cambridge, Massachusetts: MIT Press, 1973).

Ngo Vinh Long, *Vietnamese Women in Society and Revolution*, vol. I, The French Colonial Period (Cambridge, Massachusetts: Vietnam Resources Center, 1974).

Ngo Vinh Long, 'The Tasks of Reconstruction', *Vietnam Quarterly*, no. 2 (Spring 1976).

Ngo Vinh Long, 'View from the Village', *Indochina Issues*, no. 12 (December 1980).

Ngo Vinh Long, 'Agrarian Differentiation in the Southern Region of Vietnam', *Journal of Contemporary Asia*, vol. 14, no. 3 (1984).

Nguyen Dang Kieu, 'A Uniform Financial and Production Plan for Agricultural Cooperatives', *Nghien Cuu Kinh Te*, no. 10 (August 1962) JPRS no. 16 633.

Nguyen Khac Vien, *The Long Resistance* (Hanoi: Foreign Languages Publishing House, 1975).

Nguyen Khac Vien, *Tradition and Revolution in Vietnam*, edited by David Marr and Jane Werner, and translated by Linda Yarr, Jane Werner and Tran Tuong Nhu (Berkeley: Indochina Resources Center, 1973).

Nguyen Khac Vien, (ed.) *A Century of Struggle*, Vietnamese Studies no. 24 (Hanoi: Foreign Languages Publishing House).

Nguyen Khac Vien, (ed.) *South Vietnam: From the NLF to the Provisional Revolutionary Government*, Vietnamese Studies no. 23 (Hanoi: Foreign Languages Publishing House, 1970).

Nguyen Khac Vien, (ed.) *Traditional Vietnam: Some Historical Stages*, Vietnamese Studies, no. 21 (Hanoi: Foreign Languages Publishing House, 1972).

Nguyen Thi Dinh, *No Other Road to Take* translated by Mai V. Elliot, Data Paper no. 102, Southeast Asia Program (Ithica, New York: Cornell University, 1976).

Nguyen Thi Dinh. 'Toward the Sixth Party Congress', *Tap Chi Cong San*, no. 7 (July 1986); JPRS-SEA-86-193.

Nguyen Nieu, 'Correctly Coordinating and Using Administrative and Economic Methods to Adjust Economic Relationships in the Present: Improvement of Enterprise Management', *Luat Hoc* (April–June 1975) JPRS no. 66171.

Nguyen Yem, *The Thanh Oai District*, Vietnamese Studies no. 27 (Hanoi: Foreign Relations Publishing House).

Norlund, Irene, 'The Role of Industry in Vietnam's Development Strategy', *Journal of Contemporary Asia*, vol. 14, no. 1, 1984.

Ory, P., *The Annamite Commune at Tonkin* (New Haven, Human Relations Area Files, 1965).

Parsons, Kenneth H., 'Land Reform in the Postwar Era', *Land Economics*, vol. XXXIII (September 1957).

Pham Cuong, *Revolution in the Village of Nam Hong (1945–1975)* (Hanoi: Foreign Languages Publishing House, 1976).

Pham Toan, *The Ngo Xuyen Cooperative*, Vietnamese Studies no. 27 (Hanoi: Foreign Languages Publishing House).

Pike, Douglas, *Vietcong* (Cambridge, Massachusetts: MIT Press, 1966).

Polanyi, Karl, *The Great Transformation* (Boston: Beacon Press, 1965).

Polanyi, Karl, 'The Economy as Instituted Process', in *Trade and Markets in the Early Empires*, edited by Karl Polanyi, Conrad Arsenberg and Harry Pearson (Glencoe: The Free Press, 1957) Chap. 8.

Popkin, Samuel L., *The Rational Peasant* (Berkeley: University of California Press, 1979).

Prosterman, Roy L., 'Land Reform in Vietnam', *Current History* (December 1969).

Raup, Philip, 'The Contribution of Land Reform to Agricultural Development', *Economic Development and Cultural Change*, vol. XII (October 1963).

Republic of Vietnam, *Agricultural Statistics Yearbooks*, 1959–1970 inclusive (Agricultural Economics and Statistical Service) (Saigon: AESS 1960).

Republic of Vietnam, *Report on the Agriculture Census of Vietnam*,

(Saigon: Agricultural Economics and Statistics Service, Department of Rural Affairs, 1961).

Republic of Vietnam, *Vietnam Statistical Yearbooks, 1967, 1969 and 1970*. (Saigon: National Institute of Statistics 1967, 1969, 1970).

Robequain, Charles, *The Economic Development of French Indochina*, translated by Isabel A. Ward (New York: Institute for Pacific Relations, 1944).

Sacks, Milton, 'Marxism in Vietnam', in *Marxism in Southeast Asia*, edited by Frank Traeger (Stanford, California: Stanford University Press: 1959).

Sansom, Robert, *The Economics of Insurgency in the Mekong Delta of Vietnam* (Cambridge, Massachusetts: MIT Press, 1967).

Scigliano, Robert, *South Viet Nam: Nation Under Stress* (Boston: Houghton Mifflin, 1965).

Scott, James C., *The Moral Economy of the Peasant* (New Haven: Yale University Press, 1976).

Selden, Mark, 'The National Liberation Front and the Transformation of Vietnamese Society', *Bulletin of Concerned Asian Scholars*, vol. II, (October 1969).

Tap Chi Cong San (editorial), 'Revamping the Management of Basic Economic Units', *Tap Chi Cong San*, no. 6 (June 1986) JPRS no. SEA-86-171.

Thompson, Virginia, *French Indochina* (New York: Macmillan 1937).

Tran Xuan, 'Ho Chi Minh City Steps Up Small Industry and Handicraft Production', *Tap Chi Cong San*, no. 7 (July 1986) JPRS no. SEA-86-171.

Truong Chinh and Vo Nguyen Giap, *The Peasant Question*, translated by Christine Pelzer White, Data Paper no. 94, Southeast Asia Program (Ithica, New York: Cornell University, 1974).

Truong Ngoc Giau and Woodruff, Lloyd, *The Delta Village of My Thuan* (Washington, DC: Michigan State University Advisory Group, US Agency for International Development, 1970).

Turley, William S. (ed.) *Vietnamese Communism in Comparative Perspective* (Boulder, Colorado: Westview Press, 1980).

Vu Can, The NLF and the Second Resistance in South Vietnam, Vietnamese Studies no. 23 (Hanoi: Foreign Languages Publishing House).

Vu Van Hien, *Communal Property in Tonkin*, translated by Lilian Greene (New Haven: Human Relations Area Files, 1955).

Werner, Jane 'Socialist Development 'The Political Economy of Agrarian Reform in Vietnam', *Bulletin of Concerned Asian Scholars*, vol. 16, no. 2 (April–June 1984).

White, Christine Pelzer, 'Agrarian Reform and National Liberation in the Vietnamese Revolution: 1920–1957', Ph D. dissertation, Cornell University, 1981.

White, Christine Pelzer, *Debates in Vietnamese Development Policy*, discussion paper (Brighton: Institute for Development Studies, Sussex University, 1982).

White, Christine, Pelzer. *Land Reform in North Vietnam*, country paper (Washington, DC: Agency for International Development Spring Review, 1970).

White, Christine Pelzer, 'The Peasants and the Party in the Vietnamese Revolution', in Don Miller (ed.) *Peasants and Politics: Grassroots Reaction to Change in Asia*, (Melbourne: Edward Arnold, 1977).

White, Christine Pelzer, 'The Vietnamese Revolutionary Alliance', in John Lewis (ed.) *Peasant Rebellion and Communist Revolution in Asia* (Stanford, California: Stanford University Press, 1974).

Wiegersma, Nancy, 'The Asiatic Mode of Production and Vietnam', *Journal of Contemporary Asia*, vol. 12, no. 1 (1982).

Wiegersma, Nancy, 'Land Tenure and Land Reform: A History of Property and Power in Vietnam', Ph.D. dissertation, University of Maryland, 1976.

Wiegersma, Nancy, 'Regional Differences in Socialist Transformation in Vietnam', *Economic Forum*, vol. XIV (Summer 1983).

Wiegersma, Nancy, 'Women in the Transition to Capitalism: Nineteenth Through Mid-Twentieth Century Vietnam', Paul Zarembka (ed.), *Research in Political Economy*, vol. IV (Greenwich, Connecticut: JAI Press, 1981).

Woodruff, Lloyd, *Local Administration in Vietnam: Village Finance* (Washington, DC: Michigan State University Advisory Group Agency for International Development, 1963).

Woodside, Alexander B., *Community and Revolution in Modern Vietnam* (Boston: Houghton Mifflin, 1976).

NEWS MEDIA: NEWSPAPERS, NEWSLETTERS AND MAGAZINES

Bogos, Lasclo, 'The Transformation of South Vietnam', *Magyar Hirlap*, Budapest (March 1978) JPRS no, 71017, pp. 19–20.

Canh Sinh, 'Correctly Understanding the Problem of Improving the Standard of Living', *Nhan Dan* (6 August, 1963) JPRS no. 21,439, p. 53.

Casella, Alexander, 'The Case of Catch 22', *Far Eastern Economic Review* (1 November 1984) pp. 33–4.

Dao Thi Dinh, 'Training and Promoting Female Cadres', *Nhan Dan* (6 November 1962) JPRS no. 16891, p. 3.

Do Chu and Xuan Giang, 'Let's Help One Another, Not Lend Money for Interest', *Nhan Dan*, Readers' Letters Column (4 December 1984) JPRS no. SEA-85-023.

Ekonomicheskaya Gazeta, no. 28, Moscow (July 1986) p. 20. JPRS SEA-86-155, pp. 90–3.

Fraser, Stewart E., 'Vietnam Struggles With Expanding Population', *Indochina Issues*, no. 57 (May 1985) pp. 1–7.

Gellen, Karen, 'Vietnam Women: A New Agenda', *The Guardian*, New York (12 March 1986) pp. 1, 15.

Hanoi Radio, 'Economic Restoration, Production Gains Reported', (31 October 1975) JPRS no. 66182. p. 12.

Hiebert, Linda Gibson, 'Malnutrition among Children', *Indochina Issues* no. 65 (April 1986) pp. 4–5.

Hiebert, Murray, 'Call for Radical Surgery', *Far Eastern Economic Review* (22 January 1987) p. 51.

Hiebert, Murray, 'Contracts in Vietnam: More Rice, New Problems', *Indochina Issues*, no. 48 (July 1984) pp. 1–3, 6–7.

Hiebert, Murray, 'The Food Weapon: Can Vietnam Be Broken?' *Indochina Issues*, no. 15 (April 1981) pp. 1–7.

Hiebert, Murray, 'Vietnam Begins Leadership Transition', *Indochina Issues*, no. 67 (July 1986) pp. 1–5.

Huong Giang, 'Positive Changes in the Economy of Our Country Under the Illumination of Resolution 6 of the Party Central Committee', *Doc Lap*, JPRS no. SEA-84-152, p. 85.

Huu Tho 'Contractual Quota System in Agriculture Reviewed', *Vietnam Courier*, no. 9 (September 1982) pp. 7–11.

Joint Publications Research Service, 'VNA Reports Army Production Activities in South, North Vietnam', JPRS no. 67427 (June 1976) p. 7.

Nguyen Thi Kim Oanh, 'Agricultural Technician in Wrong Job', *Tien Phong* (20 May 1962) p. 2. JPRS no. 14666.

Nguyen Van Thoai, 'Agricultural Technician Rears Children', *Tien Phong* (20 May 1962) p. 2. JPRS no. 14666.

Nhan Dan (editorial) 'Improve the Quality of Socialist Transformation' (17 January, 1980) JPRS no. 75301, p. 33.

Nhan Dan, 'Irrigation Projects', (28 July 1963) JPRS no. 21217.

Nhan Dan 'Land Reorganization in Nam Bo', (October 1984) p. 1. JPRS no. SEA-84-135.

Nhan Dan 'Tien Giang Encourages Woment to Develop the Family Economy', (9 July 1986) p. 1. JPRS no. SEA-86-193, p. 60.

Nhat Linh, 'Cooperation Teams – Good and Bad Aspects', *Doc Lap* (13 June 1984) p. 5. JPRS no. SEA-84-115, p. 59.

Pham Van Tiep, 'Waste of Agricultural Technicians in Kieu An Province', *Tien Phong* (20 May 1962) p. 2. JPRS no. 14666.

Phong Ha, 'The Truth About a Village', *Dai Doan Ket* (2 July 1986) p. 6. JPRS no. SEA-86-157.

Quinn-Judge, Sophie, 'Vietnamese Women: Neglected Promises', *Indochina Issues*, no. 42 (December 1983) pp. 1–7.

Quinn-Judge, Paul, 'The Vietnam–China Split: Old Ties Remain', *Indochina Issues*, no. 53 (January 1985) pp. 1–7.

Race, Jeffrey, 'South Vietnam', *Far Eastern Economic Review*, (20 August 1970) p. 3.

Saigon Giai Phong, 'Enterprises Still "Subsidized"', (5 August 1986) p. 3, JPRS no. SEA-86-185.

Saigon Giai Phong (editorial) 'Four Months of Criticism in *Saigon Giai Phong*', (31 August 1986) pp. 1 and 4. JPRS no. SEA-86-194.

Saigon Giai Phong 'Trade Union Federation Explains to Owners Policy of Aiding Private Enterprises' (23 July 1975) pp. 1, 4. JPRS no. 65766.

Socialist Republic of Vietnam, 'Industrial Development in Southern District', Information documents in English. JPRS no. SEA-86-1512.

Socialist Republic of Vietnam Government Brief, 'Agricultural Production Progress', 16 October 1986, JPRS SEA-86-206, p. 104.

Spragens, John, Jr, 'Cautious Policy Reforms', *Indochina Issues*, no. 12 (December 1980) pp. 1–4.

Spragens, John, Jr, 'Vietnam and the Soviets, A Tighter Alliance', *Indochina Issues*, no. 51 (November 1984) pp. 1–7.

Spragens, John, Jr, 'Vietnamese Fiction Tackles the Bureaucratic Plague', *Indochina Issues*, no. 26 (June 1982) pp. 1–5.

Thien Thanh, 'To Avoid Giving "Blank Check" Contracts, Management Must Be on a Strict System of Managerial Responsibility', *Pu Nu Vietnam* 3–9, (September 1986) JPRS no. SEA-86-197.

Vietnam Courier, 'Saigon – Ho Chi Minh City', no. 59 (April 1977) pp. 1–4.

Vu Kiem. 'Member Comments on Party Congress in Nam Ha Village', *Nhan Dan* (26 August 1986) pp. 1–4. JPRS no. SEA-86-203, p. 103.

Wulff, Erich, 'Must We Make All the Old Mistakes Again?' *Southeast Asia Chronicle*, no. 76 (December 1981) p. 20.

GOVERNMENT MEMORANDA, LETTERS, UNPUBLISHED PAPERS

Archard, Douglas B., Letter to Richard Eney, Director, Land Reform Division, Military Region IV. 19 October 1971.

Callison, C. Stuart, 'Progress Report on Dissertation, the Economic, Social and Political Effects of the Land-to-the-Tiller program', Yale University, 14 February 1972 (Mimeographed).

Gittinger, Price, 'Agrarian Reform in Free Vietnam', unpublished paper, 15 September 1959.

Keane, John F., District Senior Advisor, Hoa Tan District, Go Cong Province, Report on Land Reform and Politics in Go Cong, 20 March 1971.

Ladejinsky, Wolf I., 'Field Trip Observations in Central Vietnam', unpublished government report, 2 April 1955.

MacPhail, Donald, and Vaughan, Mary, 'Comments on Stanford Research Institute Report on Land Reform in Vietnam', unpublished manuscript prepared for the United States Government, Agency for International Development.

Montgomery, John D., 'Land Reform and Political Development: Prospects in Vietnam', report writtten for United States Agency for International Development, Saigon, Revised draft, September 1967.

Porter, Gareth, 'Commodity Import Program', unpublished paper written for the Indochina Resources Center, Washington, DC, 1976.

US Agency for International Development, Vietnam, 'An Giang LTT SOS memorandum', no date.

US Agency for International Development, Vietnam, 'LTT Grievances and Disputes', a memorandum from R. A. Luedte, Land Reform Advisor to John A. Riggs, 15 April 1971.

US Agency for International Development, Vietnam, 'US Official's Attitude Toward LTT', memorandum from Donald Melville, Supervisor, Government Land Distribution Project, to Richard Hough, Assistant Director for Land Reform, 10 November 1969.

US Agency for International Development, Vietnam, 'Land Reform Memo Number 19', Associate Director for Land Reform, 10 February 1972.

US Agency for International Development, Vietnam, Office of Domestic Production, 'Review of Land Tenure Programs', production memo no. 10, 22 August 1969.

US Department of State, Airgram no. A-90. Subject: Ten Year Update of Village Studies, 2 July 1971.

Walters, Paul, An Giang Province, A Letter to Dick Eney, Directorate of Land Reform, CORDS/Military Region 4, 29 October 1971.

White, Christine Pelzer, 'Family and Class in the Theory and Practice of Marxism: 'The Case of Vietnam', Institute for Development Studies Conference, no. 133, University of Sussex, England.

White, Christine Pelzer, 'Land Reform and Revolution: Vietnam', unpublished manuscript, 1967.

White, Christine Pelzer, 'Report, Thesis Research in South Vietnam', November 1971–March 1972', (Mimeographed).

White, Christine Pelzer, 'State, Cooperative and Family in the Political Economy of Vietnamese Agriculture', paper presented at the Institute for Social Studies Seminar, 'Vietnam, Indochina and Southeast Asia: Into the Eighties', 29 September–3 October 1980.

White, Christine Pelzer, 'Vietnamese Revolutionary Alliances', unpublished manuscript, 1973.

INTERVIEWS

Porter, Gareth. Interviews written and mimeographed. Interviews with:
Au Ngoc Ho, Minister of the Economy, 1968–9. 29 September 1971.
Bui Huu Tien, in Land Reform Directorate, 1958–71. 31 August 1971.
Le Van Toan, former Chief of the Land Reform Court. 10 November 1971.
Nguyen Duy Xuan, Agricultural Advisor to the Government of Vietnam. 3 September 1971.
Nguyen Hoang Cuong, former Deputy Minister of the Economy. 16 October 1971.

Wiegersma, Nancy. Interviews with:
C. Stuart Callison, on his work in rural Vietnam on the effects of the Land-to-the-Tiller Law. April 1972.
Randy Cummings, State University of New York, Anthropology Department. On his work on villages in Chau Doc Province. August 1975.
Nguyen Xuam Kaong, US AID and former director of the Cadaster. April 1972.

Index